The Contexts of Bakhtin

STUDIES IN RUSSIAN AND EUROPEAN LITERATURE

A series edited by

Peter I. Barta
University of Surrey
and
David Shepherd
University of Sheffield

Volume 1

Russian Literature and the Classics
Edited by Peter I. Barta, David H. J. Larmour, and Paul Allen Miller

Volume 2

The Contexts of Bakhtin: Philosophy, Authorship, Aesthetics
Edited by David Shepherd

Forthcoming titles

Reconstructing the Canon: Russian Writing in the 1980s
Edited by Arnold McMillin

Iurii Dombrovskii: Freedom Under Totalitarianism, Peter Doyle

Carnivalizing Difference: Bakhtin and the Other
Edited by Peter I. Barta, Paul Allen Miller, Chuck Platter, and David Shepherd

Discourse and Ideology in Nabokov's Prose, Edited by David H. J. Larmour

Polish Literature in the European Context, Edited by Patricia Pollock Brodsky

Gender and Sexuality in Russian Civilization, Edited by Peter I. Barta

This book is part of a series. The publisher will accept continuation orders which may be cancelled at any time and which provide for automatic billing and shipping of each title in the series upon publication. Please write for details.

The Contexts of Bakhtin

Philosophy
Authorship
Aesthetics

EDITED BY
DAVID SHEPHERD
UNIVERSITY OF SHEFFIELD

Routledge
Taylor & Francis Group
LONDON AND NEW YORK

2 Park Square, Milton Park,
Abingdon, Oxon, OX14 4RN

270 Madison Ave,
New York NY 10016

Transferred to Digital Printing 2008

British Library Cataloguing in Publication Data

The contexts of bakhtin. - (Studies in Russian and European literature ; v. 2)
1.Bakhtin, M. (Mikhail), 1895-1975 2.Philology 3.Criticism - Soviet Union
I.Shepherd, David, 1958-
801.9′5′092

ISBN 90-5702-566-3 (hbk)
ISBN 90-5702-567-1 (pbk)

Publisher's Note
The publisher has gone to great lengths to ensure the quality of this reprint but points out that some imperfections in the original may be apparent

CONTENTS

INTRODUCTION TO THE SERIES

Change and difference have become the cliched watchwords of Slavic studies in recent years. There is surely no need for further cataloguing — whether celebratory or cautionary — of the transformations in the practices and potential of our discipline wrought by the political, social, and economic turmoil of the former Soviet Union and the Eastern Bloc, not to mention the sweeping changes in interpretive practices within the study of the humanities in Western countries.

A series such as *Studies in Russian and European Literature* must in large degree be a response to those transformations; it cannot, however, be reduced to their mere product or reflection, and does not set out to impress by superficial novelty. In seeking to promote a comparative approach, with particular emphasis on the ties between Russian and other European literatures, and on the relationship between Western and Eastern European cultures, the series will extend long-established paths of inquiry. There will also be continuity in the embrace it offers theory, to which Russia and Eastern Europe are no strangers.

At the same time, such a venture must recognize that much of what passes for change and difference is all too often nothing more than an exchange of negative for positive which leaves old categorizations and oppositions in place, their valencies inverted by a mechanical operation of a kind characteristic of a world and a system which are supposed to have been discredited. The demise of one conceptual framework and the concomitant vindication of another might well hold out the prospect of rapid and dispiriting ossification. *Studies in Russian and European Literature* will resist this possibility. Like its global counterpart, literary history has not yet come to an end.

Peter I. Barta
David Shepherd

PREFACE

An important impetus of much Bakhtin scholarship in the 1990s has been the realization of an apparent irony: that a body of scholarly work so tenacious in its insistence on the importance of context (historical, social, institutional, intellectual) was itself, in the course of appropriation in the 1970s and 1980s by ever-increasing numbers of self-styled "Bakhtinians", decontextualized in a manner and to a degree that represent a betrayal of Bakhtin's true significance and originality. This position has recently been articulated with characteristic directness and vigour by Caryl Emerson in her introduction to a volume edited by Amy Mandelker and entitled, symptomatically, *Bakhtin in Contexts: Across the Disciplines*. Reproving some Western scholars for their "brand of 'hurrah-collectivism' that incorporates Bakhtin's ideas into one or another suprapersonal theory", Emerson speaks approvingly of "Russian Bakhtinists" who "have long been easing out of their master's legacy a sort of neohumanism, usually liberal in spirit and often religiously informed" (Emerson 1995, 2). Further, "a full picture of 'Bakhtin in contexts' is gradually and belatedly coming to include an intellectual exchange with a scholarly community in Bakhtin's own homeland that, in the past half decade, has become unprecedentedly diverse" (5). This exchange will help reveal the key to a proper, contextualized understanding of Bakhtin and his full potential: sensitivity to "the insight — or corrective — offered [to various disciplines] by Bakhtin's profoundly antitheoretic mode of thought" (2).

The present volume, for all that its title is similar to, and no less symptomatic than, that of Mandelker's, has a somewhat different emphasis. The contributions, most of which began life as papers written for the Fifth International Bakhtin Conference held at the University of Manchester in 1991 (where the first faltering steps towards "intellectual exchange" between Russian and Western approaches to Bakhtin were taken), are concerned not only with the uses and abuses attendant upon the "appropriation" or "application" of Bakhtin, but also with the contexts to which we might need to refer in order to achieve a better understanding of where Bakhtin "came from" and where he might take us: contexts both immediate and oblique, personal and impersonal, intellectual and, crucially, theoretical. The arrangement of articles in four separately titled sections is thus intended to imply not rigid demarcation of themes, but rather shifts in dominant within a more or less constant preoccupation with Bakhtin's philosophical (especially (Neo-)Kantian) and aesthetic affiliations.

The first section, "Life, Philosophy, Philosophy of Life", opens with Iudif' Kagan's moving account of Bakhtin's personal and intellectual relationship with her father Matvei Kagan. The overview of Kagan's published and unpublished works is broadened and deepened by Ruth Coates's consideration of the similarities and differences between Kagan's and Bakhtin's thought. Nikolai Nikolaev shows how Kagan's exposure to, and subsequent exposition of, the Marburg School was important for the "Nevel School". Nikolaev's painstaking scrutiny of Lev Pumpianskii's archive suggests that that "small fraternity", notwithstanding its seeming ephemerality, was sufficiently coherent to be unprovisionally designated a "School", and that its deliberations on, *inter alia*, *Lebensphilosophie* and psychoanalysis were a vital factor in shaping Bakhtin's early thought.

Nikolaev's article includes some arguments in favour of Bakhtin's authorship of the "disputed texts", arguments for which support and refutation may be found in other Russian work published in the 1990s — and, no doubt, in work yet to appear. The section "Authorship" is concerned not with this intractable problem, but with the Bakhtinian understanding of what it is to be an author. Giovanni Palmieri explores the connections between Bakhtin's approach, principally but not exclusively in "Author and Hero in Aesthetic Activity", and Romantic and phenomenological accounts, concluding that through Bakhtin it is possible to arrive at a "*metaphysics of the author*". Tony Anemone's focus is on the relationship between Bakhtin's theories of authorship in the 1920s and the literary practice of the poet and novelist Konstantin Vaginov, and in particular his *roman à clef The Goat Song* and remarkable metafiction *The Works and Days of Svistonov*. Careful reading of these novels, Anemone suggests, leads one away from the notion that they are simply an implementation of Bakhtinian theory towards a position that assumes a dialogical relationship between two members of the Leningrad Bakhtin Circle. Marietta Chudakova, although not seeking to make a case for direct influence or interaction of theory and practice in her account of Russian writers' attempts to come to terms with new (mis)understandings of authorship before, during and after the cultural revolution of the late 1920s, nevertheless sketches in a compelling "dialogizing background" to Bakhtin's work.

The dominant of "Form and Image" is Bakhtin's contribution to the problematics of representation. Natal′ia Bonetskaia, returning our attention to Bakhtin's connections with Western philosophical aesthetics, contends that his *oeuvre* (or at least the greater part of it, for, revealingly, certain works have perforce to be dismissed as "unrepresentative") is best understood as a "logic of form". Valerii Tiupa's modelling of the "aesthetic object" in terms of both creative and receptive aesthetics is predicated on a rejection of any similarity between Bakhtinian theory and Derridean deconstruction. However, the possibility of common ground with another French theorist and practitioner of the representation of language, Paul Valéry, is forcefully argued by Angela Biancofiore. And, although like Tiupa he insists upon the Platonic and Aristotelian context of Bakhtin's thinking on representation, Alastair Renfrew is less unforgivingly negative about the role that might be played by theorists such as Derrida or Barthes in the elucidation of that thinking.

In the final section, "A Time and a Place", representation is still very much to the fore, although the spotlight shifts, initially, to the chronotope, which so often seems to mark the point at which Bakhtin crosses into the comparatively infertile territory of narratology. Bernhard Scholz seeks to enrich this ground by pursuing the Kantian connection fleetingly signalled in a footnote to "Forms of Time and of the Chronotope"; as a result it becomes possible to identify a burgeoning poetics of the fictional representation of time and place immeasurably more nuanced and sophisticated than Formalist or Structuralist models predicated on oppositions of *fabula* and *siuzhet*, *histoire* and *récit*. In Graham Pechey's article the scope of the discussion of chronotope is expanded to embrace nothing less than the "history of realism", which it was Bakhtin's ambition to outline; here the context of implicit and explicit polemic with Brecht and Lukács is very much of Bakhtin's own time and place.

It is the time and the place of our readings of Bakhtin that are the central concern of the final two articles in this section by Ken Hirschkop and Anthony Wall. Hirschkop takes issue with the widespread conflation of Bakhtin's dia- logism with cosy, liberal notions of dialogue, a conflation that strips Bakhtin's theorizing of its radical potential, reducing it to little more than a comfort-blanket for anxious critics. Similarly, for Wall the principal problem besetting Bakhtin studies is the paradox whereby a growing tendency to see Bakhtin as a "philosopher of the ideal speech situation", "a philosopher of agreement", is leading to a cacophony or babble of conflicting critical voices in which there is no proper intellectual engagement or exchange.

We have returned, then, to our starting point: conflicting, perhaps even irreconcilable versions of Bakhtin. It might be tempting to take refuge in platitudes about desirable or inevitable pluralism; but that would be to take an "antitheoretic" approach to a messy (if logical) extreme. Far better, surely, to take refuge in an oft-quoted Bakhtinian opposition, and to suggest that the contexts of Bakhtin, and of Bakhtin studies, should not be abandoned to critical anarchy, should be seen as not merely given, but actively posited. It is hoped that this volume might make a small contribution to that ongoing project.

WORK CITED

Emerson, C. 1995. "Introduction: Dialogue on Every Corner, Bakhtin in Every Class", in A. Mandelker (ed.), *Bakhtin in Contexts: Across the Disciplines* (Evanston: Northwestern University Press), 1–30.

ACKNOWLEDGMENTS

Ken Hirschkop's article was first published in *Social Text*, 30 (1992), 102–113: permission to reprint the article here is gratefully acknowledged.

Natal′ia Bonetskaia's paper was published in Russian as "Estetika M. Bakhtina kak logika formy", in K.G. Isupov et al. (eds.), *Bakhtinologiia: Issledovaniia, perevody, publikatsii* (St Petersburg: Aleteiia, 1995), 51–60.

The article by Iudif′ Kagan was published in Russian as "Liudi ne nashego vremeni", in *Bakhtinskii sbornik*, 2 (Moscow, 1992), 87–98.

Nikolai Nikolaev's article appeared in Russian as "Nevel′skaia shkola filosofii (M. Bakhtin, M. Kagan, L. Pumpianskii) v 1918–1925 gg.: Po materialam arkhiva L. Pumpianskogo", in K.G. Isupov et al. (eds.), *M. Bakhtin i filosofskaia kul′tura XX veka* (*Problemy bakhtinologii*, 1, pt. 2) (St Petersburg: Obrazovanie, 1991), 31–43.

Valerii Tiupa's paper was published in Russian as "Arkhitektonika esteticheskogo diskursa", in K.G. Isupov et al. (eds.), *Bakhtinologiia: Issledovaniia, perevody, publikatsii* (St Petersburg: Aleteiia, 1995), 206–216.

ABBREVIATIONS

The following abbreviations are used throughout to refer to works by Bakhtin and other members of the Bakhtin Circle. Page references are to the English translations only; in cases where contributors have chosen to use their own translations, references are in the style 1/83, where the first reference is to the English translation, the second to the Russian edition listed here.

Works by Bakhtin and members of the Bakhtin Circle not available in English appear in the "References" list of articles in which they are cited.

AA "Art and Answerability" [1919], in *Art and Answerability*, 1–3. Russian: "Iskusstvo i otvetstvennost′", in *Estetika slovesnogo tvorchestva*, 5–6.

AH "Author and Hero in Aesthetic Activity" [c. 1920–23], in *Art and Answerability*, 4–256. Russian: "Avtor i geroi v esteticheskoi deiatel′nosti", in *Estetika slovesnogo tvorchestva*, 7–180.

BSHR "The *Bildungsroman* and Its Significance in the History of Realism (Toward a Historical Typology of the Novel)" [1936–38], in *Speech Genres*, 10–59. Russian: "Roman vospitaniia i ego znachenie v istorii realizma", in *Estetika slovesnogo tvorchestva*, 188–236.

DLDP V.N. Voloshinov, "Discourse in Life and Discourse in Poetry: Questions of Sociological Poetics" [1926], in *Bakhtin School Papers*, 5–30. Russian: "Slovo v zhizni i slovo v poezii", in *Zvezda*, 6 (1926), 244–267.

DN "Discourse in the Novel" [1934–35], in *The Dialogic Imagination*, 259–422. Russian: "Slovo v romane", in *Voprosy literatury i estetiki*, 72–233.

EN "Epic and Novel: Toward a Methodology for the Study of the Novel" [1941], in *The Dialogic Imagination*, 3–40. Russian: "Epos i roman. (O metodologii issledovaniia romana)", in *Voprosy literatury i estetiki*, 447–483.

FCS V.N. Voloshinov, *Freudianism: A Marxist Critique* [1927], ed. I.R. Titunik with Neal H. Bruss, tr. Titunik (New York, San Francisco and London: Academic Press, 1976) (reissued as *Freudianism: A Critical Sketch* (Bloomington: Indiana University Press, 1987)); all references are to the 1976 edition. Russian: *Freidizm: Kriticheskii ocherk* (Leningrad and Moscow: Gosizdat, 1927).

FM P.N. Medvedev, *The Formal Method in Literary Scholarship: A Critical Introduction to Sociological Poetics*, tr. A.J. Wehrle (Baltimore: Johns Hopkins University Press, 1978; Cambridge, MA, and London: Harvard University Press, 1985); all references are to the 1985 edition. Russian: *Formal'nyi metod v literaturovedenii: Kriticheskoe vvedenie v sotsiologicheskuiu poetiku* (Leningrad: Priboi, 1928).

FMSS P.N. Medvedev, "The Formal (Morphological) Method, or Scholarly Salieri-ism" [1925], in *Bakhtin School Papers*, 51–66. Russian: "Uchenyi sal'erizm: O formal'nom (morfologicheskom) metode", in *Zvezda*, 3 (1925), 264–276.

FTC "Forms of Time and of the Chronotope in the Novel: Notes Toward a Historical Poetics" [1937–38], in *The Dialogic Imagination*, 84–258. Russian: "Formy vremeni i khronotopa v romane. Ocherki po istoricheskoi poetike", in *Voprosy literatury i estetiki*, 234–407.

IT P.N. Medvedev, "The Immediate Tasks Facing Literary-Historical Science" [1928], in *Bakhtin School Papers*, 75–91. Russian: "Ocherednye zadachi istoriko-literaturnoi nauki", in *Literatura i marksizm*, 3 (1928), 65–87.

LS V.N. Voloshinov, "Literary Stylistics", in *Bakhtin School Papers*, 93–152. Russian: "Stilistika khudozhestvennoi rechi", in *Literaturnaia ucheba*, 2, 3, 5 (1926), 48–66, 65–87, 43–59.

MHS "Toward a Methodology for the Human Sciences" [1974], in *Speech Genres*, 159–172. Russian: "K metodologii gumanitarnykh nauk", in *Estetika slovesnogo tvorchestva*, 361–373.

MPL V.N. Voloshinov, *Marxism and the Philosophy of Language* [1929], tr. Ladislav Matejka and I.R. Titunik (New York and London: Seminar Press, 1973). Russian: *Marksizm i filosofiia iazyka: Osnovnye problemy sotsiologicheskogo metoda v nauke o iazyke* (Leningrad: Priboi, 1929).

N70 "From Notes Made in 1970–71", in *Speech Genres*, 132–158. Russian: "Iz zapisei 1970–1971 godov", in *Estetika slovesnogo tvorchestva*, 336–360.

PCMF "The Problem of Content, Material, and Form in Verbal Art" [1924], in *Art and Answerability*, 257–325. Russian: "Problema soderzhaniia, materiala i formy v slovesnom khudozhestvennom tvorchestve", in *Voprosy literatury i estetiki*, 6–71.

PDP *Problems of Dostoevsky's Poetics* [1963], ed. and tr. C. Emerson (Manchester and Minneapolis: Manchester University Press and University of Minnesota Press, 1984). Russian: *Problemy poetiki Dostoevskogo*, 3rd ed. (Moscow: Khudozhestvennaia literatura, 1972).

PSG "The Problem of Speech Genres" [1952–53], in *Speech Genres*, 60–102. Russian: "Problema rechevykh zhanrov", in *Estetika slovesnogo tvorchestva*, 237–280.

PT "The Problem of the Text in Linguistics, Philology, and the Human Sciences: An Experiment in Philosophical Analysis" [1959–61], in *Speech Genres*, 103–131. Russian: "Problema teksta v lingvistike, filologii i drugikh gumanitarnykh naukakh: Opyt filosofskogo analiza", in *Estetika slovesnogo tvorchestva*, 281–307.

RW *Rabelais and His World* [1965], tr. Hélène Iswolsky (Cambridge, MA, and London: MIT Press, 1968; Bloomington: Indiana University Press, 1984); all references are to the 1984 edition. Russian: *Tvorchestvo Fransua Rable i narodnaia kul'tura srednevekov'ia i Renessansa* (Moscow: Khudozhestvennaia literatura, 1990).

TPA *Toward a Philosophy of the Act* [1991–92], ed. V. Liapunov and M. Holquist, tr. Liapunov (Austin: University of Texas Press, 1993). Russian: "K filosofii postupka", in *Filosofiia i sotsiologiia nauki i tekhniki: Ezhegodnik 1984–85* (Moscow: Nauka, 1986), 80–160.

TRDB "Toward a Reworking of the Dostoevsky Book" [1961], in *Problems of Dostoevsky's Poetics*, 283–302. Russian: "K pererabotke knigi o Dostoevskom", in *Estetika slovesnogo tvorchestva*, 308–327.

Key to English and Russian Collections of Works by Bakhtin

Art and Answerability: Early Philosophical Essays by M.M. Bakhtin, ed. M. Holquist and V. Liapunov, tr. Liapunov and K. Brostrom (Austin: University of Texas Press, 1991).

Bakhtin School Papers, ed. A. Shukman (Oxford: RPT Publications, 1983).

The Dialogic Imagination: Four Essays by M.M. Bakhtin, ed. M. Holquist, tr. C. Emerson and Holquist (Austin: University of Texas Press, 1981).

Speech Genres and Other Late Essays, ed. C. Emerson and M. Holquist, tr. V.W. McGee (Austin: University of Texas Press, 1986).

Estetika slovesnogo tvorchestva (Moscow: Iskusstvo, 1979).

Voprosy literatury i estetiki: Issledovaniia raznykh let (Moscow: Khudozhestvennaia literatura, 1975).

TRANSLITERATION AND TRANSLATION

Except in the case of established usage (e.g. Dostoevsky) Russian words are transliterated according to the Library of Congress system (without diacritics).

The articles by Natal'ia Bonetskaia, Marietta Chudakova, Iudif' Kagan, Nikolai Nikolaev and Valerii Tiupa have been translated from Russian by the editor.

Unless otherwise indicated, translations into English are by the authors of articles or by the editor.

ABOUT THE CONTRIBUTORS

Tony Anemone is associate professor of Russian at the College of William and Mary in Williamsburg, Virginia. The author of articles on Tolstoi, Nabokov, Vaginov, Kharms, and the literary history of the 1920s in Russia, he is currently writing a book entitled *Obsessive Collectors: The Making of Modern Russian Culture*.

Angela Biancofiore teaches Italian language and literature at the Université Paul Valéry in Montpellier. She is the editor of *Athánor*, a journal of the plastic arts, literature and philosophy, and author of *L'opero e il metodo. Da Baudelaire a Valéry* (1991), as well as of a number of articles on the theory of the literary text in general and Bakhtin in particular.

Natal'ia Konstantinovna Bonetskaia is a researcher at the Institute of World Literature of the Russian Academy of Sciences in Moscow, and author of a number of works on Bakhtin's affiliations to Western and Russian aesthetic and ethical thought.

Marietta Omarovna Chudakova is a professor at the Literary Institute in Moscow. A specialist on twentieth-century Russian literature, she is known particularly for her work on Mikhail Bulgakov, Iurii Olesha and Mikhail Zoshchenko.

Ruth Coates is currently temporary lecturer in Russian at the School of Slavonic and East European Studies, University of London. She is editor and co-translator of *The Emancipation of Russian Christianity* (forthcoming), a collection of essays by academics at the St Petersburg School of Religion and Philosophy, and is currently writing a book based on her doctoral thesis on the Christian elements in Bakhtin's work.

Ken Hirschkop is a teaching fellow in the English Department at the University of Manchester. He is editor of *Bakhtin and Cultural Theory* (with David Shepherd, 1989 and 1998), and the author of numerous articles on Bakhtin. He has recently completed a book entitled *Bakhtin and Democracy*.

Iudif' Matveevna Kagan, the daughter of Matvei Isaevich Kagan, lives in Moscow, and is a specialist on classical languages and literatures; and on twentieth-century Russian poetry. Her publications include *Marina Tsvetaeva v Moskve: Put'k gibeli* (1992).

Nikolai Ivanovich Nikolaev is a researcher at the St Petersburg State University Library. A leading expert on the work of Pumpianskii, he is the author of a number of works based on detailed archival research, and a member of the editorial team currently preparing Bakhtin's *Collected Works* for the Russian Academy of Sciences.

Giovanni Palmieri teaches Italian in a high school in Milan. His principal interests are Italian philology and literary theory. He is the author of *Invito a conoscere il futurismo* (1987, 1993) and *Schmitz, Svevo, Zeno* (1994), and has edited the works and correspondence of Italo Svevo.

Graham Pechey lectures in English at the University of Hertfordshire. Besides his work on Bakhtin, he has written a number of articles in the fields of Romantic writing, literary and cultural theory, and the postcolonial. The paper published in this volume is a shortened and somewhat differently focused version of a chapter in a book he is writing under the provisional title of *Postmodern Bakhtin*.

Alastair Renfrew is a lecturer in Russian at the University of Strathclyde. He is editor of *Exploiting Bakhtin* (1997) and a co-editor of *Face to Face* (1997), a collection of papers from the Seventh International Bakhtin Conference held in Moscow in 1995, and has written on contemporary Scottish fiction.

Bernhard Scholz is professor and chair of General and Comparative Literature at Gröningen University. His research is focused on word–image relations, poetics, and the history and philosophy of literary scholarship. He is editor of the series *Symbola et Emblemata: Studies in Renaissance and Baroque Symbolism*.

David Shepherd is professor of Russian and director of the Bakhtin Centre at the University of Sheffield. He is the editor of *Bakhtin: Carnival and Other Subjects* (1993); *Bakhtin and Cultural Theory* (with Ken Hirschkop, 1989 and 1998) and *Dialogism: An International Journal of Bakhtin Studies*, the first issue of which will appear in 1998.

Valerii Igorevich Tiupa teaches at Novosibirsk Pedagogical University. He is the author of numerous works on Russian literature, literary theory and poetics, and a founding editor of the journal *Diskurs: Kommunikatsiia — obrazovanie — kul'tura*.

Anthony Wall is professor of French at the University of Calgary. His main research interests lie in literary semiotics and the philosophy of language. Recent work on deviant forms of prose has yielded *Superposer: essais sur les métalangages littéraires* (1996). Other publications include *Hubert Aquin entre référence et métaphore* (1991) and a translation, completed with Roy Sellars, of Renate Lachmann's *Memory and Literature: Intertextuality in Russian Modernism* (1997).

Life, Philosophy, Philosophy of Life

PEOPLE NOT OF OUR TIME

Iudif' Kagan, Moscow

One of the poems written by Osip Mandelstam during his exile in Voronezh contains the following poignant lines:

> Somebody read me! Somebody lead me! Somebody heal me!
> Somebody say something on the jagged stairs!
>
> [— Читателя! советчика! врача!
> На лестнице колючей разговора б! ...]
>
> (Mandelstam 1973 [1937], 91)

I quote these words because following Bakhtin's death quite a number of accounts of conversations with him appeared in the press. But at the same time Leonid Efimovich Pinskii, an outstanding literary scholar, seems to have had good reason for saying, on 31 March 1976, at one of the earliest conferences on Bakhtin, that this most profound student of dialogue was a "silent philosopher" (*filosof-molchun*). At least that was how Pinskii, who visited him not long before he died, saw Bakhtin; and so it was, I believe, towards the end of Bakhtin's life. Bakhtin would say to my mother, when suggesting that she and I should visit him more often, "Come to see me! You are always welcome! We have memories in common!" Bakhtin also had in mind a certain common intellectual culture. His inscription on the copy of the new edition of *Problems of Dostoevsky's Poetics* which he gave to my mother reads: "To dear Sof'ia Isaakovna Kagan with respect and love, and in memory of the unforgettable Matvei Isaevich." Unforgettable.

From recently published letters and notes written by Bakhtin's Nevel friends Voloshinov and Pumpianskii, and from the extracts from Bakhtin's own testimony preserved in the records of his prosecution (see Iu.M. Kagan 1992 and Konkin 1991, 3), it is clearly evident that, first in Nevel, and later in Vitebsk and Leningrad, they had conversations which lasted all night, serious discussions of serious books on philosophy, art and theology, that they told each other about their own research and their own thinking. There were conversations, and there were people to converse with.

When I first began to work on the archives of the State Academy for the Arts (Gosudarstvennaia Akademiia Khudozhestvennykh Nauk, GAKhN), where my father had been a member of the Philosophy Department, there were times when, after the first document, the sheet bearing the signatures of those who had been present at a meeting, I found it almost impossible to read on, because virtually every name on the sheet bore witness to the terrible fate which befell those people. Sympathetic listeners and opponents alike disappeared. They were arrested, driven out of the country, exiled, prevented from carrying out what they saw as their vocation, or simply murdered... Little by little philosophy, free thought of any kind, was forced into the catacombs, and even there partners in conversation became steadily fewer. Their quality as well as their quantity changed. The continuity of thought and speech was lost. As my father wrote in his "On the Course of History" ("O khode istorii", 1920), "the word must not be treated with indifference, because the word is always more than its purely semantic meaning".

Immediately after Pasternak's funeral at the beginning of June 1960 I went to see my teacher Aleksei Losev to tell him about the ceremony in Peredelkino — who had been there, what had been said... I had known Losev for a long time, and was utterly shocked to see him weeping, struggling to hold back his sobs. He was weeping not only for Pasternak, but for himself, for a whole age which, he thought, had gone for ever. Through his tears he said again and again: "What a spirit there was then! What a spirit there was on this earth! And they've destroyed it all!" I tried helplessly to console him, telling him that no, everything had not been destroyed, that there were young people who were trying to carry on what there had been in the past, that they were reading, thinking, discussing... I knew people who were doing this. Losev replied that I was only saying this because I could not even imagine what intellectual life in Russia had been like in the late 1910s and early 1920s. And it is true that I have rarely come across people of the same intellectual calibre as Losev since.

And this is why I think that, if it is at all possible somehow to gain an idea — not from the accounts of others, but directly from people not of our time, from people who did not think "the way we do" — of what the people mourned by Losev were saying, what they wanted to say to one another and to those who they thought might respond to what they were saying, if it is possible to discover what has been preserved of their thought, then it is our duty to listen to them carefully and to try, however difficult it might be, to understand them. This is especially important because, like all free-thinking people, they were by no means always in agreement with one another. What they had in common was their departure from the officially sanctioned ideological "line", as well as an undoubted interest in a number of the same problems in the theory of cognition, aesthetics, and religious thought which were of great concern to them all.

In his article "Secret Freedom", the grandson of the philosopher Gustav Shpet, M.K. Polivanov, a physicist and cultural historian, recalled Akhmatova saying to him, during a conversation about *Doctor Zhivago*, that the times described by Pasternak were her times, but that she did not recognize a single person in the novel. Polivanov offered the following gloss on Akhmatova's comment:

> People like the characters of *Doctor Zhivago* were not to be seen in the literary and artistic society of those years, they were not to be found among the visitors to the "Stray Dog" or the circle which gathered around the "Musaget" publishing house. It is easier to imagine them in the group of young people surrounding the contributors to *Landmarks*, or, later on, in the Nevel circle from which Iudina, Bakhtin, and Matvei Kagan emerged [...] Almost all people of this kind were wiped out, or lived very inconspicuous lives. (Polivanov 1990, 107)

It is well known that Bakhtin and my father were close acquaintances between 1918 and 1921. Their circle of friends was formed in the immediate post-Revolutionary years in two small towns within the former "Jewish Pale", Nevel and Vitebsk. Nevel was my father's native town. A Jew, and the son of a not particularly wealthy merchant and tanner, he was educated first in a cheder, then in a Russian school for Jewish children. In 1909 he left Nevel and completed his grammar-school education as an external pupil. His examiner in Latin was the poet Innokentii Annenskii, whose verse my father was very fond of.[1] Upon completing his secondary education, Matvei Kagan, whose high intellectual calibre was later noted by all who knew him, went to Germany with the intention of studying philosophy at a university there. His teachers were Hermann Cohen, Paul Natorp, and Ernst Cassirer, as well as the renowned Wundt and Nicolai Hartmann, who had not yet become famous. By the time he returned to Russia Kagan was a convinced Neo-Kantian with a doctorate from Marburg University. He was glad to find new friends in Nevel, and they were glad to meet him. Their acquaintance was to prove important for the whole of their lives. Pasternak, who studied under Cohen in Marburg in 1912, wrote with rapture in *Safe Conduct*:

> the Marburg school of philosophy had two special features that won me over. First of all it was original. It dug everything down to the foundations and it built upon clear ground. [...] The Marburg school did not suffer from any terminological inertia and it turned back to primary sources, that is, to the authentic signatures left by thought in the history of science. [...]
>
> A second feature of the Marburg school derived directly from the first and consisted in its discriminating and exacting approach to the legacy of history. (Pasternak 1986 [1929–31], 40–41)

In the small town of Nevel Bakhtin, Pumpianskii and Kagan formed the nucleus of a short-lived domestic philosophy seminar referred to by contemporaries as "Kantian". By 1920–21 the only seminar participants remaining in Nevel were apparently Bakhtin and Kagan. Then Kagan left to take up a teaching post in the newly established Orel University. Bakhtin moved first to Vitebsk, then to Leningrad. Kagan set up home in Moscow, making occasional trips to Leningrad but, because of professional commitments, unable to see his old friends with any frequency. The ties between them grew weaker — although in 1929 my mother and father both played an active part, alongside their old friend Mariia Iudina, in the campaign to save Bakhtin from being sent to the Solovki hard-labour camp.

But Bakhtin and my father did not actually meet again until many years later, in 1936 and 1937. I was a child, and all I knew about Bakhtin was that he was someone my father was extremely fond of, and that my father always remembered Bakhtin was in exile and needed to be helped. I also knew that I was not to tell any of this to people outside the family. I remember their meeting in the summer of 1936 very well. We were reading Gogol′'s *Dead Souls* aloud: "Rus′, whither racest thou? Answer me. She does not answer." The doorbell rang, my father went to open the door and was away for a long time. I went after him, impatient to know what was delaying him. My father and a stranger were standing in a silent, tearful embrace on the landing of our communal apartment. The stranger was Bakhtin. We had no telephone, so his arrival was unexpected.

Somebody say something on the jagged stairs!

My father and Bakhtin met daily during that time. It was the same in the summer of 1937. Fifteen years on the two men's common interests and mutual affection were reaffirmed. Their meeting in 1937 turned out to be their last. At the end of December that year my father died as a result of an angina attack. He was 48. When Bakhtin, in violation of residence laws, came to say his last farewell to his old friend, he literally could not tear himself away from the papers which were still on my father's desk. My mother and I do not know what lay behind this intense interest. Perhaps it was a wish to learn what it was they had not had time to speak about... These were terrible days. From the mid-1920s my father had been working on economics and studying the USSR's energy resources. By the 1930s he was a well-known specialist in this field. Had he lived longer he would undoubtedly have been arrested, and we can only thank God that he died at home and did not fall into the hands of the state criminals. In his letters to my mother, who as a geologist was often away on expeditions, he would make terse reference to the trials that were going on, saying that he was reminded of Dostoevsky's *The Possessed*, Leskov's *At Daggers Drawn*, and Shakespeare's histories, and speak of his torment at his isolation, of being unable to participate in life, by which he meant to live. After his last meeting with Bakhtin, on the latter's advice he began to write down his ideas about Pushkin's poetry in the hope of publishing an article to mark the centenary of the poet's birth in 1837. Many, many years later, thanks to the efforts of Sergei Bocharov, his notes for the article were able to be published. Bakhtin wrote the "in-house reader's report" required by the publisher. In it he wrote that the impression made by Kagan's work was "refreshing". True, the Sovetskii pisatel′ (Soviet Writer) publishing house did change the title from "Motifs of Tragic Doubt in Pushkin" ("Motivy tragicheskogo nedoumeniia u Pushkina") to "Pushkin's Narrative Poems" (see Kagan 1974 [1937]). It was thought that there could be no doubt, especially tragic doubt, in Pushkin. Of course it is unfortunate that not all my father's thoughts were written down. Bakhtin insisted that I search more carefully and read my father's papers more thoroughly, as he assumed there should be notes not just about the Southern poems, but also about *Eugene Onegin*, because that was the subject of their last conversation... Alas, there are no notes about *Eugene Onegin* among my father's papers. Nor are there any notes about "A Scene from Faust", although a number of his friends recalled him reading this to them, and saying "some very interesting things".

But what happened *before* their last meeting in 1937?

We still have a copy of the Gospels given to my father in Nevel in 1918 by Boris Zubakin, who was shot in 1938 (Bakhtin admired Zubakin's poetry, and shortly before his death recited some of it to me and my. mother from memory). The inscription on the book reads:

Ancient legends are not myth.
The Lord and the world — all is semper idem.
Like Moses from Mount Horeb
We see the Promised Land.

Forgiving sorrowful mistakes
We have hatred for no person.
And, standing on the summit of mountains,
We see a council of ecumenical joy!

This poem stands apart from the rest of Zubakin's poetry. What is noteworthy is the repetition of "we", the juxtaposition of the Lord and the world, the sense that "we" are as it were called by God and able to see the future. The final lines recall what my father said so often about the essential meaning of history lying in its goal… "But the goal itself remains transcendent."

Before the poem comes Zubakin's dedication "To my Friend and Brother…"

In one of the statements made during his criminal investigation Bakhtin wrote that in an essay on Scheler he had spoken about confession: "Confession, according to Scheler, is a revelation of self before the other, making social ('discourse') something with an impulse towards its own asocial, extra-discursive limit ('sin') which was an isolated, uneliminated foreign body in the individual's inner life" (Konkin 1991, 3). Several years earlier, in 1925, my father wrote in a letter that in his view the fundamental conflict of Pushkin's narrative poem *The Robber Brothers* arose from the fact that it contained a confession. A confession of a brother to people who know nothing of brotherhood, to "the inter-national rag-tag of the rootless…" It is easy to imagine that during the Civil War and in the first years of the Revolution it was not only the Nevel circle which found a subject for deliberation and discussion in brotherhood and fratricidal feuding, retribution and confession, and repentance. Zubakin wrote "To my Friend and Brother", with capital letters; he was a Rosicrucean, and for him these words were charged with special significance. Bakhtin used to recall how Zubakin, who was very different from him and my father, would say to them "I'll tend the stove and fetch water: you talk! Just talk!"

Bakhtin probably knew my father's article on the death of Hermann Cohen. Although it was published when Kagan had moved to Moscow, it was written in 1918, and it is highly likely that the ideas it puts forward on ethics and aesthetics were discussed in Nevel. My father wrote: "In order to be autonomous, aesthetics must also have its own clear and particular *type of consciousness* [...] What is essential is not only *distinctiveness* in the objective idea of beauty, but also a methodological grounding of its *particular type* of consciousness" (Kagan 1920 [1918], 119). It was the distinctiveness and the particularity of the object of his argument that became the principal focus of his attention.

In March 1921 Bakhtin wrote to Kagan in Orel:

> Unfortunately it must be acknowledged that you are destined to remain isolated in Russia for a long time yet, and the best you can hope for is to find respect, but precious little understanding or sympathy. Absurd though it may seem, in Russia even "philosophy" is understood in a way that bears very little resemblance to the way you understand it. This is true not just in the case of ordinary people, but of our professional philosophers as well... (Bakhtin 1992 [1921], 67)

In a work by Bakhtin dating from the early 1920s and later published under the title "Toward a Philosophy of the Act" there is a passage which seems to offer a further gloss on these words:

> One can and should acknowledge that in the domain of the special tasks it sets itself modern philosophy (and Neo-Kantianism in particular) has obviously attained great heights and has been able, finally, to work out perfectly scientific methods (something that postitivism, in all its varieties, including pragmatism, was unable to do). Our time deserves to be given full credit for bringing philosophy closer to the ideal of a scientific philosophy.

Bakhtin continues:

> But this scientific philosophy can only be a specialized philosophy, i.e., a philosophy of the various domains of culture and their unity in the form of a theoretical transcription from within the objects of cultural creation and the immanent law of their development. And that is why this theoretical philosophy cannot pretend to being a first philosophy, that is, a teaching *not* about unitary cultural creation, but about unitary once-occurrent Being-as-event. Such a first philosophy does not exist, and even the paths leading to its creation seem to be forgotten. Hence the profound dissatisfaction with modern philosophy on the part of those who think participatively [...] (TPA, 19)

Any attempt to recreate the conversations which took place in a town referred to jokingly by the parties to them as "our Marburg", to surmise their thoughts, will be greatly assisted by hitherto unknown works by my father, such as his article "Sociology and the Individual" ("Sotsiologiia i lichnost′"), written in late 1918, and his "On the Course of History", begun in 1920 and forming part of his study "How is History Possible?" ("Kak vozmozhna istoriia?").[2] (The problem of "the course of history" interested Kagan as a problem in systematic philosophy.) Also noteworthy is his 1922 lecture "The Two Aspirations of Art" ("Dva ustremleniia iskusstva"); the fragment "On the Problem of Sculpture" ("K probleme skul′ptury"); and a number of other items which date from the period when Bakhtin was writing his predominantly philosophical works. Knowledge of Kagan's works will give some sense of the context of Bakhtin's (see also the article in this volume by Ruth Coates).

Before saying anything about these unknown works, I must make clear from the outset that they were not prepared for publication by their author, but are often no more than rough drafts and fragments... Mandelstam once referred to fragments as "precious scraps", since often they "end precisely where continuity is most wanted" (Mandelstam 1979a [1915], 85). In the conditions of our Russian reality (as Bakhtin put it, "beneath this unfree sky" (Bocharov 1994, 1012)) it is an occasion for celebration that despite this history and this reality fragments have been preserved in family archives.

One further "warning". Those who are familiar with Matvei Kagan's published work cannot fail to have noticed the complexity of their treatment of issues which are already complex enough in themselves. Anastasiia Tsvetaeva heard my father speaking in Berdiaev's seminar in early 1922, did not understand his paper, and said so to Zubakin, who was also present. He replied: "That's hardly surprising! He thinks in ancient Hebrew, translates it into German, and says it in Russian! But you should listen to him! He is the John the Evangelist of our times!" Aleksei Losev, who knew my father well at the State Academy for the Arts, and gave him copies of all his books, once said to me: "Matvei Isaevich could not be a great scholar. He was too good a person for that. These days a scholar must not see a great many things, and he was not capable of that..."

It is not my intention to summarize, and certainly not to offer any interpretation of, the works I have mentioned, to compare them with the works of Bakhtin, Pumpianskii, Voloshinov and Medvedev, or of other German and Russian philosophers. My hope is that works by my father which have lain hidden for many years will be published in the foreseeable future. When that happens, apart from anything else it will become clear how densely his works are written. It is because of this density that it is difficult to select separate, self-contained extracts which would offer a rapid introduction to a given work. But there are some what might be called recurrent ideas, differently elaborated in different works, which it is probably worth discussing. For example, the idea that "humanity in its historical existence does not always live all questions of culture, although all these questions are present in history in one form or another...", and "the so-called eternal problems are destined to be the object of constant interest". It was Kagan's view that "all problems exert some degree of historical influence". He wrote that history was in the goal, that "history does not only *happen*, it is posited, it becomes". He wrote: "The system of historical being will always be open, becoming. Outside of *process* historical being is unthinkable. In accordance with the goal, there will be different directions within this process." Kagan considered that Antiquity, the Middle Ages, the Renaissance, and the Reformation did not just designate particular periods, but were constantly present in history as something like structurally recurring mythologemes. He further spoke of how particular interest on the part of any one party, or in any one moment, could only lead to claims to have solved or posed the question of the course of history, how particular interest in any one of its lines could shift "into the sphere of competence of the unity of the whole path of the systematic process of history". When I came across the remark in this text that "in a systematic study of the course of history it will not be possible to ignore the significance of religion for history", I remembered the famous lawyer I.D. Levin's account to me of something said by my father during discussion of a lecture by Semen Frank in November 1921: "the Bible is more important for the historian than Herodotus!" "The goal is, as it were, justified in the striving towards the immanent historical purpose which is man's historical duty." In "On the Course of History" Kagan wrote: "Again and again we begin to live historically. This is a process open to constantly renewed possibilities... In reality, history is always beginning."

Alongside the undoubted humanism of all Kagan's works (whether their subject be economics, science, or art), alongside the constant awareness of human responsibility, we find our attention drawn to his discussion of the individual, both in "Sociology and the Individual" and in "On the Course of History", where he notes that "the phenomenon of history can never be located outside of a direct relation to man, to people", or when he says that man is a historical and social being whose goal is not merely egoistic, but socio-cultural, and that the individual in his unmediated present life is an altruistic individual. All the works listed above say a great deal about anticipation of the goal of history, about involvement in a world of higher aims. In a discussion of economics Kagan writes: "In economic life we encounter the phenomenon of *need*... Economic need cannot be said to be the purposefulness of anticipation of a historically obligatory (*dolzhnoi*) goal." I would also like to quote an extract from "Sociology and the Individual", written in Nevel almost immediately after Kagan's return to Russia from Germany:

> Marx's assertion that social labour fundamentally defines social use value is profoundly social in its sociological truth. It is symptomatic that, despite his expressed disdain for idealism and ethics, in his foundation of history Marx defines value not by labour understood generally as work, not by the work of a machine or a natural element, or even of any living creature other than man. In Marx, value is defined by human labour. Surplus value too is calculated only in terms of human labour. This is not to reproach Marx, but to note a positive aspect of his thinking.

In what reads like a conclusion of this characterization of Marx, Kagan writes: "He is far more idealistic than is generally accepted..." Kagan shows that Marxism was wrong to include culture in the economic sphere, thus making this sphere much too broad.

"On the Course of History" also discusses the concepts of culture, price, value, merit, and needs. Kagan singles out three needs: consumption, cognition, and love. The course of history is measured by the aspirations of these needs. The system of prices does not govern the system of values, but the system of prices forms a part of other systems:

> The object of our consumption may be in itself a subject for those who are able to belong, apart from their other being, to a world of a different sort — to the being of elemental existence. The product of consumption is only a means. More precisely, only an object of economic consumption is a means of history, a means of cultural human life. All the rest is more than a means...

Love is a very important category for Kagan. Love is what Bakhtin refers to as "act", active participation in the world of other people here and now:

> Interaction between people is itself a need which in itself is, as it were, teleological... Subjectively, we call this need, teleological in itself, for interaction between people love. [...] The more objective love in the subjectiveness of its necessity, the more directly purposeful beauty there is in it. But love is more than need, for it is also action.
>
> The past can be judged only for the future. [...] The other's past should be a past beloved by me... past cultures should be loved. Their death and demise are not a matter of indifference to me. Neither the *Iliad* nor Jeremiah's lament would have come about without this love for what is dying. In art death

> [*gibel′*] itself ceases to be Death. Nor does the death of one we love signify the death of love. Dante knew this better than anyone.

And, as though suddenly realizing that he had digressed, Kagan continued: "But here we are not in the field of art, even when it comes into contact with religious motifs. We are in the field of the methodology of human history and culture, the problem of decline in the course of history."

In *Safe Conduct* Pasternak wrote: "In Marburg they knew history to perfection. [...] In Marburg they looked at history through both Hegelian eyes — that is, in a brilliantly generalised fashion, but at the same time within the exact limits of commonsense plausibility" (Pasternak 1986 [1929–31], 41).

Kagan's writings on art are also important. Here we need to turn to "On the Two Aspirations of Art" and the fragment "The Problem of Sculpture". It is interesting that, when he speaks of love as action, as a need to overcome the opposition of the inner to the outer, of the subject to the object, Kagan moves to what was for him one of the most important problems, that of art and beauty:

> The work of art lives inwardly by love. It hangs in a gallery or is in an apparently passive state somewhere, but, being a work of art, lives inwardly by the need for love. And we subsequently extend this love to the whole of the external world in its elemental existence. We fill even products of consumption with the quality of beauty.

For Kagan art forms part of the unity of human culture and can be understood within the problem of systematic philosophy. "The Two Aspirations of Art" has the subtitle "Form and Content; Subjectlessness and Plot" ("Forma i soderzhanie; bespredmetnost′ i siuzhetnost′"). The paper begins with a critique of the well-known expression "tastes differ" [*na vkus i tsvet tovarishchei net*]. If we agree with this, it will be impossible to establish the identity of art. The world for Kagan is always open, always not ready, always not consummated. But art, and only art, brings about consummation. Not consummation of everything as a whole, but in the middle, in relation to the given moment:

> The consummatedness and identity of the moment in that which is concrete, the constant moment of life, is not only a *process*, not only a *path of consummation* open only to the future. It is an already open, ready, internal identity. The concrete facts of all spheres of being and culture other than art do not possess such an identity.

Nothing possesses such a degree of concreteness, such constancy, and such reality as the life of art, as a work of art.

What reigns here is connection, here the indivisibility of the Platonic eros is constant. Absolute identity, constancy of immanence — this is art.

From the objective angle the meaning of a work of art is termed *beauty*. From the other, subjective angle it must be defined as *love*. Neither angle is abstract. They are not external, not extensive. It can be said that artistic life is the beauty of love and the love of beauty. [...] *The being of art is the being of beauty. Its reason is the reason of love.*

This recalls Pasternak's

All-powerful god of love,
All-powerful god of details...

This aesthetics does not resemble, it would seem, either classical or formalist aesthetics. Both "The Two Aspirations of Art" and "The Problem of Sculpture" contain discussions of reflection: "It is not a matter of life being reflected in art. This is a mere banality which commits us to nothing. The question is, what kind of reflection is it? If you like, it is a matter of the mirror, which in this case is aesthetics." Kagan writes: "The aesthetic mirror of the meaning should prompt us to see that the reflection of reality comes from art. From art to life, and not the other way round." This quality of art is termed by Kagan the "task of purity", which is carried out by the creating artist. The concept of "purity" becomes clearer in the light of Kagan's thinking about myth, which he understands as "the anticipated consummatedness of an episode with eternal factual meaning". "Consummatedness of plot" is something like what the Formalists called *fabula*, something like "story". This conception of myth is also present in Kagan's philosophy of culture, in his aesthetics, and in his philosophy of history. "Myth is the principle and fact of a constant creative origin in anticipation of the revelation of the future in the present and the inclusion of the past in a constantly revealed eternal present, which lives by the future." Kagan's discussion of festival as the element of art required by life is interesting in this regard. "The festival is not an idle matter" [*Prazdnik delo ne prazdnoe*], he writes punningly. Art is a festival of life and a celebration of being endowed with life. "In the festival there is plenitude of achievement and of the pure force of life, something that is not given either to theory or to historical life [*byt*]." Kagan opposes this kind of festival to "being beset by idleness in the absence of festival in life, defiance of the mundane in the absence of the everyday existence of a living cultural structure". He ends his lecture, read in Soviet

Moscow in the early 1920s, with a quotation from Blok's *The Twelve* (*Dvenadtsat'*, 1918):

Oh, what a blizzard, Saviour.

But, having touched on these themes, I would like to conclude with a different quotation. In his "Toward the Philosophical Bases of the Human Sciences", a preliminary version of "Toward a Methodology for the Human Sciences", Bakhtin wrote: "The role of memory in this perpetual transformation of the past. The cognition and understanding of the past in its unfinalizability (in its non-coincidence with itself). The moment of fearlessness in cognition. [...] The corresponding moment of the humility of the cognizer" (Bakhtin 1979, 410). In my case there is also the desire to follow the commandment which requires that we honour our parents.

NOTES

1. It was of Annenskii that Mandelstam wrote that he "showed us what an organic poet should be: a ship could be built entirely from foreign planks, but it must have its own form" (Mandelstam 1979b [1922], 158).
2. "On the Course of History", which is about 60 typewritten pages long, is in Russian, and may be a new version of "Vom Gang der Geschichte", a work of 15 printer's pages which was written in German in 1915–16 but which has not survived. Part of "How is History Possible" was published: see Kagan 1921 [1919].

WORKS CITED

Bakhtin, M.M. 1979. "K filosofskim osnovam gumanitarnykh nauk" cited in notes to "K metodologii gumanitarnykh nauk", in *Estetika slovesnogo tvorchestva* (Moscow: Iskusstvo), 409–411.

________. 1992 [1921]. [Letter to M.I. Kagan of March 1921], cited in full in Iu.M. Kagan 1992, 67–69.

Bocharov, Sergey 1994. "Conversations with Bakhtin", in *PMLA*, 109/5, 1009–1024.

Kagan, Iu.M. 1992. "O starykh bumagakh iz semeinogo arkhiva: M.M. Bakhtin i M.I. Kagan", in *Dialog. Karnaval. Khronotop* (Vitebsk), 1, 60–88.

Kagan, M.I. 1920 [1918]. "German Kogen (4 iiulia 1842 g. – 4 aprelia 1918 g.)", in *Nauchnye izvestiia. Sbornik vtoroi: Filosofiia–Literatura–Iskusstvo* (Moscow: Akademicheskii tsentr Narkomprosa), 110–124.

________. 1921 [1919]. "Kak vozmozhna istoriia? (Iz osnovnykh problem filosofii istorii)", in *Zapiski Orlovskogo gosudarstvennogo universiteta*, 1, 137–192.

________. 1974 [1937]. "O pushkinskikh poemakh", in S. Mashinskii (ed.), *V mire Pushkina: Sbornik statei* (Moscow: Sovetskii pisatel'), 85–119.

Konkin, S. 1991. "Arest i prigovor: Novye materialy o M.M. Bakhtine", in *Sovetskaia Mordoviia* (26 March), 3.

Mandelstam [Mandel'shtam], O. 1973 [1937]. "What shall I do with myself, now it's January?" ["Kuda mne det'sia v etom ianvare"], in *Selected Poems*, tr. C. Brown and W.S. Merwin (London &c.: Oxford University Press, 1973), 90–91; Russian in *Sobranie sochinenii v chetyrekh tomakh*, ed. G.P. Struve and B.A. Filippov, vol. 1 (Moscow: Terra, 1991), 242–243.

________. 1979a [1915]. "Peter Chaadaev", in *The Complete Critical Prose and Letters*, ed. Jane Gary Harris, tr. Harris and Constance Link (Ann Arbor: Ardis), 83–89.

________. 1979b [1922]. "A Letter about Russian Poetry", in *The Complete Critical Prose and Letters*, ed. Jane Gary Harris, tr. Harris and Constance Link (Ann Arbor: Ardis), 156–159.

Pasternak, B. 1986 [1929–31]. *Safe Conduct*, in *The Voice of Prose*, ed. C. Barnes (Edinburgh: Polygon, 1986), 21–108.

Polivanov, M.K. 1990. "Tainaia svoboda", in *Literaturnoe obozrenie*, 1, 103–109.

TWO OF A SMALL FRATERNITY? POINTS OF CONTACT AND DEPARTURE IN THE WORK OF BAKHTIN AND KAGAN UP TO 1924

Ruth Coates, University of London

> The recognition of the holiness of culture may appear in small fraternities. There must be many of them; they will be neither Jewish nor Christian, but may lean towards both Judaism and Christianity... Their way is hard.
>
> (Kagan, JCC, 235)

There is now enough documentary evidence available to us of the relationship between M.M. Bakhtin and M.I. Kagan to show that there was a close personal bond between them which extended to their working relationship (see Iu.M. Kagan 1992, and the articles by Iudif' Kagan and Nikolai Nikolaev in the present volume). It is known that Kagan was deeply influenced by Neo-Kantian philosophy, as well as by his Jewish heritage, and that Bakhtin likewise had a lively interest in both Kant and questions of religion. How far, then, can we speak of an affinity of world-view with respect to the two thinkers? In what exactly did this affinity consist, and where, if at all, did it break down? We can of course only adequately answer these questions by analysing the two thinkers' surviving publications.

In this essay I shall refer to three texts by Kagan: "Essay in a Systematic Assessment of Religion in Time of War" (1916, hereafter SAR); "How Is History Possible?" (1919, published 1921, hereafter HHP), and "Judaism in Cultural Crisis" (1923, published 1988, hereafter JCC), and three by Bakhtin: "Art and Answerability" (AA, 1919), "Toward a Philosophy of the Act" (TPA, 1919–21, first published 1986), and "Author and Hero in Aesthetic Activity" (AH, c. 1920–23, first published 1979). The last two may have been written at any time between 1919 and 1924. I take 1924 as a cut-off point because Kagan ceased work in philosophy in that year, while Bakhtin's work also takes a new direction as he enters the late 1920s. (All translations from the Russian are my own.)

My argument is in four stages. Firstly, I outline the key conceptual oppositions shared by the two writers and the various ways in which they are employed; secondly, I show the similarities and differences in Bakhtin and Kagan's attempts to draw these oppositions into a unity; thirdly, I compare and contrast the threats perceived by both to the realization of this unity; and finally, I sketch their respective correctives to these threats, suggesting that it is here that Bakhtin and Kagan most significantly part company.

Bakhtin and Kagan employ in different ways the same set of basic oppositions as a framework for their thinking. Prominent among these is the given/posited (*dan/zadan*) opposition, characterized on the one hand by closure and stasis, on the other by openness and process. Kagan acknowledges two types of Being, of which natural being, the object of the exact sciences, exhibits all the properties of givenness, and historical being, escaping the causality of Nature by virtue of its origins in creative reason, those of positedness (HHP, 153). History is born out of Nature in the struggle of the posited to overcome the resistance of the given. Bakhtin has a more complex understanding of the given/posited dichotomy, applying it to divisions *within* the realm of human history and culture. Thus he notes a general distinction between the "given" product of cultural activity, which develops autonomously within an abstract intellectual realm, and the activity itself, which, since it is rooted in real time and space (Bakhtin's "open event of being"), is supremely "posited" (TPA, 1/83 and *passim*). The human subject displays both "given" and "posited" modes in his or her situation in Being, depending on the architectonic viewpoint in operation at any one time. In my nature as subject, in the I-for-myself, I am incomplete and developing, whereas in my capacity as object, as other, I am finalized and whole. We notice here Bakhtin's preference for the individual, personal and relational over against Kagan's more abstract, large-scale focus.

The given/posited opposition is developed by both thinkers to include their close parallels, passivity/activity and being/obligation. Kagan sees activity as an exclusively positive, passivity an exclusively negative concept. For Bakhtin, typically more subtle than this, passive and active, given and posited, interact with each other in a kind of dance of give and take, positive and negative. The value each receives depends on how it is being perceived. Thus, for example, in "Author and Hero" he insists that our self-perception as posited beings is always interpreted negatively, "in tones of repentance", and yet he is clear that process, growth and incompleteness are essential and positive aspects of being. We can only create as active beings, but peace and joy are only fully available to us when we are passive (AH, 136/120). Kagan and Bakhtin alike associate being, or "is", with givenness, and obligation, or "ought", with positedness. In "Systematic Assessment" Kagan states that all historical being functions according to the principle of Ought (*das Sollen*). Similarly, in "How Is History Possible?" he maintains that history "is conceived not in what is but in what ought to be" (HHP, 160). In "Author and Hero" our self-experience is characterized by a strong sense of obligation (*dolzhenstvovanie*) and striving ahead, whereas as objects of aesthetic contemplation we dwell in the realm of "is" (AH, 120–121/106).

Finally, there is the opposition between the immanent and the transcendent poles of reality. This is a pivotal distinction in Kagan's work, which holds that history, though immanent in the world and developing immanently, exists only by virtue of the Transcendent, the "goal" towards which all of history and culture strives (HHP, 157). Although transcendence in this sense is absent from "Toward a Philosophy of the Act" altogether, it plays an important role in "Author and Hero", where it appears in its impersonal form as the "absolute semantic future", towards which human selves are necessarily oriented in exactly the same way as history is oriented towards the goal in Kagan. Everything in us which is posited strives towards the absolute semantic future which alone can provide the ultimate aesthetic justification for our lives (AH, 121/106–107). This future is not an immanent extension of our lives but is located outside of time and space. In both Bakhtin and Kagan the Transcendent is also interpreted theistically, as we shall see later.

The common and overriding task of the two thinkers may be said to be the discovery of principles whereby the oppositions outlined above may be understood as a unity. Kagan seeks a foundation common to the historical and natural spheres of reality which can unite them organically, not merely mechanically or formally: "This unmediated-actual foundation will *as it were, lead a given sphere of reality out of itself.* It will strive to step across the limits or borders of the given reality" (HHP, 143). As a principle of historical reality this foundation will be immanent in history, and as a principle underpinning *all* reality it will be transcendent to it, thus embracing the poles of both the given/posited and the immanent/transcendent oppositions. Bakhtin shows a similar concern when he writes "the whole is called mechanical if its separate elements are joined together in time and space only by an external link, and not penetrated by the inner unity of meaning" (AA, 1/5). In "Toward a Philosophy of the Act" he again asks how one may reconcile the worlds of culture and life:

> [...] facing each other there are two worlds, absolutely not communicating with each other and impervious one to the other: the world of culture and the world of life — the unique world in which we create, cognize, contemplate, have lived, and die; the world in which the act of our activity is made objective and the world in which that act uniquely and actually flows, is accomplished. (TPA, 2/82–83)

What is needed is a single plane where the two faces of this Janus can define each other reciprocally in relation to an overarching unity.

The mediating principle proves to be similarly conceived by both philosophers, sharing common ground in the notion of human activity. For Kagan the very possibility of history is contingent upon the phenomenon of labour (*trud*), which, though rooted in natural being as physical labour, carries humanity into historical being as the common denominator of all forms of cultural endeavour: "In this respect it is correct to say that all of history rests on labour; all of history in its reality technically and culturally rests upon and is set in motion by work" (HHP, 176). Moreover, labour provides the sought-after link between immanence and transcendence, serving as the vehicle transporting us beyond this world to the realm of the Transcendent: "labour leads history, and reality generally, out of the reality of this world" (HHP, 180). Kagan stresses that the centrality of labour should not mislead us into making it an end in itself; labour is the means to the end of unity and harmony, which can only come from the Transcendent. However, since it is the indispensable mediator of unity to culture, Kagan characterizes labour as holy. Finally, work gives unity also to the personality as it draws together all the aspects of our natural/animal and cultural experience: "Work is the objectivization of our value and the merit of each and every personality, individual, man, in God" (HHP, 190).

If for Kagan history is the sum of human activity, then for Bakhtin an individual life may be seen as a complicated deed. And as for Kagan labour leads humanity out of natural and into cultural being, and out of immanent into transcendent reality, so for Bakhtin my life is an act of entering, or joining, the wider event of being: "[The world] is found by me insofar as I go out of myself in my deed–vision, deed–thought, deed–affair (*postupok–delo*)" (TPA, 57/124). The thoughts, feelings and experiences which together constitute my life are all in their turn deeds and act out the drama of entering life on a small scale. But the deed not only joins the subject to the world, it also has the potential to reconcile the products of culture with life. Bakhtin devotes twenty pages to the refutation of the all-pervasive assumption of his day that the key to the unity of culture and life may be found within one of the branches of the former, be it ethics or aesthetics or psychology. He asserts that, far from being able to incorporate life into theory, theory must be seen as only one feature of life. It is the deed alone in its performative aspect which knows and possesses life as a whole:

> the deed pulls together, relates and resolves in one single and *already final context* both meaning and fact, the general and the individual, the real and the ideal, for everything enters into its responsible motivation; in the deed there lies the way out of mere possibility into *singularity once and for all*. (TPA, 29/103)

Lastly, in my responsible action I hold all oppositions together *in my person* without eradicating them:

> I find myself in being, and I actively participate in it; I partake of both given and posited: my uniqueness is given, but at the same time it is only insofar as it is actually realized by me as uniqueness, it is always in the act, in the deed, that is, posited; both being and obligation: I am actual, irreplaceable, and therefore am obliged to realize my uniqueness. (TPA, 41/113)

We have here, then, three kinds of unity in the deed: firstly, I am united with the world; secondly, the theoretical world is drawn into the event of being; and thirdly, in acting the human agent unites in his or her person the given and posited aspects of reality.

It follows from their conception of Being as divided and in need of unification that both Kagan and Bakhtin understand the universe to be flawed. A whole world must be fought for, with the real possibility of failure. Kagan perceives this drama in consistently theological terms; for him history has "the task of overcoming the curse of the Fall" (HHP, 137). Though he never states explicitly what the Fall has resulted in and how it is to be overcome, it is implicit in every aspect of his analysis of history. In striving towards the Transcendent humanity is looking for the restoration of a lost harmony. The Transcendent is God, Providence, the Creator, Holiness, a reality of a different order lying beyond the reach of human culture. This task of overcoming the Fall depends for its success, however, on the recognition by humanity of its fundamental state of dependence on the Transcendent and its willing submission to the pursuit of God through labour. In order for the pre-Fall harmonious relationship of the immanent with the Transcendent to be restored and maintained it is essential that we accept our limitations and commit ourselves to the pursuit of the goal. Thus humility and responsibility go hand in hand:

> The heroism of culture demands from us individual responsibility before culture and history in our work. This responsibility is conditional upon our assessing ourselves humbly as creatures in need. We accept our dependence in labour, in the fact that labour is inadequate in itself as a goal. Thus labour lays claim to an heroic responsibility, and makes a humble statement about its responsibility in need before culture and history. (HHP, 179)

Faith, for Kagan, is the belief that our endeavour is not in vain but does provide a route to God.

Since humanity is free also to reject its calling, there is a real danger that human progress may be halted, may even relapse into brute Nature. The central thesis of "Judaism in Cultural Crisis" is precisely that cultural crisis arises when humanity abandons its faith in the Transcendent and its understanding of history as progress towards a goal. The creative drive loses its impetus, disintegrates, and culture slumps back into natural inertia. In "Systematic Analysis" the phenomenon of war is explained in a similar way as an event which disrupts the development of history towards the ideal of the Good and places the ethical imperative itself under threat. Thus there are forces at work in being which directly oppose unity and harmony. "How Is History Possible?" suggests that the locus of this flaw in the universe is the rebellious human spirit. We may become proud of our cultural achievements and come to see them as an end in themselves: "culture and history may become self-sufficient. Under these circumstances the death of culture from self-sufficiency is possible" (HHP, 188). Where givenness is preferred to positedness, there is loss of meaning, and death.

Bakhtin likewise has an understanding of struggle based on responsibility, though, typically, he works it out on a more concrete and personal level. Because we are each uniquely situated in being (we have no "alibi in being", as Bakhtin puts it), we bear a unique responsibility towards it which we are free either to acknowledge or evade; hence the potential for tragedy: "it is possible to ignore activity and live by mere passivity, it is possible to attempt to prove one's alibi in being, it is possible to be a pretender (*samozvanets*). It is possible to deny one's *obligation-imposing uniqueness*" (TPA, 42/113). Bakhtin's description of the pretender bears a striking resemblance to Sartre's person living in bad faith. Knowing the way things are, he or she consciously rejects the consequences for him- or herself, and in doing so perpetuates the split between the world of perpetual theoretical possibility and the world of concrete historical reality. According to Bakhtin "the whole transcendental [?] unity of objective culture is in fact dark and elemental, cut off completely from the single and unique centre of responsible consciousness." Indeed, any clarity it may seem to possess when we declare it to be autonomous is derivative; it "shines by the borrowed light of our responsibility" (TPA, 30/104). Cultural crisis for Bakhtin is thus the result of the breakdown of responsible agency. The content and performance aspects of the deed are split, and once the product has been torn away from its ontological roots the spatio-temporal aspect of the deed degenerates into mere biological subjectivity — the "deed–drive", whereas everything of objective significance becomes located in the product. The situation then exists in which "we have summoned up the spectre of objective culture, which we are unable to exorcize" (TPA, 55–56/123). The world of givenness dominates and sterilizes the open event of being.

This existential tension receives a theological underpinning in "Author and Hero". Here harmony in Being is shown to be dependent both upon the responsible fulfilment of our aesthetic obligations towards others, for which we have God as the supreme role model, and upon the recognition of our incompleteness and consequent need of the aesthetic activity of others, ultimately of God, for our justification. The basis for these prerequisites is a model of aesthetic activity whereby the hero, the one observed, stands in *need* of the author, the observer, for the gracious provision of a total aesthetic perspective on him- or herself which the hero is incapable of achieving. God, according to this model, functions as the supreme, transcendent Author/Other who can comprehend us perfectly in time and space. In a passage strongly recalling Kagan, Bakhtin describes what he perceives as a tendency in Being towards the arrogant denial of one's existential state of dependence on the Transcendent:

> We may say that this is a Fall immanent in being, and experienced from within it: it lies in the tendency of being towards self-sufficiency; this is the internal self-contradiction of being [...] the self-condensed self-affirmation of being in defiance of the meaning that gave it birth (a breaking-away from its source) [...] (AH, 124/109)

The denial follows the same pattern found in Kagan and in "Toward a Philosophy of the Act" — a preference for the complacency of givenness over our natural, but more humbling and challenging, state of positedness. And just as in Kagan culture loses its coherence and ultimately dies when cut off from its transcendent goal, so for Bakhtin "to be for oneself means still to be forthcoming (*to cease being forthcoming, to prove to be already complete here, means to die spiritually*)" (AH, 123–124/109).

The fundamental differences in the religious-philosophical perspectives of Bakhtin and Kagan become apparent through a comparison of their suggested correctives to the potential tragedy of Being, which in turn flows from their respective conceptions of God. Kagan depersonalizes his God to such an extent that, in "Systematic Analysis", he asserts that God should be understood more as a principle than a personal Being, and His role as "guarantor" of human history and cultural activity as entirely functional:

> God should not exist for the sake of Heaven and not to preserve Himself as substance, but for the sake of human, material history and human culture. In this respect God is not supposed to have created Man, but rather he should exist in correlation with historical humanity. We should not speak of the substantial existence of God, but of a divine principle. (SAR, 36)

Indeed, the exercise of an ultimate guarantee proves to be His *only* role:

> God may never be ascribed other purposes; He acts as guarantor for humanity and in no other capacity. "Allah has no need to create any longer, we are creating his world." Humanity has created the world of moral culture. And this involves the creation of God also, the only God as guarantor of the world in its culture. (SAR, 50)

Religion and faith may likewise only legitimately assert themselves where gaps occur in times of moral crisis. Other areas of progress, such as science, law and politics, manage ordinarily quite well on their own and should not be interfered with (SAR, 53). Thus Kagan at once places limits on the role of the Transcendent and in some way makes it dependent in its nature upon the very creature whose existence it is supposed to safeguard. There is moreover no provision for communication between the realms of the immanent and the Transcendent except via the medium of labour. Though holiness is imparted to culture through labour it is very much contingent upon human initiative, human striving. The emphasis is everywhere on the effort of humanity to establish a link with God, and the whole is expressed throughout in abstract terms.

Kagan's view of the nature and role of the Divine is certainly rooted partly in the Jewish conception of God, partly in Neo-Kantian philosophy ("Systematic Analysis" contains multiple footnotes with cross-references to Natorp, Cohen and Cassirer). In "Author and Hero", on the other hand, Bakhtin both exhibits a trend away from a rationalistic Transcendent towards a more personalistic world conception and draws on Christian doctrine for his understanding of unity and wholeness in the universe. While God appears as the guarantor of all aesthetic activity in His capacity as Author of the universe (AH, 206/179), He is never reduced to a principle. Indeed it is His personhood with its emotional-volitional dimension which provides the model for human initiative in relationships. There is a persistent connection between aesthetic activity and love, the act of bestowing wholeness upon a person being described as one of self-sacrifice and gracious condescension, a gift of form given freely and without preconditions on the initiative of the transcendent Other. Thus the heroes of a tragedy are "saved and atoned for by an aesthetic salvation" (AH, 71/65), and my soul, my aesthetically finalized inner life, "descends on me as a blessing upon a sinner, as an unearned and unexpected gift" (AH, 101/90). Elsewhere the terms "absolution", "benediction" and "forgiveness" are employed to express the same phenomenon whereby we are rescued from the uncertainties of positedness not by ignoring or denying it — a partial and ultimately destructive "solution" — but by being justified in spite of it. That unity is ultimately vouchsafed by a God who acts selflessly in this way to affirm Being is a source of strength for human agents, strength which comes by faith.

Thus to the theological notions of need and dependence, faith and commitment, humility and transcendence, which he shares with Kagan, Bakhtin adds the language of grace along with a range of emotions from penitence through to love and joy. The same personalization of the universe and the reduction of the divide between Creator and creation which characterizes the Christian Gospel also makes Bakhtin's world-view both more vital and more optimistic than Kagan's. But perhaps the key theological concept which Kagan lacks and Bakhtin exploits to the full is that of the Incarnation. Whenever Christ is mentioned in Bakhtin's early work it is to put Him forward as a perfect model of the ideal which he is setting out. In "Toward a Philosophy of the Act" He is said to epitomize responsible existential awareness; His coming down to earth [?] is a "great symbol of activity" (TPA, 16/93). Above all His life shows how in order to sacrifice oneself fully, to be fully selfless, one must also assert oneself to the maximum possible extent (TPA, 48/118).

In "Author and Hero" Christ combines in Himself the two acts of self-effacement described in Russian Orthodox thought as "kenotic"; not only does He divest himself of His glory to appear in the world as a sacrifice for sins (the kenotic act traditionally ascribed to the Son), but He also acts out the Father's kenotic role whereby He effaces himself in the act of creation. This latter notion finds a clear parallel in Bakhtin's understanding of the nature of human aesthetic activity:

> This [...] is the external position of the author in relation to the hero, his loving self-elimination from the field of the hero's life, his clearing of the whole field of life for him and his being, the participatory understanding and completion of the event of his life by a cognitively and ethically impartial observer. (AH, 14–15/16)

Bakhtin conceives Christ as the most self-aware historical example of aesthetic activity, consciously dividing humanity into "himself, the lover, and others, the beloved, himself, the Saviour, and all the others, the saved, himself, the one who takes upon himself the burden of sin and atonement, and all the others, the ones set free from that burden and atoned for" (AH, 56/51–52).

However, Christ is much more for Bakhtin than a good example of authentic living. He also demonstrates in himself how two opposites may be brought harmoniously together; in Christ the transcendent God *becomes* immanent. Further, the Incarnation may, I believe, inform and theologically legitimate Bakhtin's consistent preference for the concrete world of human experience against abstract concepts, for what we may term an *incarnational* view of truth. In "Toward a Philosophy of the Act" Bakhtin lays great emphasis on the necessity for theoretical truth to be incorporated into spatio-temporal reality if it is to become living and binding upon individuals. The adjective he employs in describing the alternative is highly suggestive: "But it is possible to have an unincarnated thought, unincarnated action, an unincarnated, arbitrary life as empty possibility; life on the tacit [?] basis of one's alibi in being falls away into indifferent, rootless being" (TPA, 43/114). Even where he prefers the Slavic adjective *voploshchennyi* to *inkarnirovannyi*, the Christian connotation is unmistakeable. A living truth is an embodied truth, a Word made flesh.

Finally, Bakhtin's strong sense of values as rooted in relationships also echoes Christ. He disputes the ability and the right of a disembodied spirit to take up any axiological stance (TPA, 48/118), insisting that there are no such thing as abstract values, any more than there are abstract human beings: "there is no Man in general, there is I, there is a definite concrete other: my neighbour, my contemporary" (TPA, 47/117). In becoming Man, Christ saves God from the necessary neutrality of a disembodied consciousness and allows him to participate fully in the world. Thus Christ may be said literally to embody many of the ideas closest to Bakhtin's heart.

What conclusions, then, can be drawn from their texts about Kagan and Bakhtin's intellectual relationship? In general terms, we may say that they employ a range of identical concepts with a view to the same end of establishing the framework for a unified and harmonious universe. Both perceive this universe to be in a state of becoming, heading towards an absolute ideal and yet permeated with struggle and failure. Kagan and Bakhtin alike interpret being in a religious way, and moreover monotheistically, embracing general concepts such as the Fall, human dependence (as opposed to autonomy), free will, and salvation. Bakhtin, however, differs from Kagan in significant ways, not least in the matter of philosophical style: Kagan displays a consistent concern for method and is rigorously and severely systematic, in both the broad and the narrow sense of this word, whereas Bakhtin's looser style reveals a mind less concerned with uniform presentation than with harmonizing diverse ideas and material. Both Kagan's style and the content of his work testify to the overwhelming extent to which his several years of direct exposure to Neo-Kantian philosophy in Germany influenced his thought. Unlike Bakhtin, he shows no desire to break away from the tradition in which he was educated, and is quite candid about this, openly acknowledging his debt to his teachers in his essays: especially interesting in this regard is his personal obituary to the philosopher Hermann Cohen (1920). Bakhtin, it is known, was a classicist by training and largely self-taught in contemporary philosophy. We may surmise that this left him more freedom to give rein to what seems to be his natural inclination away from the abstract to the concrete, the cognitive to the emotional-volitional, and the impersonal to the personal and relational. These preferences, I suggest, largely flow from his specifically Christian outlook, with its strong historical basis and stress on relationship. In particular, the life and death of Christ illustrate, and indeed realize, the vision of perfect relatedness developed so earnestly by Bakhtin in his early work.

WORKS CITED

Kagan, Iu.M. 1992. "O starykh bumagakh iz semeinogo arkhiva: M.M. Bakhtin i M.I. Kagan", in *Dialog. Karnaval. Khronotop* (Vitebsk), 1, 60–88.

Kagan, M.I. 1916 [SAR]. "Versuch einer systematischen Beurteilung der Religion in Kriegeszeit", in *Archiv fuer systematische Philosophie*, 31–53.

_______. 1920 [1918]. "German Kogen (4 iiulia 1842 g. – 4 aprelia 1918 g.)", in *Nauchnye izvestiia. Sbornik vtoroi: Filosofiia–Literatura–Iskusstvo* (Moscow: Akademicheskii tsentr Narkomprosa), 110–124.

_______. 1921 [1919] [HHP]. "Kak vozmozhna istoriia? (Iz osnovnykh problem filosofii istorii)", in *Zapiski Orlovskogo gosudarstvennogo universiteta*, 1, 137–192.

_______. 1988 [1923] [JCC]. "Evreistvo v krizise kul'tury", in *Minuvshee* (Paris), 6, 229–236.

THE NEVEL SCHOOL OF PHILOSOPHY (BAKHTIN, KAGAN AND PUMPIANSKII) BETWEEN 1918 AND 1925: MATERIALS FROM PUMPIANSKII'S ARCHIVES

Nikolai Nikolaev, St Petersburg State University Library

Now that all Bakhtin's early works have been published it is possible to trace the development of his ideas and terminology throughout his career, and to define, through typological comparisons, the indisputably original place occupied by his philosophy among twentieth-century theories. But for all its undoubted originality, it is equally certain that, as it emerged, Bakhtin's philosophy had historical connections with specific trends in European and Russian philosophy of the first third of the century. We are therefore faced with the task of establishing the sources, influences, and parallels bearing on Bakhtin's philosophy, or, to recall Borges's essay, of seeking "Kafka's precursors", since to date there have been only very general, and excessively vague, surmisals about the origins of Bakhtin's philosophy.

Some clarification may be provided by a detailed examination of the activities of the Nevel School of philosophy, to which Bakhtin belonged. "The Nevel School" is not a conjectural title, but one which may have been used by the School's own members. Ivan Kanaev recalled Ivan Sollertinskii, a pupil of Bakhtin and of Lev Pumpianskii, referring to himself as a member of "the Nevel School of philosophers". The Nevel School was in existence, with interruptions, from 1918, when its principal members (Bakhtin, Matvei Kagan, and Pumpianskii) came together in Nevel, most probably until 1927, when the group's regular gatherings, at which they read and discussed papers and reports on work in progress, came to an end (for a description of these gatherings, see Pumpianskii 1992 [1926]). But even after they had stopped meeting the members of the School continued to take an interest in each other's ideas for many years.

The most important and fruitful period in the history of the School, the period which evidently saw the formation of its three leading members' original ideas, was the Nevel period proper, 1918–19. This was the only period in the School's history when Bakhtin, Kagan and Pumpianskii were in constant contact. Although Kagan came to Nevel with his philosophical outlook already defined, his major published work, "How is History Possible?" was, to judge by the date of its writing, produced in the context of the Nevel School's animated debates (see Kagan 1921 [1919]). Works in Pumpianskii's archive which formed the basis of his books on Dostoevsky (1922) and Gogol′ (1922–25) also date, as we shall see, from this Nevel period. And the fact that Bakhtin's "Toward a Philosophy of the Act", written several years later, contains echoes of every word of his only extant work from the Nevel period, the brief "Art and Answerability" (1919), is just one example of evidence that it was in the Nevel period that the ideas of Bakhtin's early philosophical works were conceived.

Unfortunately it is not yet possible to describe the shared principles of the Nevel School. All that can be said is that the works of its principal members have in common a frequently declared anti-psychologistic, anti-metaphysical and anti-dogmatic thrust, and a determination to pursue pure research in the sphere of philosophical cognition. What is more clearly discernible is a philosophical tradition — the Neo-Kantianism of the Marburg School, and above all the philosophical system of its leader, Hermann Cohen. It is significant that in 1920 Kagan, in an article entitled "Hermann Cohen" dedicated to the memory of his teacher and evidently representing a summing up of discussions in Nevel of Marburg School ideas, should have written that Marburg philosophy, and thus that of Cohen, was "a necessity today for the historical development of philosophy" (Kagan 1920 [1918], 123).

The Nevel School retained this orientation towards Cohen's system throughout the whole of its existence, so much so that by 1927 it had even became an object of irony among the group's closest friends. In Konstantin Vaginov's novel *The Goat Song* a philosopher, whose prototype was Bakhtin, makes a train journey during which he has the thought that "The world is posited, not given; reality is posited, not given" (Vaginov 1991 [1927], 61). Bakhtin attested that this episode reflected his fascination with Cohen's philosophy at the time. Katerina Clark and Michael Holquist's biography of Bakhtin (which, incidentally, brings together all the available evidence about the Nevel School's activity: 1984, 54–62), Nina Perlina's work (1984), and Vadim Liapunov's commentaries to his translations of the early Bakhtin (1990) all examine in some detail the connections between Bakhtin's work and Cohen's philosophy. In Bakhtin's early work and that of other members of the Nevel School Cohen's terminology is treated as something universally accepted and requiring no clarification. This applies to concepts such as "givenness and positedness", "unconsummatedness" (of cognition), "problem", "goal" ("teleology"), "unity" (of consciousness, cognition, being, etc.), "act", "answerability/responsibility" (*otvetstvennost'*), "the relations of I and the Other", and so on. Moreover, Bakhtin's "Art and Answerability" can be seen as a paraphrase of certain themes of Cohen's *Ethics of Pure Will* and *Aesthetics of Pure Feeling*.

But in all his early works, beginning with "Art and Answerability", Bakhtin's philosophical inquiries indisputably outgrow the limits of Cohen's system and change the meaning of the Cohenist terminology used. The most obvious changes affect "answerability", which Clark and Holquist are quite right to see as the key concept in Bakhtin's work between 1919 and 1924. Materials in Pumpianskii's archive dating from the summer months of 1919 show that the publication of "Art and Answerability" in the Vitebsk journal *Den' iskusstva* on 13 September 1919 was preceded by a discussion among the members of the Nevel School about the meaning of "answerability". Pumpianskii's "Response to a Problem Posed by Mikhail Mikhailovich" ("Otvet na zadachu, postavlennuiu Mikhailom Mikhailovichem") begins "He has established unerringly the logical conditions of moral reality, which come down to the word 'answerability'" (Nikolaev 1992, 227). In these same notes and other works by Pumpianskii moral reality is also termed actual being, moral being, or serious actuality. Thus the problem of moral reality conditioned by answerability, set out by Bakhtin in "Toward a Philosophy of the Act", was being discussed in Nevel as early as the summer of 1919.

However, it can be assumed that the discussions of summer 1919 did not focus on the legitimacy of this problem as such (Pumpianskii was simply following Bakhtin's definitions), but revolved around a question noted in Pumpianskii's "Response", that of how moral being is revealed. In "Response" Pumpianskii offers his own answer in the spirit of late Symbolism

(Viacheslav Ivanov): "we may find an accessible alphabet of the real in symbols" (Nikolaev 1992, 228). "Toward a Philosophy of the Act" suggests that Bakhtin almost certainly could not have agreed with this kind of symbolic interpretation (see TPA, 53).

Kagan also had his reply, if we assume that the problem he raised of "subjective consciousness" or "ontological subjectivity" can be correlated with Bakhtin's problem of moral reality. For Kagan "the specific problem of subjective consciousness was to be approached via historical analysis" of "the system of the whole of objective culture" (Kagan 1920 [1918], 122–123). On this point Kagan shows himself to be a consistent follower of the Marburg School, for this was essentially the direction taken by Ernst Cassirer in his works of the 1920s on symbolic forms. In "Toward a Philosophy of the Act" Bakhtin discusses this sort of approach to "living consciousness" from the point of view of cultural values and finds it wanting. Bakhtin's response follows logically from the essence of moral reality as he had established it: all that is possible is a participative description or phenomenology of this reality (TPA, 34–35, 16–17, 31–32).

These discussions of summer 1919 about serious actuality and how it might be revealed prompted Pumpianskii to write, in the same year, "An Attempt to Construct Relativistic Reality on the Basis of [Gogol′'s] *Government Inspector*" ("Opyt postroeniia reliativisticheskoi deistvitel′nosti po *Revizoru*"), which begins with a discussion of an issue raised by Bakhtin and ends with an expression of gratitude to him. This sketch of a theory of the comic is closely linked with the unfinished book on Gogol′ which Pumpianskii worked on between 1922 and 1925, and which in 1972 Bakhtin strongly urged should be sought out (Pumpianskii 1984 [1922], 1986 [1925]). This book contains, incidentally, the first original philosophy of laughter in the history of the Nevel School; the second was produced in the 1930s by Bakhtin in his study of Rabelais. Had Pumpianskii been able to read Bakhtin's book on Rabelais, he might possibly have echoed what Kagan said after reading "Discourse in the Novel" in 1936: "it contains an idea similar to one that I once expressed [...] My idea was an observation made in passing [...] But Mikhail Mikhailovich has developed it to the full and made it truly significant" (Kagan 1992 [1936], 75).

One of the most difficult issues in the prehistory of Bakhtin's ideas is clarifying the sources of his two indisputable philosophical discoveries. The first of these discoveries is the problem of moral reality which we have already discussed; the second is his use of the concepts of "author" and "hero", borrowed from literary theory, as categories of philosophical analysis. Using these categories, "Author and Hero in Aesthetic Activity" continued the exploration of moral being begun in "Toward a Philosophy of the Act", and offered "a phenomenological description of the axiological consciousness of oneself and of one's consciousness of the other in the event of being" (AH, 188). That such an exploration of moral being could be carried out in the sphere of aesthetics had already been effectively established by Cohen's philosophy: at one point Cohen states that the content of aesthetic consciousness is morality (Cohen 1904, 452; cf. TPA, 27, 61–62).

But within the Nevel School the first non-traditional examination of author–hero relations (with reference to literary history) was Pumpianskii's *Dostoevsky and the Ancient World* (1922; originally a paper delivered in 1921 to the Free Philosophical Association: see Igeta 1986). However, in Pumpianskii's Nevel manuscripts on Dostoevsky dating from the first half of 1919 this problem is not dealt with, although all the other major themes of the book are already present. Nor is the problem dealt with in other extant works by Pumpianskii from the first half of the 1920s. It may be assumed that the problem of author–hero relations as it is dealt with by Pumpianskii (the hero escaping from the author's power) emerged during, and was occasioned by, the actual writing of the book. It is significant that it was Pumpianskii's treatment of this particular aspect of the problem that Bakhtin referred to in a lecture on Turgenev's *Fathers and Children* on which R.M. Mirkina made notes in the mid-1920s (see Averintsev and Bocharov 1979, 405 n.3). Naturally the approach in Pumpianskii's book, replete as it is with historiosophical generalizations, is different from the methodologically impeccable application of the categories of "author" and "hero" in Bakhtin's theoretical philosophy. Therefore nothing definitive can be said as yet about the two thinkers' possible influence on each other. What is important is simply that the formulation of the problem took place within the same philosophical school.

Both Pumpianskii's 1919 manuscripts about Dostoevsky — his paper "Dostoevsky as a Tragic Poet" ("Dostoevskii kak tragicheskii poet") and "A Brief Contribution to a Debate about Dostoevsky" ("Kratkii doklad na dispute o Dostoevskom") — make reference to Bakhtin. These references show that Bakhtin's idea for his book on Dostoevsky goes back to at least 1919, i.e. the Nevel period.

The next materials in Pumpianskii's archive with a Bakhtin connection date from 1924–25, when, following Bakhtin's arrival in Leningrad in the spring of 1924, the Nevel School began to meet again. The presence in Pumpianskii's archive of notes on Bakhtin's lectures and contributions to the

School's meetings can be explained by his wish to keep a record of new, hitherto unknown work by Bakhtin for subsequent consideration and discussion. His archive contains no records for 1920–25 of lectures or papers by any individuals other than members of the Nevel School, and the majority of such records concern Bakhtin. The reliability of Pumpianskii's account of Bakhtin's ideas is confirmed by the numerous correspondences between his notes and Bakhtin's early work.

The first major record, most probably made in July 1924, is of a series of lectures by Bakhtin on "Hero and Author in Artistic Creation" ("Geroi i avtor v khudozhestvennom tvorchestve") (Nikolaev 1992, 233–234). There are notes on the first lecture only, and they include a plan, a methodological introduction, and the first chapter. Judging by the title of the lecture series and the content of Pumpianskii's note, the lectures were based on "Author and Hero in Aesthetic Activity", which Bakhtin had written in Vitebsk; we can now see that the provisional title given to that work by its editors when it was first published in 1979 is very close to the original. Pumpianskii's note gives us some idea of how the lost beginning of "Author and Hero" may have looked. The fact that this work was new to the members of the Nevel School allows it, and the closely related "Toward a Philosophy of the Act", to be dated to 1922–24. At the same time Pumpianskii's note, judging from numerous parallels, can also be seen as an outline of Bakhtin's "The Problem of Content, Material, and Form in Verbal Artistic Creation", written in 1924 for the journal *Russkii sovremennik.* Thus we may conjecture that this article, the first work in Bakhtin's philosophy, is a reworking of the lost beginning of "Author and Hero". Indeed, it is possible to single out certain conceptual layers of the article which lead directly back to the text of "Author and Hero". If this conjecture is correct, then the very fact that Bakhtin should have reworked his own text under the influence of external circumstances, and the manner in which he did so, constitute a further argument in favour of his authorship of books and articles published under the names of his friends.

The fact is that the article "The Formal (Morphological) Method, or Scholarly Salieri-ism", published under the name of Pavel Medvedev and dated October–November 1924 (FMSS), is a further reworking of "The Problem of Content", or rather of those sections that deal with the critique of the general principles of the "Formal School" from the standpoint of philosophical aesthetics. It can be assumed that, following the failed attempt in autumn 1924 to publish "The Problem of Content" in *Russkii sovremennik,* the resourceful Medvedev, already well known in official Leningrad literary circles, offered (as a way of making money) to rework the critical section of the article and publish it under his name in the Leningrad journal *Zvezda*. Thus it was that, entirely by chance, Bakhtin assumed the identity of Medvedev in official literary scholarship.

But it fell to Valentin Voloshinov to represent Bakhtin in official philosophical scholarship; and this time, in all probability, it was a conscious decision. Thus the article "Beyond the Social: on Freudianism" appeared under Voloshinov's name in *Zvezda* in 1925. In this article, however, in contrast with "Scholarly Salieri-ism", the analysis was conducted, entirely in the spirit of the times, in the conceptual language of sociology. The appearance of this article followed the Nevel School's discussion of psychoanalytical ideas in the winter of 1924–25. This is shown by the presence of works by Freud and other psychoanalytical theorists in the "Lists of Books Studied, Read, or Scanned" by Pumpianskii in these winter months. (These lists, incidentally, allow us to monitor Pumpianskii's reading and work month by month between 1920 and 1925.) We may also assume that Bakhtin completed the article on Freudianism by January 1925. The final section, which contains a critique of Otto Rank's *The Trauma of Birth* (1924), is clearly a supplement to the main body of the article. Meanwhile Pumpianskii wrote an article entitled "Toward a Critique of Rank and Psychoanalysis" ("K kritike Ranka i psikhoanaliza"), most probably in January 1925 and, as was his usual practice, immediately after reading Rank's book, which had in all probability only just become available to the members of the Nevel School, and thus also to Bakhtin, causing the latter to supplement his already completed article with the critique of Rank (see Voloshinov 1925, 211–214).

In my view sterile discussion of Bakhtin's total or partial authorship stands in the way of an answer to a far more important question: what was it in Bakhtin's early philosophy (or in the preceding philosophical tradition) that allowed him to begin using sociological language, and voluntarily at that, at a time when no other serious thinkers in Moscow or Leningrad even considered doing so? (Reference to the circumstances of the times is unconvincing, for Aleksei Losev would begin publishing his books as late as 1927.) And if at first the writing of works in sociological language was a marginal occupation alongside Bakhtin's energetic involvement in the activities of the Nevel School, from roughly 1926 onwards, beginning with the article "Discourse in Life and Discourse in Poetry", published in *Zvezda* in 1926, he produces works written exclusively in this language (four books and several articles). (No evidence exists of any other works, even lost works, written in his former philosophical language.) And it was in these books and articles of the 1920s that he formulated the fundamental Bakhtinian ideas (dialogue, another's speech, etc.) which were to bring him such renown in the 1960s, when they proved unexpectedly modern.

And it is significant that Pumpianskii, who did not complete his own transition to sociological and class-based positions until approximately 1927, should have highlighted above all, in his annotations on three of Bakhtin's books (*The Formal Method in Literary Scholarship*, *Marxism and the Philosophy of Language*, and *Problems of Dostoevsky's Art*), their wholly original, even creative, development of a sociological idiom which in "Beyond the Social", for instance, had been merely cosmetic. Moreover, because it was not possible to use traditional philosophical terminology, even if it were given a new interpretation, Bakhtin was obliged to create new concepts by borrowing from other areas of scholarship. Only in the Dostoevsky book did he complete the process of creating that peculiarly Bakhtinian language whose sociological aspect was wholly translatable. And translate it is what Bakhtin did with his Dostoevsky book (this shows that a similar translation of the other books of the 1920s is also possible). If the first edition of 1929 patently bears a veneer of sociologism, as do Bakhtin's other books of this period, then in the 1963 edition we have a completely different book. And although the translation was achieved with minimal adjustments, the sociological veneer has vanished.

But it would be wrong to think that this forced change in Bakhtin's philosophical language was triumphal and painless. It was a difficult, dramatic process which from the outside (as it is described in Vaginov's *The Goat Song*, whose characters are based on members of the Nevel School) looked like a renunciation and betrayal of all that was best in Bakhtin. If in the early works "Toward a Philosophy of the Act" and "Author and Hero" Bakhtin's consistently anti-metaphysical position led him to rule out of consideration a whole set of traditional philosophical ideas and concepts (such as the gnoseological subject), then the price of his shift to sociological language was the exclusion of his own ideas and concepts from the sphere of his reflections.

Nevertheless, although the problematics of Bakhtin's later books changed and became narrower in scope, and although his language changed, the conceptual system of his early works constantly shows through from deep beneath the surface of this language, often in extensively altered form. Moreover, it is even possible to discover fragments which clarify his early philosophical texts. Thus the overview in *Freudianism* of the major works by representatives of "philosophy of life" can be seen as a bibliography for "Toward a Philosophy of the Act" (see *FCS*, 12–15; cf. Voloshinov 1925,

186–188, where Russian thinkers such as "Stepun, Frank, to some extent Losskii" are named as representatives of "philosophy of life"). In the Nevel period, 1918–19, Bakhtin's thinking on the problem of moral reality conditioned by answerability was most probably based on Cohen. In 1922–23, when he was working on "Toward a Philosophy of the Act", he also took some of his bearings for his treatment of the same problem from works dealing with "philosophy of life" by Simmel, Rickert and Scheler. In *Freudianism* Simmel's "Individual Law" (1914) is singled out as fundamental. A number of articles by Simmel and Rickert dealing with problems and concepts discussed in "Toward a Philosophy of the Act" ("experience", "the world of culture and the world of life", "areas of meaning with autonomous laws", "the whole of life as a complex act", "meaning", "values and evaluations", "the crisis of the contemporary act") were translated in the Russian edition of the philosophy yearbook *Logos*. The translators of these articles created a comprehensive Russian terminology for the "philosophy of life" outlined therein (see Simmel 1910, 1911–12 and 1914; Rickert 1910, 1912–13, 1914).

In July 1924 Pumpianskii also made notes on Bakhtin's paper "The Problem of Grounded Peace" ("Problema obosnovannogo pokoia"), in which some of the themes of "Toward a Philosophy of the Act" and "Author and Hero" are treated from the point of view of the philosophy of religion (see Nikolaev 1992, 234–236).

Of greatest interest are the notes on six lectures given by Bakhtin in October and November 1924 (Nikolaev 1992, 236–244). In the course of a discussion of the early sections of Kant's *Critique of Pure Reason* these lectures provide a critical survey of fundamental problems in European philosophy. In many ways this survey is a generalized version of the views on European philosophy found in "Toward a Philosophy of the Act" and "Author and Hero". Particularly noteworthy is Bakhtin's identification of the aesthetic basis of most philosophical doctrines and systems.

Pumpianskii's last Bakhtin records, dating from October and November 1925, are fragments of a dispute between Bakhtin and Mikhail Tubianskii, an active participant in the Nevel School's Leningrad meetings (Nikolaev 1992, 244–245). The theme of this dispute, the meaning of Miracle and Revelation, and Bakhtin's replies were obviously of great importance to Pumpianskii — this is the only explanation for his having kept a record of them.

Both documents date from the period in the winter of 1925–26 when the Nevel School was studying theological issues. The books on theology in

Pumpianskii's "Lists" up to 20 December 1925 provide evidence of the School's work on theology, mentioned by Pumpianskii in his letter to Kagan of 1926, where he also attests to his own theological outlook — "the Eastern Orthodox Church" (Pumpianskii 1992 [1926], 74).

There is nothing to suggest other than that Bakhtin shared this theological outlook. And this is the point at which we might ask how that outlook was reflected in Bakhtin's philosophy. However, searching for the Orthodox origins of any philosophical system is just as pointless as searching for its class basis. A more appropriate question to ask would therefore be to what extent Bakhtin's philosophy belongs to the Russian religious-philosophical tradition — or, more specifically, how it correlates with early twentieth-century Russian religious philosophy.

Bakhtin undoubtedly belongs to the Russian philosophical tradition when he states in "Toward a Philosophy of the Act" that the architectonics of the single and unique event of life (i.e. being in its concrete reality) is expressed by the whole meaning of Christian morality (TPA, 16–17, 27, 75). This is the basis of his critique of "philosophy of life" and traditional philosophical cognition, which is unable to grasp the conditioning of moral reality by answerability that Bakhtin discovered. Early twentieth-century Russian religious philosophy in its turn would seem to have distanced itself from the Western theoretical philosophy of the day (including Cohenism). But its adherents, relying essentially on different stages in Western European philosophy (late Romanticism and Schellingism), aspired to the creation of an actual philosophy of life, a kind of secular theology which in their view corresponded to the postulates and the dogmas of the Eastern Church's Byzantine tradition.

On the basis of Bakhtin's views as expressed in Pumpianskii's notes on his "Lectures", it can be said that, whereas the Russian religious philosophers saw it as their task to problematize the cognition of the concepts of Christian morality, Bakhtin set himself the task of problematizing moral reality itself. This inevitably led to a critical attitude on the part of Bakhtin and other members of the Nevel School towards contemporary Russian religious philosophy, with its unrigorous metaphysical and dogmatic way of thinking.

But the divergences between Bakhtin and contemporary Russian religious philosophers are clearer in their respective evaluations of specific cultural phenomena. If Pavel Florenskii, proceeding from the notion of the correspondence of the phenomenon to acknowledged and unquestioned value, defines the poetry of Blok, which he admired, as a vision of demons (*besovidenie*), and Losev saw Rabelais's laughter as satanism, then Bakhtin's evaluations, in his lecture on Blok as recorded by Mirkina (Bakhtin 1993 [1920s], 155–163) and the Rabelais book, are characterized by a trusting acceptance which stems from the very essence of his philosophy.

But even when discussing problems similar to those which occupied Russian religious philosophers — in Pumpianskii's note of his dispute with Tubianskii, or in "The Problem of Grounded Peace" — Bakhtin examines them from the standpoint of the philosophy of religion. Only the absence in Russian philosophical culture of a remotely serious tradition of philosophy of religion can explain the fact that some parts of "Author and Hero", those devoted to the philosophy of religion, are sometimes perceived as religious philosophy. Perhaps Bakhtin's place in Russian culture is so unusual, even unique, because he was probably one of the few Russian Orthodox thinkers who confronted philosophy of religion. Unfortunately the only basis on which we can judge Bakhtin's philosophy of religion are the fragments in Pumpianskii's notes.

It is thus my view that Bakhtin's early philosophy will be fully and properly understood only after it has been examined in the context of the development of the Nevel School, and after the origins of its conceptual system have been studied in detail.[1]

NOTE

1. The author wishes to express his sincere thanks to E.M. Isserlin, Pumpianskii's widow, for kindly allowing him access to the scholar's archive.

WORKS CITED

Averintsev, S.S., and S.G. Bocharov 1979. "Primechaniia", in M.M. Bakhtin, *Estetika slovesnogo tvorchestva* (Moscow: Iskusstvo), 384–415.

Bakhtin, M.M. 1993 [1920s]. "Lektsii ob A. Belom, F. Sologube, A. Bloke, S. Esenine (v zapisi R.M. Mirkinoi]", in *Dialog. Karnaval. Khronotop* (Vitebsk), 2–3, 138–174.

Clark, K., and M. Holquist 1984. *Mikhail Bakhtin* (Cambridge, MA and London: Harvard University Press).

Cohen, H. 1904. *Ethik des reinen Willens* (Berlin: Bruno Cassirer).

Igeta, S. 1986. "Iwanow–Pumpianski–Bachtin", in *Przeglad Humanistyczny*, 6, 131–140.

Kagan, Iu.M. 1992, "O starykh bumagakh iz semeinogo arkhiva. (M.M. Bakhtin i M.I. Kagan)", in *Dialog. Karnaval. Khronotop* (Vitebsk), 1, 60–88.

Kagan, M.I. 1920 [1918]. "German Kogen (4 iiulia 1842 g. – 4 aprelia 1918 g.)", in *Nauchnye izvestiia. Sbornik vtoroi: Filosofiia–Literatura–Iskusstvo* (Moscow: Akademicheskii tsentr Narkomprosa), 110–124.

________. 1921 [1919]. "Kak vozmozhna istoriia? (Iz osnovnykh problem filosofii istorii)", in *Zapiski Orlovskogo gosudarstvennogo universiteta*, 1, 137–192.

________. 1992 [1936]. [Letter of 7 August to S.I. Kagan], cited in full in Iu.M. Kagan 1992, 75.

Liapunov, V. 1990. "Notes , in *Art and Answerability: Early Philosophical Essays by M.M. Bakhtin*, ed. M. Holquist and Liapunov, tr. Liapunov and K. Brostrom (Austin: University of Texas Press), 231–256.

Nikolaev, N.I. 1992. "Lektsii i vystupleniia M.M. Bakhtina 1924–1925 gg. v zapisiakh L.V. Pumpianskogo", in L.A. Gogotishvili and P.S. Gurevich (eds.), *Bakhtin kak filosof* (Moscow: Nauka), 221–251.

Perlina, N. 1984. "Mikhail Bakhtin and Martin Buber: Problems of Dialogic Imagination", in *Studies in Twentieth-Century Literature*, 9/1, 13–28.

Pumpianskii, L.V. 1922. *Dostoevskii i antichnost'* (St Petersburg: Zamysly).

________. 1984 [1922]. "Gogol'", in *Trudy po znakovym sistemam*, 18 (*Uchenye zapiski Tartuskogo gosudarstvennogo universiteta*, 664), 125–137.

________. 1986 [1925]. "*Vechera na khutore bliz Dikan'ki*; O *Zapiskakh sumasshedshego* Gogolia", in *Prepodavanie literaturnogo chteniia v estonskoi shkole* (Tallinn), 100–126.

________. 1992 [1926]. [Letter to M.I. Kagan of 1926], cited in full in Iu.M. Kagan 1992, 73–74.

Rickert, H. [Rikkert, G.] 1910. "O poniatii filosofii", in *Logos* (Moscow), 1, 19–61. In German: "Zur Begriff der Philosophie", in *Logos* (Tübingen), 1 (1910–11), 1–34.

________. 1912–13. "Tsennosti zhizni i kul'turnye tsennosti", in *Logos* (Moscow), 1–2, 1–35. In German: "Lebenswerte und Kulturwerte", in *Logos* (Tübingen), 2 (1911–12), 131–166.

________. 1914. "O sisteme tsennostei", in *Logos* (St Petersburg and Moscow), 1/1, 45–79. In German: "Vom System der Werte", in *Logos* (Tübingen), 4 (1913), 295–327.

Simmel [Zimmel'] G. 1910. "K voprosu o metafizike smerti", in *Logos* (Moscow), 2, 34–49. In German: "Zur Metaphysik des Todes", in *Logos* (Tübingen), 1 (1910–11), 57–70.

________. 1911–12. "Poniatie i tragediia kul'tury", in *Logos* (Moscow), 2–3, 1–25. In German: "Der Begriff und die Tragödie der Kultur", in *Logos* (Tübingen), 2 (1911–12), 1–25.

________. 1914. "Individual'nyi zakon. K istolkovaniiu printsipa etiki", in *Logos* (St Petersburg and Moscow), 1/1, 201–249. In German: "Des individuelle Gesetz: Ein Versuch über das Prinzip der Ethik", in *Logos* (Tübingen), 4 (1913), 117–160.

Vaginov, K.K. 1991 [1927]. "Kozlinaia pesn'", in *Kozlinaia pesn'*: *Romany* (Moscow: Sovremennik), 12–161.

Voloshinov, V.N. 1925. "Po tu storonu sotsial'nogo: O freidizme", in *Zvezda*, 5, 186–214.

Authorship

"THE AUTHOR" ACCORDING TO BAKHTIN ... AND BAKHTIN THE AUTHOR

Giovanni Palmieri, Milan

DECLARATION

In all of Bakhtin's writings there is no one work that contains a single organic theory of the author; rather, one can identify the main points of his theory scattered like fragments throughout his works. It is up to the critic to reconstruct genetically, as it were, his theory, which is what I intend to do.

PROMETHEUS: ROMANTIK

Odd as it may seem, Bakhtin's basic ideological assumptions in his early writings belonged to the Symbolist and Romantic schools of aesthetics. In particular, I am referring to the Promethean conception of a demiurge with a god-like capability of creation. Indeed, as Bakhtin wrote, "an author is the uniquely active form-giving energy" (AH, 8). And also: "the individual human *subiectum* experiences himself as a creator only in art" (PCMF, 316). We read still more about this in a text written in 1961: "The author, like Prometheus, creates [...] living beings who are independent of himself and with whom he is on equal terms" (TRDB, 284).

Lessing, Herder, Goethe and Moritz, who were all well known to Bakhtin, had reshaped the old Prometheus myth (cf. Walzel 1932), focusing their attention more on the relationship between the artist and his work than on that between the work of art and the outside world. Alongside the Romantic aesthetics of German Idealism we find the theurgic conception of art and the artist typical of Orthodox Christianity and widely reflected in the works of the Russian Symbolist poets. It is not by chance that the Romantic myth of the author was born in a Neoplatonic environment, and was first expounded as a theory in the well known 1st-century BC treatise on rhetoric *On the Sublime*.

Moreover, Bakhtin's whole conception of language as a creative and vital activity, as dialogic *energeia* as opposed to *ergon*, is directly derived from Humboldt and Novalis, while the privilege Bakhtin granted to totality as against its parts had its origins in the Romantics' biological vitalism — as we will see later.

A critical analysis must not fail to take into account the Romantic–existentialist component and the slight vitalistic vein in Bakhtin's works, because these characteristics, together with a strong Orthodox Christian religious sensibility, constitute the cultural-dialogical background to the whole of Bakhtin's aesthetics. To this scenario we must add the rationalism of German philosophy and a tendency to go beyond intuitionism by applying a personal interpretation of Husserl's phenomenology to the most diverse problems of literary theory.

IMAGES

According to Bakhtin, the author is exotopic (in a position of *vnenakhodimost'*) not only to the characters and the narrative world, but also to himself, or rather to that part of himself he manages to communicate in the text. In order to express himself, the author must objectify himself; here Bakhtin applies the philosophical concept of self-reflection — or "pure apperception", as Kant called it — to the writer. This notion can be traced back to Scholasticism, whose philosophers had in turn inherited the concept from Aristotle. In basic terms the problem is this: Man can think, but he can also see himself thinking — that is, can see himself as a thinker, or thinking being, in his thoughts. Kant, who was Bakhtin's starting point, poses the problem of the ethical knowledge that man can have of his objectified self. Kierkegaard and Husserl both deal with the notion of self-reflection, although from very different points of view.

For a literary theorist such as Bakhtin, the problem lies in determining the ways in which the author can think of himself, express himself and represent himself in the text. What, for example, is the relationship between the author, his textual discourse and his characters' discourse? Linked to these questions is the axiological problem that the characteristics that make moral evaluation possible are part of the text itself, and as such are evidently the author's own creation. Indeed, it is not always possible to distinguish between those values and moral judgements that belong properly to the author's "personal" discourse and those that are part of the characters' ideology.

Let us start with a series of selected quotations about the image of the author from "Author and Hero in Aesthetic Activity":

> [The image I have of myself] lacks any inner cogency, for I do not stop experiencing myself from within myself, and this self-experiencing remains with me or, rather, I myself remain *in* it and do not introduce it into the mentally represented image of myself. [...] my *self*-representation is contrived and does not correspond to any actual perception. The most essential part of my actual experience of myself is excluded from outward seeing. (AH, 37)

> I can to some extent perceive myself through my outer sense, and thus render myself in part an object of my desiring and feeling — that is, I can make myself an object for myself. But in this act of self-objectification I shall never coincide with myself — *I-for-myself* shall continue to be in the *act* of this self-objectification, and not in its product, that is, in the *act* of seeing, feeling, thinking, and not in the *object* seen or felt. I am incapable of fitting all of myself into an object, for I exceed any object as the active *subiectum* of it. (AH, 38)

> I myself as *subiectum* never coincide with me myself: I — the *subiectum* of the act of self-consciousness — exceed the bounds of this act's content. (AH, 109)

So when the author thinks of himself in order to represent himself in the text, he builds an image of himself that can never coincide with his real self; he will never match his self-representation as a global author.

This notion, another central point of a possible theory of the author, strictly depends on the idea of exotopy or outsideness (*vnenakhodimost'*): the author, in his globality as a person, will never coincide with the image of himself he has created in the text and therefore will also be exotopic to himself. It is easy to demonstrate how Bakhtin's conviction is a theoretical and literary adaptation of what Kant stated about the self of pure apperception in the *Critique of Pure Reason*: since "I think" is the condition for all other representations, it cannot represent itself as well (see Kant 1956 [1787], 94). Here Bakhtin applies some logical extensions of Kant's paralogisms of pure reason to the subject that produces the text which, since it is capable of self-representation, cannot at the same time coincide with this representation. Bakhtin's adaptation of Kant's ideas derives from Paul Natorp's interpretation of Kant in the second edition of his *General Psychology*, published in 1912. Explaining Kant's notion of the pure self, Natorp wrote:

> The self as the ultimate connexional centre communal to the content of which it is conscious is not similar to the content; on the contrary, it is not even comparable to it [...] the self is not characterized by a relationship similar to that between the contents of the self. No content is aware of the self in the way the self is aware of the content. This is why the self is only ever similar to itself [...] This means *it in turn can never become a content.* [...] This is precisely why it is impossible to give any further description of it [...] In other words, any "representation" of it we may create would make it into an "object". But the moment you think of it as an object, you necessarily stop thinking of it as the self. [...] Being something you are aware of means being the object of a self and this "being an object" cannot in turn be objectified. (Natorp 1912, 3–5 [I, §3], 27–29, 32–33 [II, §3, §5])

The conceptual affinity between Bakhtin's ideas and the "psychological" paraphrase of Kant's notions in Natorp's essay is so evident that it is tempting to speak, in this case, of a direct source. It is interesting to note that almost all of the passage discussed by Natorp is also referred to by Husserl in the fifth part of his *Logical Investigations*, where he discusses Kant's pure ego (see Husserl 1970 [1913 (1909)], vol. 2, 548–551 [§8]). We know from Nina Perlina's study of Bakhtin's cultural background that the Russian philosopher Matvei Kagan (1889–1937) studied in Germany with Cohen and Natorp himself; on his return home he, Bakhtin and a group of friends organized a Neo-Kantian seminar (see Perlina 1989; see also the articles in the present volume by Nikolai Nikolaev, Iudif' Kagan and Ruth Coates).

REFLEXIVE OUTSIDENESS AND PHENOMENOLOGICAL CONFIRMATIONS

We now come to another central issue in the theory of the author we are trying to reconstruct. Bakhtin made it clear from the start that in the text the author *must* (note the emphatic imperative) objectify himself in order to be able to offer us an image of himself, a persona that can be a narrative voice as well as an alter ego in the guise of a "character". The author, however, can also express his attitude to that persona or self-image he has built; that is, he can judge it, he can poke fun at it, he can describe it, and so on. In this case he doubly reflects himself and, as a result, his words are doubly voiced. With my own words I can comment on my own words from a different point of view, that is, exotopically. In semiological terms we could call this a metanarrative potential that is, however, never expressed directly, is not registered linguistically, but rather remains implicit within rhetorical strategies such as parody or satirical allegory.

We are all familiar with the Russian literary manner in which a leaning towards parody is almost *de rigueur*: *skaz*, in which the word "not only represents, but is *itself* represented" (DN, 336). Bakhtin mentions the short stories of Gogol′ and Leskov, to which we might add the stylistic polyphony of Babel′'s *Red Cavalry*. But here is how Bakhtin reformulated the problem of reflexive outsideness in theoretical terms:

> To express oneself means to make oneself an object for another and for oneself ("the reality of consciousness"). This is the first step in objectification. But it is also possible to express one's relationship to oneself as object (the second stage of objectification). In this case one's own word becomes an object and acquires a second — its own — voice. (PT, 110; translation modified)

This, taken from an essay written in the early 1960s, seems to echo what Bakhtin had already said in "Discourse in the Novel", where he maintained that "Behind the narrator's story we read a second story, the author's story; a story about what the narrator narrates, and also about the narrator himself" (DN, 314; translation modified).

This shows once again how philosophical issues are applied to literary theory — in this case the Scholastic notion of "double reflection", which in turn derives from Aristotle. According to St Thomas Aquinas, "because our minds are self-reflective, we can also reflect on our understanding and understand, in a secondary sense, the abstract species by which we understand" (Aquinas 1989 [1265–74], 134; q. 85, a. 2). In other words, the intellect conceives or thinks of itself by means of a reflected act, but it can also — in an act of double reflection — think of itself as capable of thinking of itself. In terms of literary theory, the author, in an act of first-degree reflection, constructs an objectified image of himself but, in an act of second-degree reflection, he can also judge or express his relationship with that image.

The philosophical problem of double reflection was also dealt with by Husserl, who is known for his interest in Scholasticism:

> The [*cogitatio*] can at any time become [intentional]: to its essence belongs in principle the possibility of a "*reflexive*" *directing of the mental glance* towards itself naturally in the form of a new *cogitatio* [...] In other words, every *cogitatio* can become the object of a so-called "inner perception", and eventually the object of a *reflexive* valuation, an approval or disapproval, and so forth. (Husserl 1931 [1913], 123 [§38])

The linguistic and conceptual affinities between the two writers seem to indicate that Bakhtin adapted or applied Husserl's ideas on the problem of self-reflection to the field of literary theory; moreover, critical opinion has long acknowledged the relationship between the Russian theorist and the father of phenomenology. Many passages clearly indicate the extent of Bakhtin's intellectual debt to Husserl; two will suffice to illustrate the point:

> What in life, in cognition, and in performed actions we call a determinate object acquires its determinateness, its own countenance, only through our relationship to it: it is our relationship that determines an object and its structure, not conversely. (AH, 5)

> And an artistic representation, an "image" of the object, may be penetrated by this dialogic play of verbal intentions that meet and are interwoven [...] If we imagine the *intention* of such a word, that is, its *directionality toward the object*, in the form of a ray of light, then the living and unrepeatable play of colors and light on the facets of the image that it constructs can be explained as the spectral disposition of the ray-word, not within the object itself (as would be the case in the play of an image-as-trope, in poetic speech taken in the narrow sense, in an "autotelic word"), but rather as its spectral dispersion in an atmosphere filled with the alien words, value judgments and accents through which the ray passes on its way toward the object [...] (DN, 277; translation modified)

To Bakhtin the very nature of the art object — dependent as it is on a creative process — must have looked similar to the way in which any event, seen from a phenomenological perspective, is radically compromised by its subjective representation.

THE DIANOETIC PRESENCE OF THE AUTHOR

The ideological aspect of the text and therefore the dianoetic presence of the author in the narrative world are ever-present themes in Bakhtin's aesthetic thought. They mainly concern the author's implicit discourse on the narrative universes and on the characters' actions. From what standpoint does the author know, judge and evaluate the ideas and actions of the "actors" he himself has put on the stage? Who do the axiological components revealed by the narrative structures of the text belong to? To the author, to the characters, to the exemplariness of the narrative story, or to all three of these components interactively?

Bakhtin clearly indicates that his approach to the text is neither naive nor directly ethical:

> The artist does not intervene in the event as an immediate participant in it, for then he would become somone who is engaged in cognition and who acts ethically. The artist assumes an essential *position outside* the event as a contemplator who is disinterested [...] (PCMF, 281–282)

The position described here of being basically external to the event once again points to the exotopy of worlds and the different positions of the *author* and the *hero*. The author's judgement will never, therefore, be able to enter the narrative world *directly*. This does not mean, however, that the creator of the work cannot sympathetically relive the events and co-evaluate them by constructing axiological codes. It is the author's indirect empathy with the content of his work that allows this act of co-evaluation, this fixing of values. As Bakhtin puts it: "This *situatedness outside* (but not indifferentism) allows artistic activity to unite, give form to, and consummate the event *from outside*. [...] What is needed is an essential axiological position outside the cognizing consciousness and outside the obligated and act-performing consciousness" (PCMF, 282; translation modified).

However, the external axiological position the author must take up is not synonymous with moral neutrality, that is, with indifferentism in the Kantian sense of the term; its moment of transition occurs within the form. "I become active in the form", we read, "*and through form I assume an axiological position outside content as cognitive-ethical directedness* [...] Thus, form is the expression of the active, axiological relationship of the author-creator and of the perceiver (the co-creator of the form) to content" (PCMF, 306; translation modified). In other words, the moral judgements made by the exotopic author are all indirect and, although they are directed at the content, they are only expressed through the form, that is, the relationship between the author and his work. The reader finds them in the text but on a formal level which is external to the narrative content. Bakhtin upheld this idea, maintaining that the author, the world and the characters are *built with language*: by relating to them with his words, which are exotopic and indirect, the author relates to their particular linguistic expression, and indeed the images he creates of them are not seen as empirical subjects but rather as *speaking consciousnesses*. The author thus creates his own image of the characters' linguistic choices, that is of their linguistic ideology.

Similarly, he also builds an image of himself as a linguistic consciousness, as a speaking voice on which he can reflect, if at all, by self-objectification. The writer's self-awareness, therefore, assumes an exclusively linguistic character. As a consequence, all the values fixed in the text are always — and only — embodied in verbal representation and depend not on the characters' actions but rather on the relationships between two linguistic consciousnesses that have come into contact: that of the author and that represented by his narrative world.

We must not forget that, according to Bakhtin, the author judges ideologically or fixes values *only* by expressing himself as a linguistic consciousness as well. This is why the creator of the work can never directly impose ideological values, but can only put them forward indirectly, as a bearer of values. These values, moreover, necessarily figure as part of other people's consciousness; the author's judgement is always a reflection of his ideological standing or of the particular genre in which it is written — the bare narrative facts can never reveal it.

This is how Bakhtin expresses this concept, again in Husserlian terms: "In form I *find myself*, find my own productive, axiologically form-giving, activity, *I feel intensely my own movement that is creating the object*, and I do so not only in primary creation, [...] but also during the contemplation of a work of art" (PCMF, 304). In this phenomenological and Kantian opposition to any scale of ethics based on content Bakhtin reveals his debt to Max Scheler. Scheler, a Christian philosopher with a phenomenological orientation, maintains that there is a strict gnoseological interdependence between *values* as given eternal essences intuited by the emotions and the *things* or the *events* in which values manifest themselves. Only love, by which Scheler meant an intentional act, acts as a trigger to reveal the values intentioned in the consciousness.

Similarly, according to Bakhtin, the creator's love of his work of art, or creation, leads him to a co-evaluating discovery of the values that will be embodied, as we have seen, in the form. Towards the end of "The Problem of Content" Bakhtin writes: "The aesthetic object is a creation that includes its creator within itself. The creator finds himself in it and feels intensely his own creative activity in it. Or put differently: it is a creation as it appears in the eyes of the creator himself, who created it freely and lovingly [...]" (PCMF, 316; translation modified). The presence of Scheler's motif of love as a revealer of values is not a mere coincidence, as another passage, this time from "Author and Hero", illustrates: "aesthetic consciousness [...], as a loving and value-positing consciousness, is a consciousness of a consciousness: the author's (the *I*'s) consciousness of the hero's (the *other*'s) consciousness" (AH, 89).

INDIRECT SPEECH AND THE DEATH OF THE AUTHOR

One of the most important consequences of the necessarily exotopic position of the author is what Bakhtin called "indirect speech". The creator of the work of art cannot express himself in it in a direct way. We have already seen that, in order to express himself, the subject, according to Bakhtin, must first think of himself. But in the very act of thinking of himself he undergoes a process of interior self-isolation; that is, he inevitably puts himself in a position from which he cannot communicate anything about himself. In Bakhtin's words, "The most essential part of my actual experience of myself is excluded from outward seeing" (AH, 37). This coincides precisely with Kierkegaard's negation of direct speech: just as the subjective thinker cannot communicate his own experience directly — that is, within his own existence — so the author, according to Bakhtin, cannot express himself directly. What, then, is he to do?

The only option available is to split oneself, to separate oneself, to exotopize oneself, to give oneself a double voice. The image of the author as Bakhtin intended it is no more or less than the indirect speech of another voice. In a nutshell, the author must make himself polyphonic, he must represent himself dramatically as a character; in so doing he inevitably cedes his words, his "property rights", as it were, since they can never be uttered directly, as his own. Bakhtin's statement is quite unequivocal:

> Any direct meaning or expression is false, especially when pathos-laden.
>
> We see the ground being prepared here for a radical scepticism toward any unmediated discourse and any straightforward seriousness, a scepticism bordering on a denial of the very possibility of a direct word that is not false. This scepticism was to find its most profound expression in Villon, Rabelais, Sorel, Scarron and others. (DN, 401; translation modified)

Villon's name is even more relevant today: recent studies of this author have revealed that behind this *nom de plume* lurked a cultured, sophisticated poet who had created a fictitious character and given him the historical name of Villon (see Villon 1991).

Speaking of the *primary* or real *author*, that is, about the author as a living being, Bakhtin writes, in even more Kierkegaardian terms:

> The primary author, if he expresses a direct word, cannot be simply a *writer*. Nothing can be said in his own person by a writer (in this case the writer turns into a commentator, a moralist, a scholar, and so forth. Therefore, the primary author clothes himself in *silence*. (N70, 149; translation modified)

> The writer is a person who is able to work in language while standing outside language; who has the gift of indirect speaking. (PT, 110; translation modified)

The argument formulated by Bakhtin to deny the author the possibility of direct speech is entirely that of Kierkegaard. According to the Danish philosopher, the thinker as subject cannot choose any "form" *directly*: "In the same degree that the subjective thinker [...] is not himself either poet or ethicist or dialectician, his form cannot be that of either directly" (Kierkegaard 1941 [1846], 319).

One of the most radical consequences of the use of indirect speech is the death of the author, of the self that is represented by his or her name and as such is the legal guarantor of the work of art. The dying process begins with the progressive distancing from his own words which the author inevitably undergoes by representing himself as a character; it is a short step from here to the adoption of a pseudonym, at which point the author points a gun at his own head. When the author opts for total anonymity, he pulls the trigger. On this issue Bakhtin writes: "Is not any writer [...] always a 'dramaturge' in the sense that he directs all words to others' voices, including to the image of the author (and to other authorial masks)?" (PT, 110). In another passage he even welcomes the "striving to depart from one's own words, with which nothing essential can be said. I myself can only be a character and not the primary author" (N70, 149).

Of course, the impossibility of communicating his own discourse directly led Kierkegaard — in an attempt to avoid the short circuit of a subject forced to transform itself into an object — to a giddy polynomy which inevitably manifested itself as anonymity, or at least as the absence of any defining, all-embracing name. There can be no real name if there is no real author, and there can be no real author if direct speech is impossible. Every one of us remains trapped in his own inviolable secret self, and the words which would express our subjectivity are forever in retreat, to the extent that a certain sense of self is indicated by their very absence.

Bakhtin, who regarded Kierkegaard's pseudonyms as author–characters created by the primary author, writes about the author–hero relationship: "the author lacks any unitary countenance [...] This type includes [...] some of the heroes of [...] Kierkegaard" (AH, 20). Bakhtin himself signed books that he did not feel were totally "his own" with various heteronyms. And yet, in spite of his ideology, his politics, and his sense of pragmatics, it seems legitimate to claim that Bakhtin's choice was motivated by his desire to adhere to forms of indirect speech.

A SUMMARY

As a temporary conclusion, it is possible to maintain that the exotopic position of the author posits itself, according to Bakhtin, against a complex, polyphonic series of relationships involving:

a) the author's own world;

b) the narrative world;

c) the reader's world;

d) the author's own discourse, that is, the language of the self;

e) alien discourse, that is, the discourse of others;

f) himself as author and living being;

g) himself as the creator of the work;

h) himself as a created image;

i) himself as the image created by the reader;

j) the characters as interacting linguistic consciousnesses;

k) the narrator, the narrative style and the chosen genre;

l) his own point of view (that is, a reflected moral judgement within the text) on all of the above.

The author, who, as we have seen, can never be represented in his entirety, remains both to himself and to the reader a "phenomenological residue" which cannot be further represented. Therefore, as the author must necessarily be assumed to exist and as such is indivisible and holistic, he seems to be *a priori* material, to use Husserl's terminology. Given our slim access to knowledge or analysis of the author through his works, then, the author, according to Bakhtin, must be accepted *a priori*; the reader can only perceive what the author gives of himself in his relationships with his work and the images he creates of himself. Even the axiological codes and the ethical-gnoseological aspects present in the text as the author's discourse are rightly considered by Bakhtin as internal formal structures.

An uncreated creator, the living author is more than can be gleaned of him from the text, not only by the reader but even by the author himself, as he only offers part of himself in the text, always reflecting in the creative process a self-unity which however remains permanently out of reach. Bakhtin's work, developing an extremely coherent global theory within a fascinating rhapsodic structure, conformed therefore to what can almost be described as a *metaphysics of the author*.

WORKS CITED

Aquinas, St Thomas 1989 [1265–74]. *Summa Theologiae: A Concise Translation*, ed. T. McDermott (London: Eyre and Spottiswoode).

Husserl, E. 1931 [1913]. *Ideas: General Introduction to Pure Phenomenology*, tr. W.R. Boyce Gibson (London: George Allen & Unwin Ltd.; New York: Macmillan).

________. 1970 [1913 (1909)]. *Logical Investigations*, tr. J.N. Findlay (London: Routledge and Kegan Paul; New York: The Humanities Press).

Kant, I. 1956 [1787]. *Critique of Pure Reason*, tr. J.M.D. Meiklejohn (London: J.M. Dent & Sons Ltd.; New York: E.P. Dutton & Co. Inc.).

Kierkegaard, S. 1941 [1846]. *Concluding Unscientific Postscript*, tr. D.F. Swenson and W. Lourie (Princeton: Princeton University Press).

Natorp, P. 1912. *Allgemeine Psychologie nach kritischer Methode* (Tübingen: J.C.B. Mohr [Paul Siebeck]).

Perlina, N., 1989. *Funny Things are Happening on the Way to the Bakhtin Forum* (Washington, DC: Kennan Institute For Advanced Russian Studies, Occasional Paper 231).

Villon, F. 1991. *Lascito, testamento e poesie diverse*, ed. M. Liborio (Milan: Rizzoli).

Walzel, O. 1932. *Das Prometheussymbol von Shaftesbury zu Goethe* (*Wortkunst: Untersuchungen zür Sprach- und Literaturgeschichte*, 7) (Munich).

CARNIVAL IN THEORY AND PRACTICE: VAGINOV AND BAKHTIN

Tony Anemone, College of William and Mary

Although the works of Konstantin Vaginov (1899–1934) were mentioned as a possible influence on Mikhail Bakhtin's theory of the novel as long ago as 1971 (Revzina 1971, 161), the complex relationship between Bakhtin and Vaginov, one of the leading writers of his generation and an active participant in Bakhtin's Leningrad circle, has not yet received the scholarly attention it deserves.[1] Clearly, this is part of a larger problem in Bakhtin scholarship: for despite the privileged role of polyphonic discourse and dialogism in Bakhtin's life and thought,[2] and despite distinguished work in precisely this direction by Holquist, Clark, Perlina and others, we still lack a sufficiently detailed (and dialogical) understanding of Bakhtin's relationship to the cultural milieu of Leningrad in the 1920s. And while Vaginov's novels and poems, for example, have, on occasion, been discussed by Bakhtinians, these readings have, so far, failed to recreate the complex dialogue with the age in which both Vaginov and Bakhtin participated. Thus, Katerina Clark and Michael Holquist read Vaginov's novels and poems as a semi-fictionalized portrait of Bakhtin and the Leningrad circle, while Leonardo Paleari reads Vaginov's novels as a more or less direct application of Bakhtin's theory of carnival and menippean satire to Russian life in the 1920s.[3] What is needed, then, is a thoroughly contextualizing approach to Bakhtin's dialogue with his age, an approach that can transcend the traditional literary-historical construction of one-way influence from teacher to student, or theory to practice, and recreate the multi-faceted dimensions of Bakhtin's development within the intellectual and cultural horizons of early twentieth-century Russia.

The relationship between Bakhtin's theory of the novel and Vaginov's novels is but one small piece to this puzzle. In this essay, I would like to suggest a more complex and, I hope, more truly dialogic view of the relationship between Vaginov and Bakhtin in the 1920s, one that goes beyond the role of the carnivalesque in Vaginov's novels. My central argument is that, in very different ways, Vaginov and Bakhtin confronted similar problems about the nature of literature and the fate of culture in post-Revolutionary Soviet society. While their solutions differ in many ways, the dialogue and polemic that can be reconstructed from their works form one element of the complex cultural and intellectual context from which the ideas we today associate with Bakhtin's name developed.

We can begin this inquiry with the problem of menippean satire. In his *Problems of Dostoevsky's Poetics*, Bakhtin describes the menippea as a serio-comic work of mixed genre, which combines poetry and prose, fantastic and adventure plot elements, with inserted narratives, often used parodically. Its style is marked by the maximum possible contrast and variety, juxtaposing high philosophical and/or religious seriousness with low, "slum naturalism" and a concern with topical and current events, issues, and personalities. The ideological center of the menippea, according to Bakhtin, is the testing of a philosophy, an idea or a version of some truth which is "embodied in the image of a wise man, the seeker of this truth". Finally, the menippean satire often includes elements of social utopia, usually in the form of the hero's dreams or journeys to unknown lands (*PDP*, 113–121).

Vaginov's novels, it has been argued (most forcefully in Paleari 1981), exhibit all the defining characteristics of the menippean satire as described by Bakhtin. For example, like the classical menippea, Vaginov's 1928 novel *The Goat Song* (*Kozlinaia pesn'*, in Vaginov 1989; hereafter *KP*) focuses on the adventures of a "wise man," by name Teptelkin, in whose person the central ideological issues of the text are embodied. The truth that is sought, and tested, in this particular hero's tragi-comic adventures among the bohemian intelligentsia of Soviet Leningrad, concerns the meaning of the Revolution and the fate of the Russian intelligentsia and Russian culture in the post-Revolutionary period. Vaginov's representation of this quest combines the stylistic, structural, and thematic elements of the menippea: the quest takes place on three planes, heaven, the earth, and hell, as his characters move between the ivory tower of culture, the banal realities of Soviet life, and the hell of artificially altered states of consciousness. Issues of high philosophical and historiographical seriousness, such as the meaning of the Revolution in Russia, the historical fate of the old intelligentsia, and the nature of art in the modern world, are debated in inappropriate locales (what Bakhtin called "slum naturalism"). Further, Vaginov's contemporary menippea juxtaposes current events, topical issues and real persons with legendary and mythological actions and characters. The text is full of allusions to important contemporary figures, and, in the vision of the future rebirth of culture, it exhibits elements of a social utopia. In the hallucinatory vision of *The Goat Song*'s second main character, the autobiographical unknown poet, the novel even includes a journey to the underworld, a typical action in the classical menippea. Emphasizing the sharp contrasts, abrupt shifts of tone, and oxymoronic combinations of the menippea, Vaginov's novel juxtaposes serious discussions of the meaning of art and the recurrent cycles of history with naturalistic sketches of the lives of the Petersburg bohemia of artists, drug addicts, prostitutes, collectors, and criminals. Abnormal and extreme psychological states — dreams, insanity, intoxication, obsession — are used to explore the complexities of consciousness and the mysteries of personality. Various kinds of doubles (e.g. Philostratus–Teptelkin, Misha Kotikov–Kostia Rotikov) are used to break down a "monologic" view of consciousness, as inserted texts and poetry, usually used parodically, tend to "dialogize" the narrative.[4]

On a more abstract level, Vaginov's novels exhibit many of the elements of the carnivalesque principle that dominates in the menippean satire. According to Bakhtin, carnival, which presents an inverted image of the "normal world", is characterized by the systematic violation of normal conduct (eccentricity) and language (profanity), and the rejection of all hierarchical structures of authority. The basic meaning of carnival is contained in the ritualistic "*mock crowning and subsequent decrowning of the carnival king*" and is described by Bakhtin as "the pathos of shifts and changes, of death and renewal" which reinforces the "*joyful relativity* of all structure and order, of all authority and all (hierarchical) position" (*PDP*, 124). Related to these various types of freedom, carnival produces an image of a world set free from the normal limitations of time and space, where the past communicates freely with the present (*RW*, 255–256).

Signs of carnival are, indeed, everywhere present in Vaginov's world. Representatives of the dominant pre-Revolutionary classes are consistently presented as "ritually decrowned", and their former prestige, power and sex appeal usurped by the triumphant working class. In *The Goat Song*, for example, the former tsarist general Golubkov has been reduced to playing the piano in a music hall, while his daughter Natasha has forsaken her fiancé, the Junker Kovalev, for the muscular charms of the "new Soviet man"

Kandalykin (*KP*, 118–122). The decadent sexual practices of Vaginov's characters make a mockery of traditional ethical norms (*KP*, 28–31 and *passim*), while questions of philosophical and historical world-view are debated, not only by elite scholars and artists, but also by ordinary people on the streets of Leningrad (*KP*, 10–11, 52). Art and Culture are themselves subjected to fierce argument between proponents of a "high" art for an initiated elite and supporters of a "kitsch" or popular art which, by the novel's end, seems to have the upper hand.

Bakhtin's notion of a specific carnivalesque chronotope (see FTC, 146–151, 167–224, and *passim*) presents a framework for understanding another central theme in *The Goat Song*, the heroes' futile attempts to overcome temporal and spatial limitations through a synchronic vision of World Culture.[5] The boundaries between the present and the past of Western Civilization, between Petersburg, Rome and Alexandria, are constantly blurred, or even erased, for Vaginov's obsessed artists and critics, whose alienation from the present is symbolized by anachronistic and anatopic[6] images from the culture of the past. When we first see Teptelkin, for instance, on his way to the communal kitchen for a pot of hot water, he is "surrounded by nymphs and goats" (*KP*, 9). Shortly before he commits suicide, the unknown poet's madness is conveyed by a transcendent vision which occurs, significantly, amidst the classical statues of Petersburg's Summer Garden: "'I am endowed with knowledge,' he thought again. 'I am connected to Rome. I know the future. I often don't exist at all, often I am one with nature, and then I appear in the guise of a man'" (*KP*, 182). In their nocturnal wanderings, Vaginov's characters are often accompanied by figures from the past, including Teptelkin's alter ego Philostratus, the symbolic representative of the last generation of pre-Christian Hellenistic intellectuals, and thus of the inevitable extinction of the pre-Revolutionary intelligentsia in the Soviet era (*KP*, 12).

Despite the strong evidence of a carnivalesque principle at work in Vaginov's novels, Paleari's argument that Vaginov's prose represents a practical application of Bakhtin's theory of the novel raises at least two problems. Although Bakhtin was working on his Dostoevsky book in the mid-1920s, that is, at the same time that Vaginov was writing *The Goat Song* (Clark and Holquist 1984, 238–239), his analysis of carnival and menippea did not appear in the first edition of this book. In fact, Bakhtin did not discuss carnival and menippea in print until after Vaginov's death, first in the 1937–38 essay "Forms of Time and of the Chronotope in the Novel", then in the Rabelais dissertation of 1940, and, finally, in the second, 1963 edition of the Dostoevsky book. On the other hand, because of the difficulty of dating the development of Bakhtin's concepts (Morson and Emerson 1990, 3), it is by no means impossible that ideas which Bakhtin did not publish until after Vaginov's death had been raised initially in the discussions of the Bakhtin Circle in the mid-1920s. In other words, while Vaginov's prose may have been influenced by his acquaintance with Bakhtin's thinking about the novel in the mid-1920s, this is by no means a proven fact. At the same time, we should not ignore the possibility that Vaginov's broadly "carnivalesque" prose influenced Bakhtin's thinking about the modern relevance of a supposedly "archaic" literary genre such as the menippean satire.

Another problem with Paleari's argument concerns the degree of carnivalization in Vaginov's prose. Rather than truly carnivalesque, with associations of joyful ambivalence and rebirth through death, Vaginov's satire is profoundly pessimistic. Rather than enacting a straightforward and joyful rite of liberation and rebirth,[7] Vaginov's satire seems to celebrate death as the only possible response to the crisis of Russian culture in the post-Revolutionary period. Rather than being reborn in the crucible of carnivalesque laughter, Vaginov's heroes are stripped of their illusions and delusions through the corrosive effects of the author's laughter. As Dmitrii Segal persuasively argues, Vaginov's prose functions as a kind of literary anti-talisman (*anti-okhrannaia gramota*), a literary monument to the impossibility of preserving the cultural legacy of the past and preserving it intact for the future (Segal 1981, 231). According to Segal, all Vaginov's novels are dedicated to illustrating art's inability to package and preserve the cultural legacy of the past for the future. In fact, the culture that the heroes of *The Goat Song* dedicate themselves to saving is, in the course of the novel, revealed as already corrupt and not worth preserving. The novel's trajectory describes its heroes' gradual disillusionment with their role as self-appointed defenders of culture from contemporary barbarism and their eventual reconciliation with the vulgar realities of Soviet life. Its central action takes place under the sign of transformation and metamorphosis: as the author is transformed into a "three-fingered monstrosity", the scholar and critic Teptelkin becomes the Chairman of his House Committee (Domkom), tsarist General Golubkov's daughter Natasha marries Kandalykin, the epitome of triumphant Soviet philistinism, while Misha Kotikov, the would-be biographer of the poet Zaevfratskii, becomes a dentist. Several characters avoid this degenerative transformation by choosing death or silence: thus the unknown poet and Mariia Petrovna, Teptelkin's wife, commit suicide, while the philosopher, supposedly modelled on Bakhtin, elects to stop writing books that nobody reads. Rather than liberating carnivalesque masks which they can put on and take off at will, these transformations are finalizing events in the lives of these characters: despite their desires, none of Vaginov's heroes will experience the elusive renewal promised by carnival. The novel ends, then, with an apotheosis of death: the death of individuals, the death of an entire class, and the end of a two-thousand-year cycle of cultural development. The dream and hope that the Russian Revolution, like the Christian revolution two thousand years before, would lead to a new cycle of cultural development, are unfulfilled: "My dream has ended", as the author says in the first of the novel's Forewords. Vaginov's carnival, in other words, works in ways antithetical to Bakhtinian carnival as traditionally understood. Again, the possibility that the relationship between Vaginov and Bakhtin in the 1920s may be best understood as an on-going polemic concerning the future of Russian culture needs to be re-examined and taken more seriously than it has in the past.

Another issue in Vaginov's prose closely related to Bakhtin's work of the 1920s is the techniques and effects of representing living people in a work of art. The central action of Vaginov's second novel, first published in 1929, *The Works and Days of Svistonov* (*Trudy i dni Svistonova*, in Vaginov 1989; hereafter *TDS*), describes the novelist Svistonov's "translation" of Ivan Ivanovich Kuku into Kukureku, the main character of his — not Vaginov's — novel. Kuku is a pompous but harmless nonentity, a hanger-on who lives at the margins of Leningrad's literary establishment, whose ambition is, in fact, to become the hero of a novel. Lacking true artistic talent, yet equipped with a surplus of aesthetic sensibility, he insists on viewing his life as a work of art. Since his every action is explicitly calculated for the effect it will make on others, Kuku is described as a character with no self of his own (*TDS*, 229). Kuku is obsessed with what Bakhtin would call his "I-for-others" and, simultaneously, completely unaware of his "I-for-himself". Because of his self-absorption, Kuku remains ignorant of how others actually perceive him, and his misunderstanding of the true meaning of Svistonov's aesthetic representation leads directly and inexorably to his demise.

A careful reader of Bakhtin will recognize the similarities between this problem and Bakhtin's discussion, in his unfinished philosophical manuscript of the early 1920s "Author and Hero in Aesthetic Activity", of the ethical issues involved in creating an image of a living person in a work of art. In describing the significance of point of view in a work of art, Bakhtin writes the following: "it is only in a life perceived in the category of the *other* that my body can become aesthetically valid, and not in the context of my own life as lived for myself, that is, not in the context of my self-consciousness" (AH, 59). Kuku's attempt to transform his life into a work of art is doomed to failure, Bakhtin would argue, because he misunderstands the necessary role of a dialogic mediation between self and other in art: in other words, he ignores the difference between life and art. Despite the apparent relevance of passages like this to Kuku's misguided attempt to live life as an artist creates art, the conclusion that Bakhtin's text provides a simple gloss to Vaginov's novel would be, as we shall see, a gross oversimplification.

Rejoicing that Svistonov has depicted him in his novel — "Our friend Svistonov has immortalized me" (*TDS*, 273) — Kuku gradually discovers the high cost of aesthetic immortality. In a parodic conflation of the myths of Pygmalion and Narcissus, Kuku's life is rendered redundant and meaningless when the image of his beloved double, Kukureku, comes to life in Svistonov's novel! Humiliated and embarrassed at the public exposure of his personal and aesthetic insignificance, Kuku is, in effect, crushed by seeing himself, for the first time, from an external viewpoint: for the first time he truly sees his "I-for-others" represented and objectified in a complete and finalized form. In a desperate attempt to reassert control over his life, Kuku changes his appearance and his style of living but, whatever he does, he finds that his life has already been lived for him and that he is merely repeating actions and scenes from Svistonov's novel. Nothing remains for Kuku but death, and he therefore disappears from the novel. The irony, of course, is that Kuku's fondest hope has always been for his life to take on the form of literature: what he now seems to find unbearable is the consciousness of finality in the finished, aesthetic image of himself that he reads in Svistonov's novel.

Bakhtin's treatment of the same problem in "Author and Hero", where he repeatedly associates the aesthetic image of a person with that same person's death, is tantalizingly close to Vaginov's: "Memory of someone else's finished life (although anticipation of its end is possible as well) provides the golden key to the aesthetic consummation of a person. An aesthetic approach to a living person forestalls his death, as it were — predetermines his future and renders his future redundant" (AH, 107). He even goes on to argue that, in order to create an aesthetically satisfying and convincing image of a person, the novelist must imagine that person's death: "Of essential significance for accomplishing the aesthetic consummation of a human being is the anticipation of his death. Indeed, the anticipation of death constitutes a necessary moment in the aesthetically valid form of the other's interior being, in the form of his soul" (AH, 130). For Bakhtin, the foreknowledge of a literary hero's death is simply part of the necessary "surplus" vision of an author, and is treated strictly from the viewpoint of the author. Bakhtin never looks at the relationship from the viewpoint of the hero, nor does he discuss the effect of this "anticipation" of the hero's death on the living consciousness of the literary prototype. One way of conceptualizing the relationship between Vaginov and Bakhtin, one could argue, is to read Vaginov's novel as an attempt to rethink Bakhtin's model of the relationship between author and hero from the viewpoint of the hero. In other words, while Bakhtin concentrates on the hero within the text, Vaginov focuses on the hero outside the text, that is, the prototype for the literary hero. Vaginov, then, rewrites Bakhtin's version of the dialogical relationship between authors and heroes into a more complex triangular relationship between author, hero and prototype. Further, the ethical responsibility of the author is conceived, in Vaginov's novel, as directed as much towards the hero's prototype (the hero in life) as towards the hero in the text.

Bakhtin's discussion of the ethics of responsible action helps to explain Kuku's despairing realization that his life has been rendered meaningless by Svistonov's representation of it in his novel. One of the differences between the self and the other, according to Bakhtin, is that while we can imagine another "fully consummated in time", this is impossible in relationship to the self: "The consciousness of being fully consummated in time (the consciousness that what *is* constitutes *all* there is) is a consciousness with which one can do nothing or with which it is impossible to live" (AH, 121). Bakhtin clarifies what is essentially a point about ethics and freedom later on in the same text, when he writes:

> The aesthetic approach to another's interior being predetermines the other [...] To be able to see one's interior portrait is the same as to see one's exterior portrait: it is a looking-in from outside into a world in which I am in principle absent and in which there is nothing I can do as long as I remain myself. That is to say, my aesthetically valid inner countenance is a kind of horoscope, with which, once again, there is nothing I can do. If someone really knew his horoscope, he would find himself in an inwardly contradictory and incongruous situation: the seriousness and the risk of living would be impossible; the proper position for performing an action would be impossible. (AH, 130).

By "the proper position for performing an action", Bakhtin means a position from which we can both freely choose our actions and accept responsibility for them. Prior knowledge of one's future renders this crucial ethical dimension of action (i.e. taking responsibility for our actions) impossible. In this sense, at least, Kuku is precisely correct: Svistonov's representation of him has made it impossible for him to act in an ethically responsible way in the future.

In *The Works and Days of Svistonov*, Vaginov goes well beyond the gloomy conclusions of *The Goat Song* concerning the nature and the possibilities of art in the contemporary world. In a crucially important moment of insight and confession, Svistonov describes literature as the process of translating people from this world to "the next world" and as the "afterlife" (*zagrobnoe sushchestvovanie*, *TDS*, 235) of these characters. At one point in the novel, we even see Svistonov visiting the city cemetery in search of names for the heroes of his novel (*TDS*, 300–302). Eventually, however, Svistonov comes to understand that as literature populates "the next world", it simultaneously depopulates this world, leaving only death and desolation in its wake. If the dominant theme of *The Goat Song* was the gradual degeneration of the author, his heroes, and even culture itself which accompanies the realization of the terrible truth that Petersburg and its new "Hellenists" have nothing in common with their beloved "world of bright spirits", *The Works and Days of Svistonov* illustrates how art itself destroys the lives of the author and his hero. In the final image of the novel, Svistonov himself disappears into the world of his novel: "Wherever Svistonov appeared, he saw his heroes. They had different names, different bodies, different hairstyles, different manners, but he recognized them immediately. In this way, Svistonov entered into the world of his novel" (*TDS*, 333). Both author and hero discover death and isolation in art.

Where Vaginov describes Svistonov's novel as the process of translating people from this world to "the next world" and as the "afterlife" of these characters (*TDS*, 235),[8] Bakhtin compares literary representation to a funeral. In a striking metaphor of the role of memory in art, Bakhtin writes: "Memory begins to act as a gathering and completing force from the very first moment of the hero's appearance; the hero is born in this memory (of his death), and the process of giving form to him is a process of commemoration (commemoration of the departed)" (AH, 131). The role of memory in aesthetic representation, crucial to both Vaginov and Bakhtin, is, in both cases, associated with death. While Kuku hopes that literary representation will confer the gift of eternal memory to its subject, and Svistonov thinks that it confers immortality on its creator, Bakhtin describes art as a struggle between memory and death: "In this sense, we could say that death is the form of the aesthetic consummation of an individual [...] The deeper and the more perfect the embodiment, the more distinctly do we hear in it the definitive completion of death and at the same time the aesthetic victory over death — the contention of memory against death [...] Throughout the entire course of an embodied hero's life, one can hear the tones of a requiem" (AH, 131).

Rather than resolving the paradox of the "aesthetic victory over death" in which "one can hear the tones of a requiem", Bakhtin sums up the "aesthetically creative relationship" of author to hero in the following way:

> The aesthetically creative relationship to the hero and his world is a relationship to him as one who is going to die (moriturus): it is the act of setting a saving consummation of him over against his own directedness to meaning. To accomplish this, one must clearly see in a human being and his world that which he himself is in principle incapable of seeing in himself, and do so while remaining in oneself and living one's own life in earnest; one must be able to approach him not from the standpoint of a lived life, but from a different standpoint — from a standpoint that is active outside a lived life. (AH, 190)

Vaginov's treatment of the relationship of author (Svistonov) to hero (Kuku) seems to have been written with Bakhtin in mind. Again the association with death provides an obvious connection. When, for example, Kuku begs Svistonov to destroy his manuscript, Vaginov writes that "Svistonov felt that it was not a person standing before him, but something like a corpse" (*TDS*, 278). In order to adopt the "aesthetically creative relationship" of author to hero, Svistonov adopts an unethical instrumental attitude towards the living prototypes of his heroes: "For Svistonov people weren't divided into good and bad, pleasant and unpleasant. Rather they were either necessary or unnecessary for his novel" (*TDS*, 319–320). Finally, Svistonov's world turns into "a collection of interesting freaks and monsters, and he was something like the director of this cabinet of curiosities" (*TDS*, 321).

Vaginov seems to be exploring some of the conclusions, unforeseen by Bakhtin, of an "aesthetically creative relationship of author to hero". An attitude that may be aesthetically productive turns out to be, on closer examination, ethically disastrous. Svistonov's attitude towards Kuku "as one who is going to die" has destructive consequences for both of them. The result of seeing his "aesthetically valid inner countenance" makes ethically responsible action impossible for Kuku. Similarly, Svistonov's absolute privileging of literature over life "liberates" him from the necessity of adopting an ethically responsible position vis-à-vis his heroes. In other words, Bakhtin's vision of an "aesthetically creative relationship of author to hero" is shown by Vaginov to result in an ethically untenable situation, and a critique of literary discourse as unethical and tyrannical.

In the absence of documentary evidence, it is presently impossible to provide categorical answers to questions of influence, chronology and priority in the works of Vaginov and Bakhtin. As products of similar backgrounds and the same cultural and intellectual milieu of Leningrad in the 1920s, Bakhtin and Vaginov were naturally drawn to similar issues and problems. Their close association in the Leningrad Bakhtin Circle in the mid-1920s created the context for a dialogue that was continued in the novels, essays and books produced in the following years. Those Bakhtinians who might be tempted to reject out of hand the possibility of Vaginov's influence on Bakhtin would do well to remember the words of a leading reader of Bakhtin, who has written that "Those who take seriously the validity of polyphonic discourse cannot make an exception for Bakhtin, and ignore the significance of another person's utterance within the framework of Bakhtin's own intellectual development" (Perlina 1989, 5). To do so means not only to view Bakhtin in an unnatural intellectual vacuum, but also explicitly to abandon his dialogic model of communication. Rather than trying to claim Bakhtin's unique responsibility for a new approach to the history and theory of the novel, the task of Bakhtin scholarship should be to illuminate the complex, many-sided dialogue with the age which can be read in his works. Happily, this has been an important theme in much recent Bakhtin scholarship. The sometimes polemical relationship between Bakhtin's theory and the novelistic practice of Vaginov represents one significant element of this dialogue which deserves additional study.

NOTES

1. In "The Ideas of Mikhail Bakhtin in their Historical and Cultural Context" ("Idei M.M. Bakhtina v istoriko-kul'turnom kontekste"), summarized in Revzina 1971, the Russian critic A.A. Dorogov first argued that Bakhtin and Vaginov are best understood as participants in an extended polemic with the Formalist aesthetics developed by the OPOIaZ group. While the Formalists emphasized the linguistic context of the work of art, both Bakhtin and Vaginov emphasize the reception of literary and linguistic phenomena within a specific social context. And as the Formal School is often seen as a post factum theoretical rationalization for the poetics of Russian Futurism, Bakhtin's theory can be connected, according to Dorogov, to the poetic practice of the post-Futurist OBERIUTY and, especially, of Konstantin Vaginov. Although Dorogov's approach has the definite advantage of locating Bakhtin and Vaginov firmly within the larger cultural context of Leningrad in the 1920s, his generalizations are so broad as to conceal most of the distinctive details of both Vaginov's and Bakhtin's works.

2. Clark and Holquist describe the Leningrad Bakhtin circle in the following way: "[The members of the Bakhtin circle] were also the products of a nexus of shared values. Bakhtin and his friends valued above all variety, difference, free inquiry, dialogue, debate. They believed in being free of conventional norms and the traditional bounds of a given discipline and in pursuing a life of the mind that was as rich and lively as possible. In their different ways they were almost all independent spirits who cared little to conform to the expectations of their peers, whether of the right or the left, of the Soviet establishment or of its opposition. And so when they met, it was for spirited discussion. Each sought to learn something from the discourse of others who worked in different intellectual fields. Their debates ranged over the religious and philosophical systems of the East and West, of the ancients and moderns, and over topics from the humanities to the natural sciences" (Clark and Holquist 1984, 116).
3. For example, Clark and Holquist read Vaginov's 1926 poem "Dva pestrykh odeiala" as a description of the room in which Bakhtin wrote his Dostoevsky book, while the novel *Kozlinaia pesn'* is treated as a satirical and somewhat exaggerated depiction of the members of the Leningrad circle in the mid 1920s (Clark and Holquist 1984, 99, 115–119). In his 1981 article "Literature and Life in the Novels of Konstantin Vaginov", Paleari reads Vaginov's novels as "an experimental menippea" set in the world of the elite intelligentsia of Leningrad in the 1920s. Dominated by an ambivalent irony, Vaginov's prose represents, according to Paleari, an application of Bakhtin's theory of the novel to the post-1917 history of the Russian intelligentsia. Although Paleari's essay represents an exciting and often persuasive reading of Vaginov's prose from a Bakhtinian perspective, it is flawed by Paleari's ahistorical and non-dialogical tendency to construe influence as a one-way street, leading directly from Bakhtin's theory of the novel to Vaginov's practice (see Paleari 1981, 166–170).
4. By presenting the cultural achievements of the novel's heroes, including the autobiographical unknown poet, in an ironic light, Vaginov forces readers to confront their feelings about the passing of the pre-Revolutionary intelligentsia.
5. According to Dmitrii Segal, Vaginov's profound pessimism concerning the possibility of recreating and preserving the culture of the past through art represents the central difference between him and Mandel'shtam: see Segal 1981, 209, 211–219, 242–244.
6. For the definition and use of the concept of anatopy and its relationship to chronotope in Bakhtin's works, see Morson and Emerson 1990, 48, 369.
7. Morson and Emerson argue that the version of carnival presented in the Rabelais book is, in many ways, inconsistent with much of Bakhtin's thought. They argue that the less anarchistic discussions of carnival of, for example, the essay "Towards a Prehistory of Novelistic Discourse" and the second edition of the Dostoevsky book, are more nuanced and useful: see Morson and Emerson 1990, 89–96, and *passim*.

8. This provocative definition of literature as the "afterlife" of its heroes is also interesting in its rejection of dialogic speech within the work of literature. Indeed, what kind of dialogue can an author have with characters he is transporting to the next world? Vaginov develops this theme in the lives of his heroes, for example, in the curious relationship between Svistonov and his deaf mistress. Here is how Vaginov describes Svistonov's thoughts as his deaf companion sleeps: "He felt safe. She would not eavesdrop on his thoughts, would not give away the secrets of his work. He could talk to her about anything. She was the ideal listener" (*TDS*, 264).

WORKS CITED

Clark, K., and M. Holquist 1984. *Mikhail Bakhtin* (Cambridge, MA and London: Harvard University Press).

Morson, G.S., and C. Emerson 1990. *Mikhail Bakhtin: Creation of a Prosaics* (Stanford: Stanford University Press).

Paleari, L. 1981. "La Letteratura e la Vita nei Romanzi di Vaginov", in *Rassegne Sovietica*, 5, 153–170.

Perlina, N. 1989. *Funny Things are Happening on the Way to the Bakhtin Forum* (Washington, DC: Kennan Institute For Advanced Russian Studies, Occasional Paper 231).

Revzina, O.G. 1971. "Nauchnaia zhizn'", in *Voprosy iazykoznaniia*, 2, 160–162.

Segal, D. 1981. "Literatura kak okhrannaia gramota", in *Slavica Hierosolymitana*, 5–6, 151–244.

Vaginov, K.K. 1989. *Kozlinaia pesn'. Trudy i dni Svistonova. Bambochada* (Moscow: Khudozhestvennaia literatura).

AUTHOR AND HERO IN RUSSIAN LITERATURE OF THE SOVIET PERIOD

Marietta Chudakova, The Literary Institute, Moscow

In the years immediately following the October Revolution literature's need for a replacement for the old hero from the intelligentsia burdened by profound psychological analysis, the "hero who spends all his time thinking, thinking" (Tynianov 1924, 292) became bound up in complex ways with two differently directed pressures emanating from society. First, there was the insistence that a hero from the people should be brought on to the literary stage, a hero who was not given to reflection or self-analysis (the self-analysis in which heroes and authors alike had been so well schooled by the great Russian novelists), but one who acted, and acted on the basis of his social intuition. It is worth noting that this change of hero was not actually carried through in Russian literature until the 1960s, despite the dual (intra-literary and external, ideological) pressure to do so. In 1936 Mikhail Zoshchenko would write, in an article symptomatically entitled "Literature Must be of the People":

> Our literature is too concerned with the "experience" and "restructuring" of the intellectual, and not enough with the "experiences" of the new man. Our tradition of intelligentsia literature is continuing, in which the principal subject of art is the psychological experiences of the intellectual. This tradition must be broken, because we cannot go on writing as though nothing has happened in our country.

> This is where a discrepancy arises. And in my view this is our main vice when it comes to making literature of and for the people. [...] But this does not mean that matters to do with the intelligentsia should be taken off the literary agenda altogether. It would be wrong to think that the people are interested only in themselves and only want to read about themselves. Again, it is a matter of proportion. (Zoshchenko 1936)

The other pressure from society (or more specifically from official ideology, with the support of the political authorities) was an even stronger demand that writers should not only provide answers to questions about their personal position within the new society — in effect about their loyalty to the new regime — outside their literary works, by filling in questionnaires especially designed for the purpose, but should also put these answers actually *inside* the literary work. This proved hugely destructive for Russian literature.

So the "Soviet" writer faced official demands for a new hero, different from him in every respect. These demands were met by Zoshchenko, who made a selfless effort to merge with his *hero* and his *reader* through his manner of writing, and perhaps also by the uncertain author of *The Quiet Don* (*Tikhii Don*, 1928–40; doubt has been cast against Mikhail Sholokhov's authorship of this novel). Simultaneously these same official institutions pushed the authors under their tutelage to exhibit their own "restructuring" (*perestroika*) by duplicating themselves in their characters. Thus the opposition of "I" and "the other", which, as Katerina Clark and Michael Holquist have pointed out, Bakhtin was the only one to formulate in terms of authorship (see Clark and Holquist 1984, 63–94) became more or less the key opposition in Russian literature of the Soviet period, and gave rise to a series of intricate configurations.

The figure of the *reader* began to loom larger. The author's sense of his reader lost its spontaneity. Individual, intimate contact with a reader who, although impersonal and indeterminate, was within this indeterminacy sufficiently individual for each author, vanished as the reader became a purely ideological construct, a controlling instance ("the reader won't understand that"). The reader became one with the hero, effectively entering the work in the guise of the "positive hero". Portrayal of such a hero became a special task which affirmed the author's special relationship with the hero and with the reader; the author set about trying to ingratiate himself with both. So at the same time as Bakhtin was developing his idea about the autonomy of consciousnesses within the literary work and about a hero's consciousness not enslaved by the author's, the literary process of the 1920s and 1930s and subsequently saw the dictatorship of the literary *hero and reader* over the *author* gathering strength.

This was a particular kind of shift beyond the boundaries of art and into society, a move which, apart from its prime cause, had literary forebears: we should not forget the established avant-garde orientation towards shaping or building life (*zhiznestroenie*) as the ultimate task of art. And in a certain sense literature (which gradually became what we call "Soviet" literature, itself just part of the literature of the Soviet period) did indeed begin to "build life".

Elsewhere, in the great bulk of literature (where the writer was moved by the necessity, of which he was to a greater or lesser extent conscious, of "disarming himself") the hero became a point of *surrender* for the writer (cf. the title of Arkadii Belinkov's undeservedly neglected study of Iurii Olesha, *The Surrender and Ruin of a Representative of the Soviet Intelligentsia* (Belinkov 1976). This took several forms. The first was the author's *alienation* from a hero organically close to him, an almost literal disowning/disavowal (Mechik in Aleksandr Fadeev's *The Rout* (*Razgrom*, 1927), where the author demonstrates how the reflective intellectual must inevitably turn out to be a traitor). The second was self-irony (a whole swathe of 1920s literature, in which authors such as Sergei Zaiaitskii, N. Shestakov and many others gave their heroes autobiographical features simply in order to subject their own lives to mockery. Finally, this surrender was expressed through an unhealthy feeling of simultaneous intimacy and repulsion. Viktor Shklovskii, who was able to see the construction of a literary work with merciless clarity, wrote of Olesha's *Envy* (*Zavist'*, 1927):

> The piece is wrongly constructed, because the point of view used throughout the novel is that of the negative heroes, Ivan Babichev and Kavalerov.
>
> But at the same time this is the strongest feature of the novel, and the hero cannot be refuted because he is in charge of the work's style. [...]
>
> Since the work's style is associated with Kavalerov and not with Andrei Babichev, then its heroes are Kavalerov and Ivan Babichev, since they have the work's stylistic excellence on their side. Olesha's fine prose is vitiated by this incorrect, careless resolution of the principal problem posed by the plot, this tension between plot and style. (Shklovskii 1933, 118–119)

Olesha's novel, "vitiated" from one point of view, offers a kind of oscillogram illustrating unusually vividly the author's inner struggle with himself, with his consciousness as embodied in his heroes.

Panteleimon Romanov was one of the few writers in the second half of the 1920s able to publish a work portraying a hero from the intelligentsia in which the author traces sympathetically, from the outside, the struggle in the hero's consciousness. The hero of *The Right to Life* (*Pravo na zhizn'*, 1928), who is also a writer, is reproached by an editor for failing to merge with the image of his author (hero?!):

> The editor opened the proofs on his desk, perused them in silence for a while, then looked up at Ostankin and said:
>
> "Where is your face to be found in here?"
>
> Bewildered, Ostankin passed his hand mechanically across his cheek.
>
> "Your own face is absolutely nowhere to be seen!" Rudakov went on. "The subject matter is entirely about the Revolution and the workers, but when you can't see the author's own face, then it simply doesn't ring true for the reader — it's as though you are writing about those things because 'that's the way to write' these days."
>
> *"My writing is absolutely sincere," said Ostankin, his face reddening.*
>
> "I don't doubt it! But the more sincerely you write, the more the reader, if he cannot see your face, will take it as artificial and ingratiating, will wonder why it is that suddenly no-one can take a single step without writing about the Revolution or the workers."
>
> Ostankin stood behind Rudakov's chair and felt as though not just his cheeks, but his ears were beginning to burn, as though scorched by the wind. [...]
>
> "But what is it that I have done wrong?" he asked himself in bewilderment. "I feel as though I really have been found guilty of something — but I have done absolutely nothing wrong."
>
> And indeed he really did not know what he could be guilty of in the eyes of the Republic of the Soviets, what crime he could have committed against it.
>
> But there was no doubt that he had done something wrong. (Romanov 1970 [1928], 14–15)

Thus the "others'" voices in the individual's consciousness discovered by Dostoevsky become the voice of society; the way in which their sense of "guilt" before society corroded the consciousness of Soviet authors is here portrayed by Romanov with a detachment which by the late 1920s was already rare. By the early 1930s attempts at such detachment had come to an end:

> I have been fed in equal measure by the milk of two epochs. For me, one of the most interesting heroes at the present moment is the individual of thirty-

> five years of age. It is in the heart of this individual that a ceaseless struggle between the old and the new is taking place, it is his heart that young people should be sent to study: where else can one observe with such clarity, at its very source, the process by which the individual of a new historical epoch comes gradually and painfully to maturity? (Rykachev 1935 [1931], 86)

The portrayal of this struggle had by now become clichéd.

Let us return to the early 1920s. Sergei Tret′iakov argued that in Soviet society anyone ought to be able to become an *author*; everyone ought to be able to write a short notice for a newspaper. The author in the familiar sense of the word was declared defunct, and the literary hero was to all intents and purposes identified with the reader. Thus the whole author–hero–reader triad (or, more in the spirit of those years, *troika*) was changed, and a closed circle was formed: every person was to learn to portray his neighbour in a work to be read by that neighbour.

A different position was adopted by Shklovskii, whose views were close to those of Lef (the Left Front of the Arts), and its theories of "literature of fact". Like Tret′iakov, Shklovskii was eager to resist the emergence of a "Red Lev Tolstoi" portraying "fictitious" heroes (i.e. the literary heroes of the Russian classics) by proposing that these heroes be replaced by real figures, and in the first instance by the author himself, but a workaholic author with a *second*, "working" profession which he would be able to introduce into his works.

Literature supplanted what Bakhtin, in "Author and Hero in Aesthetic Activity", called "confessional self-accounting" (*samootchet–ispoved′*) (see AH, 138–150), replacing it with false confessions (before the people, the authorities, and so on). Shklovskii put himself forward as hero and continued to write in the first person even when this form had fallen entirely, or almost entirely, out of use. (The use of the first person is virtually the only thing that *holds together* some of Olesha's stories and sketches of the 1930s.)

Mikhail Bulgakov also offered his version of author–hero relations. Bulgakov overcame the outsideness of the author in relation to his hero by making author and hero identical. In contrast to the old "psychological" novel, the author of *The White Guard* (*Belaia Gvardiia*, 1924–29) placed at its centre a hero almost bereft of any philosophy, not inclined to abstract thought, making him a kind of vacuum into which a whole series of historical and other ideas belonging to the author himself are drawn with great force. The novel was constructed on the assumption that a certain type of reader would know the way of life represented in it, the characters, and the nature of their outlook on the world, which was close to that of the author himself. In *The Master and Margarita* (*Master i Margarita*, 1929–40) Bulgakov discovered a position from which the author could view his own fate from outside (cf. Bakhtin in "Author and Hero": "It is possible to love one's fate *in absentia*, or without actually seeing it, but we cannot contemplate our fate as a necessary, internally unified, and fully consummated artistic whole, the way we contemplate the fate of a hero" (AH, 176)). This personification of the author in his hero was a form of vigorous resistance to what was taking place.

This was how the author (from Shklovskii to Nikolai Ostrovskii and Bulgakov, both of whom "were afraid" to introduce their "I" openly) sought to represent *himself* in a literature which had been imperiously invaded by alien consciousness. Bulgakov's identification of himself with his hero was accompanied by the reappearance in literature of the concepts of sin and repentance in place of quasi-sin, quasi-repentance and quasi-confession. It was the impossibility of a directly confessional form, of an open portrayal of one's "I", that led to its being placed in the shell of the "other"; in this sense Ostrovskii's *How the Steel was Tempered* (*Kak zakalialas' stal'*, 1932–34) and *The Master and Margarita* have something in common. In *The Master and Margarita* and Pasternak's *Doctor Zhivago* (*Doktor Zhivago*, 1958) the "I"/"other" diad is a different way of looking at one's fate after death from that encapsulated in the line "No, I shall not die altogether" from Pushkin's "I Have Raised a Monument to Myself" ("Ia pamiatnik sebe vozdvig nerukotvornyi", 1836). The author merged with the hero, and the hero was brought close to Christ — Christ made man, a continuation of the Russian kenotic tradition. As Clark and Holquist put it, "Ultimately, Bakhtin's thought is a philosophy of creation, a meditation on the mysteries inherent in God's making people and people's making selves, with the activity of people creating other people in literary authorship as a paradigm for thinking at all levels of creating" (Clark and Holquist 1984, 80; on Bakhtin and kenoticism see 84–87).

By the late 1920s the mystery of creation had become an important literary theme; at the end of the first period in Soviet literature, this theme flowered with a sickly luxuriance in the fertile soil of Russian literaturocentrism. The author identified himself with his poet–hero, while, as has already been said, bringing the hero close to the subject of the Second Coming.

Let us move on to look at a few examples of things said by various writers of the Soviet period about the reader and reading. First, Bulgakov in *Black Snow* (*Teatral'nyi roman*, 1936–37):

> I did not sleep all night, walked round the room, looked at the banknotes in the light, drank some cold tea and imagined to myself bookshop counters. People were crowding into the shops and asking for this issue of the magazine [containing my story]. In their homes people were sitting under their lamps reading it. (Bulgakov 1967 [1936–37], 36)

In February 1953 Pasternak wrote to Nikolai Aseev:

> The distinction between contemporary Soviet literature and all that preceded it seems to me to be above all that it is bedded down on rock-solid foundations irrespective of whether it is read or not read. It is a proud, self-confiding and self-sufficing phenomenon, sharing with other pillars of state their immutability and infallibility.

Genuine art, on the other hand,

> nurtures a modest desire to be the reader's dream, the object of his longings, and is in need of his responsive imagination, not in the form of amicable condescension but as an integral element on which the artist is dependent for his formation. (Pasternak 1990 [1953], 196)

Finally, Aleksandr Tvardovskii, poet and editor of the prominent liberal journal *Novyi mir*, in a 1965 article on the émigré writer Ivan Bunin: "The fact that our prose literature is without the active, indispensable form of dissemination which is unofficial reading aloud is a result of the noticeable decline in its culture" (Tvardovskii 1965, 228).

For Bulgakov the experimental prose of the early 1920s and consummately Soviet prose belonged in the same compartment of "literature" (a literature which in his work, from "Cuff Notes" ("Zapiski na manzhetakh", 1923–24) to *Adam and Eve* (*Adam i Eva*, 1931) was placed in opposition to "printed" literature, "books"). This compartment contained works which could be *read* only with a specific aim in mind, and only once. Bulgakov himself wrote "books" addressed directly to his reader and intended to be read and re-read.

Thus the author in "Soviet" literature merged with the authorities, and the hero with the reader and also with the authorities. Hero and author attempted to win themselves over: what took place on the pages of books was not a dialogue of sovereign consciousnesses, but something akin to a *nanaiskaia bor'ba*, a wrestling bout between two people acted out by one person. In other works of the Soviet period the author merged with the hero and looked at himself from the side through the eyes of his future reader.

A separate theme is the disappearance of the reader by the mid-1930s, the disappearance from the literary dynamic of the notion of reader response, and the narrowing down, at a specific moment, of the contemporary reader to a *single* reader — a devoutly wished for partner in conversation (Bulgakov's letter to Stalin, 1992 [1931]), a double of the poet and more or less ideal reader (Pasternak's letter to Stalin, dated by Lazar′ Fleishman to 1935 (1991 [1935]), and the first poem in his cycle "The Artist" ("Khudozhnik"), dated 1 January 1936.

In 1953 Il′ia Erenburg wrote, in an article which played a crucial role in the literary thaw of that year: "But a writer cannot correct his heroes' lives as a proof-reader corrects proofs" (Erenburg 1953, 175; on the importance of this article for the thaw, see Svirski 1981, 74). So it was that a new era in Russian literature began with what reads like an account of Bakhtin's theory for non-specialists. Now the author had to find all three — hero, reader, and himself — at the same time. Finding himself proved to be the most difficult, and has not been achieved until now, in the post-Soviet era.

WORKS CITED

Belinkov, A.V. 1976. *Sdacha i gibel′ sovetskogo intelligenta: Iurii Olesha* (Madrid: Ediciones Castilla).

Bulgakov, M.A. 1967 [1936–37]. *Black Snow: A Theatrical Novel*, tr. M. Glenny (London: Hodder and Stoughton).

________. 1992 [1931]. [Letter to Stalin of 31 May 1931], in *Manuscripts Don't Burn: A Life in Letters and Diaries*, comp. J.A.E. Curtis (London: Collins Harvill), 125–128.

Clark, K., and M. Holquist 1984. *Mikhail Bakhtin* (Cambridge, MA and London: Harvard University Press).

Erenburg, I.G. 1953. "O rabote pisatelia", in *Znamia*, 10, 160–183.

Pasternak, B.L. 1990 [1953]. [Letter to Nikolai Aseev of 5 February 1953], cited in E. Pasternak, *Boris Pasternak: The Tragic Years, 1930–60*, tr. M. Duncan (London: Collins Harvill), 196.

________. 1991 [1935]. "Pis′mo Stalinu", in *Russkaia mysl′* (28 June), *Literaturnoe prilozhenie*, 12, vi.

Romanov, P.S. 1970 [1928]. *Pravo na zhizn′, ili problema bespartiinosti* (Letchworth: Prideaux, 1970).

Rykachev, Ia.S. 1935 [1931]. "Chelovek tridtsati piati let", in *Slozhnyi khod* (Moscow: Sovetskii pisatel′), 86–118.

Shklovskii, V.B. 1933. "Mir bez glubiny. (Iurii Olesha)", in *Literaturnyi kritik*, 5, 118–121.

Svirski, G. 1981. *A History of Post-War Soviet Writing: The Literature of Moral Opposition* (Ann Arbor: Ardis).

Tynianov, Iu.N. 1924. "Literaturnoe segodnia", in *Russkii sovremennik*, 1, 291–306.

Tvardovskii, A.T. 1965. "O Bunine", in *Novyi mir*, 7, 211–233.

Zoshchenko, M.M., 1936. "Literatura dolzhna byt′ narodnoi", in *Literaturnyi Leningrad* (20 April).

Form and Image

BAKHTIN'S AESTHETICS AS A LOGIC OF FORM

Natal'ia Bonetskaia, The Institute of World Literature, Moscow

One of the crucial problems in Bakhtin studies is the question of the unity of the thinker's work. Indeed, looked at together his writings give the impression of being a heterogeneous collection of works with no obvious connection between them. The early, purely philosophical works stand alongside books of literary scholarship; from studying the world of a Russian Christian writer Bakhtin moves to an apologetic investigation of the low culture of the Western Renaissance; Marxism supplants an orientation towards Neo-Kantianism; and so on. Despite this lack of homogeneity in terms of their content and the world-views which they reflect, all Bakhtin's works are undoubtedly connected by the unity of his creative personality, a unity which any reader will sense intuitively. This self-evident fact needs to be substantiated: a method must be found, and a language developed, which will allow all Bakhtin's works to be described as products of the same creative consciousness.

In methodological terms there are probably many ways of attaining this goal. Personally I find it most fruitful to isolate within Bakhtin's conceptual framework certain key or pivotal categories and trace their evolution throughout his career — something I have already done with the category of *authorship* (see Bonetskaia 1985). Similarly, we could view the whole of Bakhtin's work as an elaboration of the concept of *dialogue*, seeing the early works as a "pre-dialogical" phase and identifying within them the seeds of dialogue; the Dostoevsky book could be seen as a theory of dialogue in the strict sense of the word; and the Rabelais book as a discussion of dialogue dying out. But in this article I want to try to present Bakhtin's work as a coherent whole using the category of *aesthetic form*. However numerous the reservations one might have about this approach, it is a valid one in that Bakhtin's field is general aesthetics, the philosophy of art, and the category of form is a key to this field's meaning (this is of course true of any system belonging to the Kantian tradition, within which the category of form has particular significance). This approach will show that in Bakhtin's understanding form possesses a specific dialectic, is a logically "coming-to-be" (*stanoviashchaiasia*) category, and that the essential purpose of Bakhtin's principal works is to describe the various stages in a logic of form. The following works will be singled out for discussion: "Toward a Philosophy of the Act"; "Author and Hero in Aesthetic Activity", together with "The Problem of Content, Material, and Form in Verbal Artistic Creation"; *Problems of Dostoevsky's Poetics*; and *Rabelais and His World*. From the point of view of a theory of form Bakhtin's other works are to my mind unrepresentative, the articles on novelistic discourse, for example, demonstrating the application of the idea of dialogue to the analysis of novelistic style. The articles and books to be examined, on the other hand, are landmarks in the evolution of Bakhtin's outlook, and at the same time "chapters" in his "aesthetics", his distinctive philosophy of form.

We must first show how the problem of aesthetic form is posed by Bakhtin. His work in this field is in the mainstream of the thought of the time. In particular, in the early twentieth century the Russian cultural consciousness had developed a notion of the artist as a tragic personality: there was a belief in the fatal guilt attached to any creative work. The poet's guilt was considered similar to that of a murderer, in that the creation of artistic form was always an act of limiting, and in some ways even killing, the vital impulse behind it. Hence Aleksandr Blok in a poem on precisely this theme, "The Artist" ("Khudozhnik", 1913), uses the image of a cage imprisoning a free bird. Form in its relation to life — this is the perspective in which Bakhtin, too, poses the problem of the aesthetic. "The problem of the aesthetic is precisely to explain how the world may be thus paralysed [by form]", Bakhtin stated in the 1920s (Nikolaev 1992, 234). At this time it was essentially just a matter of finding a new way of asking the old, and perhaps eternal, question about the mystery of art. In the age of classical aesthetics beauty was defined as an expression of infinite content in finite form

(Schelling), or as the manifestation of the spirit in sensual images (Hegel). The principle of art, of form, was always characterized as contradictory; the late nineteenth and early twentieth centuries were different only in that in the minds of the thinkers of the time this contradiction was accentuated to the point that it became an irresolvable opposition. The problem of the aesthetic (and more broadly of all cultural value) was treated in terms of tragedy by Simmel, whose views we must assume to be one of the sources of Bakhtin's intuitions: Simmel's "On the Concept and Tragedy of Culture" was published in Russian in 1911–12. Simmel wrote of the hostility between the living spirit and the spirit frozen in value. He saw the tragedy of culture as lying in the divorce of value from the spiritual life which engenders it (the same intuition lies behind the existentialist idea of objectivization extinguishing spirit). Simmel lacked the experience described by Blok of the emptiness accompanying the act of creation, an experience compared by the tragic poet to what is felt by a murderer, but he still had an acute sense of the deadening aspect of form, and saw the meaning of death as giving form to life (see Simmel 1910–11). Another philosopher, this time a Russian frequently referred to by Bakhtin, Fedor Stepun, also drew a connection between creation and the tragedy of the artist trying unsuccessfully to capture in artistic form the limitless plenitude of lived experience (see Stepun 1910 and 1913). And Rickert identified the coupling of the idea of life to that of value or form as the task for the philosophy of the future (see chapter 11 of Rickert 1920, which was published in Russian in St Petersburg in 1922). Finally, Nietzsche is surely dealing with the same issue when, in *The Birth of Tragedy*, he identifies the essence of understanding ancient drama as seeing Dionysian ecstasy behind the severe countenance of Apollo.

So by the beginning of the twentieth century the fundamental question of aesthetics was being posed with peculiar starkness: indeed, in the Nietszchean terms which were so fashionable at the time, comprehending the mystery of form would mean understanding that Apollo and Dionysus were hypostases of a single deity. But in Bakhtin's terms the problem was posed in the following way: *how can spirit be given form, represented*, if it is in principle transcendent of space and time, incompatible with any kind of objectiveness or reification? It is important to point out that Bakhtin did not admit the possibility of any "alternative existence", any incarnation or symbolic manifestation of spirit. Bakhtin thinks of spirit (the subjective human spirit, an active individual "I") in the same terms as Max Scheler, who gave the name "spirit" to the centre from which all the individual's acts emanate and which is outside the spatio-temporal world and thus cannot be objectified (see Scheler 1928). In his treatment of spirit Bakhtin is also very close to the existentialists. His aesthetics thus tackles the most difficult question of all — how to give form to that which cannot in principle be given form, how to image forth that which is essentially without image, how to consummate the infinite. These difficulties did not exist for the founders of classical aesthetics. Both Hegel and Schelling conceived of the embodiment of spirit in artistic forms, but saw nothing problematic in the actual intuition of the incarnation of an incorporeal principle. According to Hegel, everything in the world is a stage or aspect of incorporeal spirit, which in general only rarely resides with itself; and if, according to Schelling, the image expresses an infinite idea, he has not the slightest doubt about the possibility of such "expression". But Bakhtin does not move even a single step away from the idea of the spirit as something outside the world (*vnemirnost' dukha*); such a rigorous position invites comparison with Judaism's essential and fundamental (*printsipial'nyi*) refusal to countenance any suggestion that the Absolute might be represented, incarnated, or limited. Nevertheless, for all that he remains true to this initial existential intuition, Bakhtin offers a dazzling solution to the problem of aesthetic form, a solution which required a lifetime's labour and the totality of his written work. But we must begin at the beginning, and examine the relevant writings in their correct order.

"TOWARD A PHILOSOPHY OF THE ACT"

This is not a work about aesthetics. It is about how to create a *prima philosophia*, a doctrine of being, being defined as an *act* (*postupok*). But if Bakhtin's system as a whole is viewed as an aesthetics, then pre-aesthetic intuitions can be glimpsed here. The act, for Bakhtin, has two aspects: an internal, existential aspect, which Bakhtin here calls *answerability* and which is what he will later define as spirit; and an external aspect — the *goal* of the act, its valuative or axiological, meaning-governed (*smyslovoi*) aspect. "Toward a Philosophy of the Act" states that the act has an *author*, and this is the terminological foundation of Bakhtin's aesthetics. The act (*postupok*) may be understood as an artistic act (*akt*), with the author thus becoming a creator of form. But "Toward a Philosophy of the Act" does not move Bakhtin's aesthetics beyond this point.

"AUTHOR AND HERO IN AESTHETIC ACTIVITY" AND "THE PROBLEM OF CONTENT, MATERIAL, AND FORM IN VERBAL AESTHETIC CREATION"

These two tracts from the early 1920s develop Bakhtin's aesthetics in the narrow sense, as a doctrine of *form* as such. The creation of form is for Bakhtin the *finalization* or *consummation* of one person (the *hero*) by another (the *author*); what is *aesthetic* is the event of communication between them. Different types of form are generated in accordance with the quality of this communication. The qualitative nature of this communication leads to different gradations of the aesthetic, different types of form. If in Hegel's system spirit manifests itself with different degrees of plenitude (*adekvatnost'*) at different stages of art, in Bakhtin's early aesthetics the existence of a spectrum of artistic forms is a function of the degree of perfection of the dialogue between author and hero, depends on how fully the *freedom* of both participants is realized in this dialogue. In Bakhtin's aesthetics, as in Hegel's, there is a particular logic to the development (*stanovlenie*) of form.

Language would seem to demand that we see "form" as the form of the *hero*. But in "The Problem of Content" Bakhtin associates the principle of *form* with the author, and *content* with the hero: form, the author's aesthetic activity, "descends [...] from outside" upon a content belonging to being, the hero (PCMF, 282). But form is not, of course, an author. Neither hero nor author, form — a traditional boundary — finds itself drawn into the event of communication; the variety of possible types of communication gives rise to different aesthetic forms. Form is not the communicative *event* itself, but its only stable moment, the one which determines its quality and overcomes its dynamism. In Bakhtin's anti-metaphysical aesthetics form is seemingly the only bearer of clear definition: in Bakhtin's eyes neither author nor hero possesses any substantiality.

So the creation of form is a matter of the consummation of an individual — but the individual is trichotomous, a unity of body, soul and spirit. In "Author and Hero in Aesthetic Activity" Bakhtin uses the commonly accepted concept of aesthetic distance (defined as "outsideness" (*vnenakhodimost'*) or "surplus of vision" (*izbytok videniia*)) and views the events of the consummation of the hero by the author principally in respect of body and soul, in space and time. What is the nature of the communication here, what forms are produced? In space and time the hero is absolutely passive; in not resisting authorial "consummation", he behaves like an *object* (*veshch'*). In essence, the hero here is dead, so that we have a clear instance of the connection made by Simmel between form and death. There is as yet no question of the aestheticization of the properly human: from the standpoint of body and soul as such the human being is not set apart from the natural world. Strictly speaking we might say that, in the section on the consummation of the body and the soul, Bakhtin is developing a conception of *sculptural* and *musical* forms; we could if we wished see in Bakhtin the beginnings of a theory of a system of the arts (one which on principle would not, it is true, include architecture); but from the very beginning Bakhtin's aesthetics develop teleologically towards a theory of *literature* as the properly *spiritual* art.

In "Author and Hero" Bakhtin is approaching such a theory. Having examined how the body and soul are consummated, he raises the question of how the properly human principle (*nachalo*) of the hero might be given form. But he does not speak of *spirit*, returning instead to the ideas of "Toward a Philosophy of the Act" and setting himself the immensely difficult task of showing that the *event* represented by the *act* of the individual may also be aestheticized, consummated. This is Bakhtin's attempt to reply to Simmel, Stepun, perhaps even Blok, and their supposition that the dynamism and profundity of reality cannot be enclosed in form, that any attempt to do so can only deaden life. Bakhtin wishes to overcome philosophically what was thought of as the "tragedy of creation". Taking the primary element of ethical life, the act, he intends to show how it will enter the image of the hero, how it can be given form. But this problem is not conclusively resolved in "Author and Hero". Remaining within the conceptual framework of "Toward a Philosophy of the Act", Bakhtin speaks about giving form to only the external aspect of the act — "the hero's meaning-governed attitude in being", which "is isolated out of the event of being and consummated aesthetically" (AH, 138). Bakhtin is clearly still true to the (essentially existentialist) intuition according to which the *innermost essence* of the act, life as such, can be neither objectified nor, therefore, given form. "Author and Hero" thus leaves an impression of incompleteness, leaves us with no explanation of whether or not the third, and properly human, principle of the individual, the *spirit*, can be "consummated".

Just what, from the point of view of Bakhtin's general aesthetics, is the typology of literary characters described in the section of "Author and Hero in Aesthetic Activity" entitled "The Whole of the Hero as a Whole of Meaning"? What is the logic of the move from *confession* to *lyricism*, and thence to the "*classical*" and "*romantic*" *character*, "*type*", "*lives of saints*"? This sequence of artistic forms is arranged by Bakhtin to reflect the hero's increasing resistance to the author's consummating activity. Life indeed resists attempts to fetter it with form. Only body and soul can be absolutely passive. But if the hero occupies a meaning-filled (*osmyslennoe*) place in being, he attempts to assert his meaning-governed position in opposition to the author's. He may succeed in this to varying degrees — hence the ladder of literary forms, with the "romantic character" at the top. This is to a certain extent the most perfect form of all, indicating on the one hand the hero's successful liberation from the author: in the forms which precede it in Bakhtin's logical sequence — the lyrical hero, for instance — the hero's emancipation is considerably weaker. But on the other hand, this liberated meaning of the hero still does not become a thing in itself (as in the "type" or the "saint's life"), but is still open to authorial intentions. The author–hero relations in the case of the "romantic character" are optimal and approaching the dialogic. The "romantic character" is the most "vital" form, the form imbued more than any other with spirit. In this position (which Bakhtin of course expresses much more guardedly) there is a curious echo of Schellingian and Hegelian aesthetics, the apotheosis of romantic, i.e. Christian art, spiritual art proper. But it must be reiterated that Bakhtin avoids the concept of "spirit" and operates only with the phenomenological category of "sense/meaning" (*smysl*). "Author and Hero", in failing to answer the question about the aestheticization of the spirit, of the individual's deepest being, cries out to be taken further.

PROBLEMS OF DOSTOEVSKY'S POETICS

Here Bakhtin's general aesthetics moves forward; this is the crucial stage in Bakhtin's logic of form. *Problems of Dostoevsky's Poetics* is a continuation of "Author and Hero", in that for Bakhtin Dostoevsky offered a solution to the problem of the aestheticization of spirit, "was able to *see* spirit in a way in which previously only the body and soul of man could be seen" (TRDB, 288). What this means is that the unobjectifiable, unreifiable spirit of the hero can be made manifest by means of the dialogical poetics created by Dostoevsky. The hero of Dostoevsky's novels is the next step after the "romantic character" in the development of literary form; this is a move from "pre-dialogue" to dialogue proper, from the hero's partial freedom to his total emancipation. For Bakhtin, if Dostoevsky had any precursors, then these were to be found only in the literature of Romanticism. But on the other hand there is, in one sense, a gulf between "Author and Hero" and *Dostoevsky*. *Dostoevsky* contains a qualitatively new (dialogic) intuition which allowed Bakhtin to pose the question of how to "give form" not only to "meaning", but also to "spirit". In the move from "Author and Hero" to *Dostoevsky* there is a shift in terminology, a rethinking of "form" and "the aesthetic", and, crucially, at the stage of *Dostoevsky* the wall between art and life comes crashing down, aesthetic distance is abolished, and the idea of the ineradicably tragic quality of creation is breached. Bakhtin truly claims that Dostoevsky has created a qualitatively new form of verbal art.

Just what is the form represented by Dostoevsky's novels? In speaking of the *dialogue* of author and hero which is the essence of this form, Bakhtin presents things as though it is a matter of an event in life rather than one of artistic creation. We should, incidentally, note at this point that the idea of creativity as *creation out of nothing* is absolutely alien to Bakhtin. In this sense the hero is in no way *created* by the author: the author's activity is merely the *consummation* of a content present in being. But there is no longer any "consummation" in *Dostoevsky*! The author possesses no ontological advantage over the hero, both are on the same level of being and interact on an equal footing. With regard to Dostoevsky's poetics it is thus impossible to speak of form in the old sense, in the sense it has in "Author and Hero" — form as a boundary created through the activity of consummation. A new form of art is born — the *polyphonic novel*, which achieves something never achieved by sculpture, music, or any other form of verbal art. For Bakhtin the Dostoevskian novel, being life itself, transcends the bounds of literature to become an autonomous type of art. The conception of form lying behind *Dostoevsky* is Bakhtin's reply both to the aesthetics of the beginning of the twentieth century, and, for example, to Rickert, who stopped when faced with the problem of reconciling form with life. The form of novelistic dialogue does not deaden life, it is itself living life; this is the culmination and the most important insight of Bakhtin's aesthetics.

But, being life itself, the dialogic form is therefore the most perfect of forms, for it aestheticizes the essence of the human being, spirit, which cannot be aestheticized in any other way. It is my view that in reaching this crucially important position whereby the revelation of individual spirit is achieved in dialogue Bakhtin was influenced by Buber's *I and Thou*, which he evidently knew well. In "Author and Hero in Aesthetic Activity" Bakhtin comes very close to the notion of dialogue, but there is as yet no properly dialogic intuition. At the same time, the anthropology of "Author and Hero" is directed towards the concept of spirit, circles tantalisingly around it, and it requires only the slightest of pushes for Bakhtin's thought to be qualitatively transformed and for a new aesthetic conception linking spirit and dialogue to be born from the heart of "Author and Hero". This push was apparently provided by Buber's book. "The colossal illusion", wrote Buber, is to think that "spirit exists in man. Actually spirit exists [...] between man and that which is not man" (Buber 1959 [1923], 93). According to Buber the spirit is between I and Thou, it reveals itself only to another spirit, the spirit is only in dialogue, and the spirit *is* dialogue. It is perfectly possible that Buber's influence led directly to Bakhtin's contemplation of the possibility of author–hero dialogue. The problem of aestheticization of spirit raised in "Author and Hero" is thus resolved at a stroke. And the search for an aesthetic form corresponding to this new situation must take as its starting point the "romantic character"; the move from here to Dostoevsky's poetics, with its organic link to Romanticism, is a perfectly natural one. The intense struggle of ideas in Dostoevsky's novels was described in the terms of Bakhtin's aesthetics with exceptional philosophical beauty.

So life as understood by Bakhtin in the 1920s is the life of the spirit, and the life of the spirit is dialogue; it is in this sense that Dostoevsky's dialogical novels are life itself. If the argument about perfect form as the form which manifests spirit is taken further, then there is an unexpected echo, in Bakhtin's highly idiosyncratic aesthetics, of classical aesthetics. Thus Schelling stated that "the fullness of form annihilates form itself", that "the indwelling spirit of nature", life, "is beyond form" (Schelling 1845 [1807], 14, 10). Hegel wrote that "*free concrete spirituality*" — the content of Christian art — cannot be the object of sensual contemplation, cannot be reduced to bodily form, and as it were overcomes this form (Hegel 1975 [1835], 80–81). According to Goethe, "a perfect work of art seems [...] to be a work of nature" (Goethe 1980 [1798], 29). Aesthetic perfection for classical aesthetics signified a move beyond form, and substantial joining of the work of art with the element of life. This is precisely the move that we find in Bakhtin: the polyphonic novel overcomes, by bringing it to perfection, the old novel form, and this break is nothing less than a move into life. Hegel and Schelling see the most perfect form in romantic art; for Bakhtin aesthetic perfection is Dostoevsky's "realism in the highest sense".

To sum up the argument so far: the notion of form in Bakhtin develops in the direction of increasing endowing with spirit (*odukhotvorenie*) of form, of bringing art closer to life. Beginning with concrete (*veshchestvennaia*) sculptural form, Bakhtin then gives it a vital impulse (rhythmical musical form), makes it meaning-bearing (a series of literary forms), then introduces the spiritual principle proper into it (Dostoevsky's polyphonic novel). This is how, step by step, Bakhtin tackles the central, eternal problem of aesthetics — the problem of form and life, which in the twentieth century has acquired a tragic resonance. Yes, form does suppress, place limits on life, says Bakhtin's aesthetics, but the degree of "deadness" of forms varies greatly, art is not entirely subject to the power of fate, it seeks emancipation and finds an outstanding means of escape in polyphonic poetics: here there is aesthetic perfection, and along with it life itself, wholly unfettered. Such is the logic of Bakhtin's aesthetics. The final outstanding question is the place of Rabelais's poetics in this series of aesthetic forms.

RABELAIS AND HIS WORLD

First: how can the form described in *Rabelais and His World* be characterized in Bakhtinian terms? Form is the result of the interaction of author and hero; but, according to Bakhtin, Rabelais's novel has *neither* hero *nor* author as individuals. The hero, the individual human being, is dissolved in Rabelais's world in the body of the people, while the author does not have his own voice in the novel: Rabelais's last word is the people's word, claims Bakhtin (*RW*, 453). The author of *Gargantua and Pantagruel* is a mouthpiece of carnival, a passive medium for the elemental life of carnival. To put it another way, he is possessed by the spirit of carnival, and through him carnival steps on to the pages of the novel free of subjective mediation. According to *Rabelais*, this novel about giant-kings *is* the elemental life of carnival itself.

Let us compare this conclusion with the main thrust of *Dostoevsky*. For Bakhtin Dostoevsky's novel was a dialogue of author and heroes, and nothing less than life itself — spiritual life, a struggle of ideas. It is clear that for Bakhtin, Rabelais's novel is also life. If Dostoevsky achieved through his poetics the union of art with life, then Rabelais achieved the same thing. But "life" is not the same thing in *Rabelais* as it is in *Dostoevsky*. In *Dostoevsky* life is an existential dialogue, the life of the spirit as understood by Bakhtin. In *Rabelais* life as carnival is the triumph of a vitality of the lowest order. Carnival is the quintessence of the life of the flesh, the of the "material bodily lower stratum" run riot. This is also a spirituality, but the spirituality of the lowest reaches. Rabelais's novel is for Bakhtin the play of the unincarnated spirits of bodily elements, a play wholly unfettered by the artist's will. There is not a single individual among Rabelais's characters: Rabelais's poetics rules out the representation of free spirit. It is directed instead towards the portrayal of beings which in occultism are called larvae (spectres), shells, the portrayal of the denizens of the lowest levels of the invisible world. So if *Dostoevsky* is dedicated to the form which correlates to the highest level of life, *Rabelais* speaks of the aestheticization of vitality of the lowest kind.

In moving from *Dostoevsky* to *Rabelais* Bakhtin seems to ask: if the polyphonic novel reproduces the life of the spirit, cannot a form, a poetics be found which will convey the life of the flesh? Clearly, in asking this the thinker is taking the next step in his resolution of the problem of the aestheticization of life. *In his aesthetics Bakhtin wishes to embrace with form the entire fullness of life*. But form cannot withstand such pressure from life. *Dostoevsky* describes perfect form, but even here it is no longer form in the proper sense, not a boundary, not a consummated whole. When the internal pressure of life on form increases, form disintegrates. In essence, Rabelais's novel as conceived of by Bakhtin does not possess aesthetic form and is not a fact of art. It is simply a piece of carnival being, transplanted on to the pages of a book and marked with the meaningless name "Rabelais". In the categories of Bakhtin's aesthetics Rabelais's novel is formless. Having associated form with the interaction of author and hero, and established its dependence on individuality, when he turns to a work where authorship is of a different, monumental type, Bakhtin effectively denies that this work possesses form (it is worth noting that the saint's life or hagiography, a product of medieval forms of authorship, also eludes classification in terms of Bakhtin's aesthetics). The logic of form in Bakhtin's aesthetics is thus completed: life in its striving to manifest itself in art, having found the optimal form for doing so, then breaks all and any barriers of aesthetic definition. And in this *logic of form* all Bakhtin's works are interconnected; taken together they form a harmonious aesthetic system.

WORKS CITED

Bonetskaia, N.K. 1985. "Problema avtorstva v trudakh M.M. Bakhtina", *Studia Slavica Academiae Scientiarum Hungaricae* (Budapest), 31, 61–108.

Buber, M. 1959 [1923]. *I and Thou*, tr. R.G. Smith (Edinburgh: T. & T. Clark).

Goethe, J.W. von 1980 [1798]. "On Truth and Probability in Works of Art: A Dialogue", in *Goethe on Art*, ed. and tr. J. Gage (London, Scolar Press), 25–30.

Hegel, G.W.F. 1975 [1835]. *Aesthetics: Lectures on Fine Art*, vol. 1, tr. T.M. Knox (Oxford: Clarendon Press).

Nikolaev, N.I. 1992. "Lektsii i vystupleniia M.M. Bakhtina 1924–1925 gg. v zapisiakh L.V. Pumpianskogo", in L.A. Gogotishvili and P.S. Gurevich (eds.), *Bakhtin kak filosof* (Moscow: Nauka), 221–251.

Rickert, H. 1920. *Die Philosophie des Lebens: Darstellung und Kritik der philosophischen Modeströmungen unserer Zeit* (Tübingen: J.C.B. Mohr [Paul Siebeck]).

Scheler, M. 1928. *Die Stellung des Menschen im Kosmos* (Darmstadt: Otto Reichl Verlag).

Schelling, F. 1845 [1807]. *The Philosophy of Art: An Oration on the Relation between the Plastic Arts and Nature*, tr. A. Johnson (London: John Chapman).

Simmel [Zimmel'], G. 1910–11. "Zur Metaphysik des Todes", in *Logos* (Tübingen), 1 (1910–11), 57–70. In Russian: "K voprosu o metafizike smerti", in *Logos* (Moscow), 2 (1910), 34–49.

________. 1911–12. "Der Begriff und die Tragödie der Kultur", in *Logos* (Tübingen), 21–25. In Russian: "Poniatie i tragediia kul'tury", in *Logos* (Moscow), 2–3 (1911–12), 1–25.

Stepun, F.A. 1910. "Tragediia tvorchestva (Fridrikh Shlegel)", in *Logos* (Moscow), 1, 171–196.

________. 1913. "Zhizn' i tvorchestvo", in *Logos* (Moscow), 3–4, 71–126.

THE ARCHITECTONICS OF AESTHETIC DISCOURSE

Valerii Tiupa, Novosibirsk Pedagogical University

By bringing together a number of Bakhtin's works from various periods we can build up a picture of the implicit kernel of a semio-aesthetic conception. It is probably only now that the necessary conditions for this conception's full potential to be realized are in place: the international growth of semiotics and theories of information and communication on the one hand, and on the other the revival within Russian culture of the philosophical traditions of the "Silver Age", and in particular of philosophical aesthetics. The first of these prerequisites is "strong" and beyond dispute, while the second is "weak", since there is a frequent tendency even among followers of Bakhtin to dismiss aesthetics as an obsolete form of knowledge. But for me this second prerequisite is actually the more crucial. Let us recall that, as Bakhtin himself put it in a challenge to neo-positivist tendencies in the twentieth century, "Deprived of the basis provided by systematic philosophical aesthetics, poetics becomes unstable and fortuitous in its very foundations" (PCMF, 260).

But it does not just come down to a question of Bakhtin's authority. Aesthetic nihilism — as in the French semiology of *écriture*, for example — leads the critic to a position from which the dividing line between, say, Chekhov's literary works and his private letters, which for all that they are superb examples of the epistolary art do not belong to the sphere of aesthetic discourse, becomes indiscernible. This aberration of aesthetic vision is radically pessimistic in its view of the destiny of art as a cultural phenomenon. But its pessimism by no means signals the decline of art and artistic quality as such, but merely marks the decline of the avant-garde paradigm of artistic quality, "the historical exhaustion of modernism" (Makhlin 1990, 122).

Another important topic which needs to be discussed at this early stage in our argument is the compatibility of the "early" and the "late" Bakhtin. I am convinced that this is a non-existent opposition. Bakhtin's thought is architectonic, it knows no *stages* of development (*stanovlenie*). Its progression from one work to the next has nothing in common with dialectic "negation of negation". It is a deepening and a making explicit of intellectual intuition, a clarification and illumination of the obscure depths of intuition which elude logical knowledge. It is a sustained scrutiny of certain facets of the primordial coherence of spiritual content which reveals itself to individual reflection and is experienced as a *gift*, a beneficent gift requiring that the content be concretized in response.

This is where we see the deep division between thinkers such as Bakhtin, Mikhail Prishvin or Teilhard de Charden on the one hand, and Jean-Paul Sartre, Roland Barthes or Jacques Derrida on the other. The common ground which has led Western students of Bakhtin to compare him with Derrida (see MacCannell 1985, Holquist 1986) is the uncompromising opposition of both to *authoritarian* consciousness, the hostility of their thought to any forms of external obligation and coercion. But beyond this there is a crucial divergence between the *isolation* of consciousness concerned above all else with its own *freedom* from any "other", and the *convergence* ("dialogism") of Bakhtinian consciousness, concerned with its own internal *answerability* before the "other". If for Bakhtin every creative act is essentially dialogical, in Derrida's view creation is merely a "substitute" for dialogue in a situation of the "absence of the other" (see Derrida 1981 [1972]).

It is obvious that freedom and responsibility, answerability, are indivisible. The measure of responsibility — as a counterbalance to obligation or "the ought" (*dolzhenstvovanie*) — is defined by the degree of freedom: external obligation deprives me of freedom to the same extent that it frees me from internal responsibility for my actions and intentions. Yet freedom and responsibility are nevertheless differently directed intentions and can easily become hypertrophied. The hypertrophying of the intention of personal freedom in the consciousness of Barthes gave him a craving to free his thought as it is today from the power, again of his own thought, but as it was yesterday, and thus already "other". The hypertrophying of the intention of personal responsibility in Bakhtin's consciousness led him to remove his name from the remarkable works which are ascribed to Voloshinov and Medvedev, who probably did not fully correspond to Bakhtin's image of himself as "other", as transcendent to his earthly being.

When one is dealing with a thinker such as Bakhtin, the time and circumstances in which a particular work was written are no longer of fundamental importance. But on the other hand the theoretical constructions of such a thinker may display what Sergei Averintsev has called "lacunae". These do not become explicit because of the demands of "making the first approach to the reality" of the spiritual object, but this may be compensated for (*vospolnit′*, a Bakhtinian word) up to a point if we proceed from the general context of the thought which gave rise to the lacunae (see Averintsev 1981, 10–11). In what follows I shall attempt to draw attention to one such lacuna in Bakhtin's philosophy of culture, a theory of aesthetic discourse.

The contemporary understanding of discourse as a "communicative event" (see van Dijk 1988, esp. 8–9) was already fully present in Bakhtin's theory of the utterance. In the early 1950s Bakhtin even expressed regret that linguistics lacked a term which could convey this (PSG, 71); "discourse" (*diskurs*, as opposed to *slovo*, the word used extensively by Bakhtin) was subsequently to become just such a term. Bakhtin's model of the utterance includes three components, three aspects of the communicative event: the *subject* (S), the *object* (O) (the "objective referentially semantic aspect" of the utterance, which in its intentionality is determined by the subject), and the *addressee* (A) (Figure 1). It is of crucial importance that Bakhtin con-

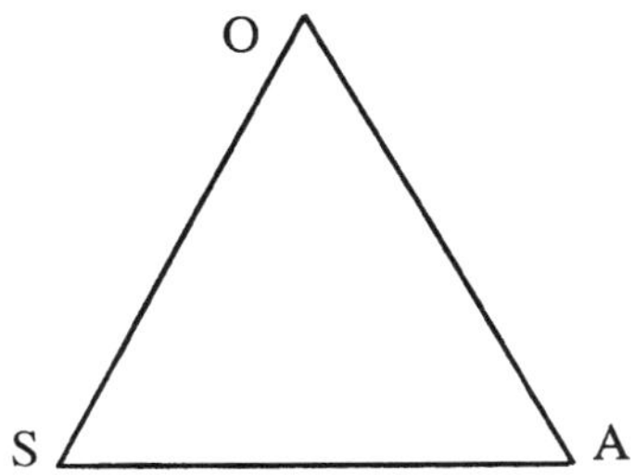

Fig. 1

ceives of the work of art alongside other types of utterance, in that it has a text, in the broad sense of "any coherent complex of signs" (PT, 103). This approach to the work of art as a specific mode of utterance sends us back to Bakhtin's earliest works on aesthetics, and in particular to the concept of the "aesthetic object", which cannot be identified either with the text of the work of art in its objective givenness or with the phenomena of consciousness (see PCMF, 300).

Bakhtin's model of the work of art also comprises three aspects: the *text* (T), the *consciousness* (C) which occupies an aesthetic position with regard to this text, and the aesthetic *object* (O). "There are two empirically present-on-hand constituents in artistic creation: the external material work [the text] and the psychic process of creation and perception" (PCMF, 300). The aesthetic object, defined as "*the content of aesthetic activity (contemplation) directed toward a work*" (267) is fundamentally and essentially [*printsipial'no*] not reducible to these "constituents" (see Figure 2).

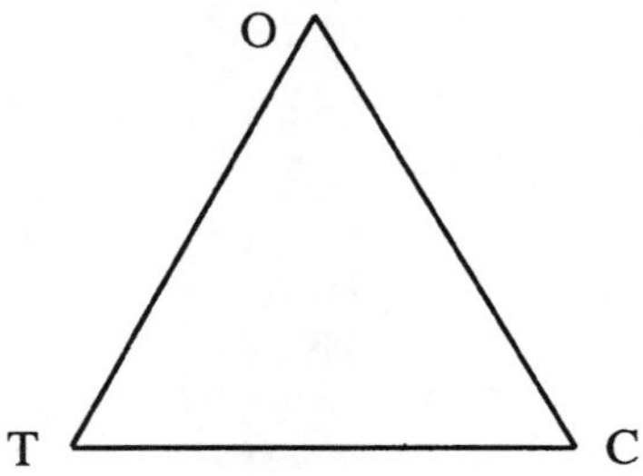

Fig. 2

At first sight the only similarity between these two models is their tripartite character; they are different in that the first contains two opposed consciousnesses (subject and addressee), while the second does not distinguish between these two consciousnesses. However, if we apply Iurii Lotman's idea of "autocommunicativeness" as a defining characteristic of the artistic text (see Lotman 1992 [1973]), then it is fairly easy to read Bakhtin's model of the aesthetic act as a model of a particular type of discourse, an auto-communicative event. This is not meant to suggest that the sphere of aesthetic relations can be limited to autocommunicative acts of consciousness. That would be to adopt a deconstructivist stance alien to Bakhtin's manner of thinking.

"Author–reader" in Bakhtin's late texts is a version of the "I–Other" pairing fundamental to his philosophy which is every bit as important as "author–hero" in the early works. But the heuristic task of bringing to light the hidden mechanisms of aesthetic activity required recourse to autobiographical creation, to a situation which obliged the creating artist "in oneself [...] [to] see another, and do so utterly" (AH, 17). A similar division into self-as-author and self-as-other (reader) which is a condition of autocommunication is the defining moment of art, the moment of creative reflection which separates creation by an individual author from folklore and myth. What is needed is a general model of the architectonics of discourse which assumes autocommunication as a particular instance.

In order to combine our two triangles we have still to clarify the position of the "text" in the model of the utterance. The text's position is categorically not between "subject" and "addressee", as good old Romanticism or the latest deconstruction might lead us to think. In a consistently Bakhtinian model of discourse the text and the subject of the utterance are one and the same aspect of the communicative event, since it is the change of subjects, which "fram[es] the utterance and creat[es] for it a stable mass that is sharply delimited from other related utterances", that is conceived of by Bakhtin as the "absolute boundary" of the work (PSG, 76).

The rationale for this identification of text and subject is that the author as a subject — in particular an *aesthetic* subject — in any given sphere of culture exists only in the form of a text. He cannot be identified with the real biographical individual who wrote this text. The subject of discourse is not the speaking or writing individual in his own right, but "the active position of the speaker in one referentially semantic sphere or another" (PSG, 84). The same individual as a bearer of, and participant in, culture is constantly split in two, as it were: "the listener becomes the speaker", while "any speaker is himself a respondent to a greater or lesser degree" (PSG, 68, 69). The biographical author, the subject possessing authorial rights during the process of writing, constantly distances himself from the intratextual position of the utterance's subject, displacing himself to the point of view of a hypothetical addressee, and constantly comes back, "into the text". The subject of discourse is ultimately just one of the functions of the communicative event, the *creative* function. In this respect, functionally, the subject *can* be identified with the text. The artistic text, for example, is the only form in which the aesthetic subject, "the author not as an image, but as a function" (PT, 112), can have a complete existence.

The addressee of discourse is similarly not an actually present individual. He is an "active responsive position" (PSG, 86) in a particular cultural sphere. He is a pole of fully perceiving consciousness, regardless of whose this consciousness might be, including the consciousness of the writer of the text himself. In the case of art it is here, and not in the text, that phantoms such as "the image of the author", "the image of the hero", "the image of the world", and, finally, the "work" itself, and so on are revealed as psychic realities of discourse.

"The person who participates in understanding constitutes part of the understood utterance" (PT, 123), in that the "anticipated response, in turn, exerts an active influence on my utterance" (PSG, 95). The addressee (in particular the aesthetic addressee) is nothing other than a second function, correlative with the first, of the communicative event; the addressee is the *receptive* function of discourse.

The question of the correlation between the creative structure of the artistic text and the receptive structure of the artistic phantom is clearly becoming the key question of contemporary literary theory and aesthetics, which runs the risk of an irreconcilable split into separate aesthetics of "creation" and "reception". Bakhtin's category of the "aesthetic object" may offer us crucial assistance in finding an answer to this urgent question.

Like the subject and addressee, the object of discourse (and not just aesthetic discourse) cannot be identified with a thing actually present. It "has already been articulated, disputed, elucidated, and evaluated in various ways [...] The speaker is not Adam, and therefore the subject of his speech itself inevitably becomes the arena where his opinions meet those of his partners (in a conversation or dispute about some everyday event) or other view-points, world views, trends, theories and so forth" (PSG, 93–94). In other words, the "referentially semantic content of the utterance" is a mental structure, an ideal (quasi-real) object belonging to a specific sphere of social consciousness. It is "only" a reflection, "only" a refraction of actual things and relations. But actual objects (*ob"ekty*) are spiritually inert, whereas the object (*ob"ekt*) of discourse is spiritually active, dialogically tense, yieldingly unyielding to the consciousnesses which bear upon it. Ultimately in its "subjectness" it yields to neither the addressee nor the subject of discourse itself, it gravitates towards the pole of "personality", not that of "object" (*veshch'*) (to use the personalist polarization so fundamentally important to Bakhtin). Only this understanding of the object of discourse could have given rise to Bakhtin's conception of the Dostoevskian hero.

The object of discourse is intentional, it requires the subject as an immutable condition of its own realization, as a guarantee of its objectivity. But the subject too requires the object to the same degree and on the same grounds. As the initiating party to the communicative nexus, the subject positions itself vis-à-vis the object in a relation of answerability before the "architectonic task" (PCMF, 271) of realizing its object. Discourse as a complex spiritual whole contains as its "referentially semantic content" an infratext, a transtextual "architectonic task" characterized by an *imperative* function inherent to this particular type of creative–receptive activity. This is what I consider to be the nature of the mental object, in particular the aesthetic object. For "no reality in itself, no *neutral* reality, can be placed in opposition to art"; on the plane of the objects of utterances, "*reality can be contraposed to art only as something good or something true in opposition to beauty*" (PCMF, 276).

The model of discourse which can be derived from Bakhtin can indeed be imagined as a particular kind of "triangle" of the communicative (and this includes the autocommunicative) event: the "word exists for the speaker in *three* aspects: as a neutral word of a language, belonging to nobody; as an *other's* word, which belongs to another person and is filled with echoes of the other's utterance; and, finally, as *my* word" since it is "imbued with my expression" (PSG, 88; first emphasis added). The "points" of this triangle are: the creative structure of the text; the receptive structure of the phantom–work (the work as a kind of "ultratext"); and, finally, the mental structure of the infratext, which may be correlated to the Word, belonging to nobody, of a translinguistic, intersubjective consciousness.

It is to this latter structure that we should assign Bakhtin's category of the "superaddressee", of whom it is said "he is a constitutive aspect of the whole utterance, who, under deeper analysis, can be revealed in it" (PT, 126–127). This idea alone, which is incompatible with the idea of "deconstruction", places Bakhtin at such an obtuse angle in relation to Derrida that there can be absolutely no question of likening them one to the other, or of accepting (even within the narrow limits of a theory of laughter) Dragan Kujundzic's thesis that the two "coincide in their strategies" (Kujundzic 1990, 289). The strategy of deconstruction is the death of Bakhtin's tri-aspectual word. By acknowledging the word as only "mine" or "the other's", and by rejecting the aspect of unassimilated *collective* discourse (*sobornoe slovo*), deconstruction rules out any possibility of a dialogic encounter between "my" consciousness and "the other's".

The addressee is inconceivable outside of his correlation with the subject of the utterance. A hypostatized "superaddressee" (ideal receiver) inevitably presupposes a hypostatized "supersubject", a kind of ideal author. Thus intersubjective originary images or *eide* of the subject (*es*: a transtextual superauthor) and the addressee (*ea*: a transtextual superreader) are peeled away from the imperative nucleus of the "referentially semantic content" of discourse. This makes the object of discourse (OD) not a referent external to the discourse itself (this is a widespread misconception), but a mental *potential* of the given communicative event. The object of any discourse, including even scholarly or scientific discourse (see Heisenberg 1959), belongs to the spheres of potential being of the *eide* and awaits concretization, awaits the communicative event which is the encounter of the consciousnesses of a real subject and a real addressee. The object of discourse, which bears within it ideal originary images of subject and addressee, is the spiritual and creative potential of such an encounter.

A similar "peeling away" can also be observed at the two other points of our triangular model of the architectonics of discourse. Within the text is revealed an object of the text (for example, Eugene Onegin in Pushkin's novel of the same name) which is in no way identifiable with the "referentially semantic content" of this novel as a communicative event, that is, with the object of discourse. Also within the text we can see its hypothetical (*uslovnyi*) addressee, no less fictitious than the hero. The communicative event of the encounter between the consciousnesses of the real author and a real reader takes place "over the head" of this intratextual addressee: a reader capable of an aesthetically complete perception of the irony of Pushkin's text will never identify himself with the "reader" who "is already expecting the rhyme 'rose'" (Pushkin, *Eugene Onegin*, canto 4, stanza 42). But however distantiated the object of the text (*ot*) and the addressee of the text (*at*) from the subject of discourse (SD), they are still, like the fictitious subject of the text (the narrator or story-teller), sloughs or "scales" of this very same creative subject. They are born of the figure of the author in just the same way as the supersubject and the superaddressee are products or sloughs of the infratextual object.

Finally, at the third point of discourse as "work", i.e. a text functioning in an individual consciousness, the receptive potential of the addressee of discourse (AD) serves as a source of subjective images, *phantoms* of the object (*pho*) and the subject (*phs*) — what are generally referred to as the "image of Onegin" and the "image of the author" in Pushkin's novel, for instance. But the reader's co-creativity is not a matter of producing an actual Onegin, or of identifying Pushkin's Onegin; it is a matter of "seeing", together with Pushkin, the *eidos* of creative discovery uniquely realized in Pushkin's text. The communicative event is not an appropriation of the text by the addressee, or a withdrawal by the perceiving consciousness into itself, or indeed a submission to the will of the author of the utterance; it is an ascent to the infratext, a movement outside the self into the intersubjective space of the encounter of consciousnesses (the "noosphere").

These clarifications made, we can now construct a model of a "tripled triangle" which in my view reproduces more fully Bakhtin's architectonics of discourse (not only aesthetic discourse) (Figure 3).

The specific character of *aesthetic* discourse is determined by three constitutive moments, corresponding to the number of aspects of the communicative event, which allow us to demarcate this form of the human intellect's cultural life from all others. The first of these moments is that the communicative function of speech is significantly weakened in the artistic text — in some cases weakened to the point of total blockage. The constructive role here belongs to the mental function, i.e. the function of "thought emerging" (PSG, 67), not of the communication of thought already complete. This peculiarity of writerly activity was termed by Bakhtin "the gift of indirect speaking" (PT, 110).

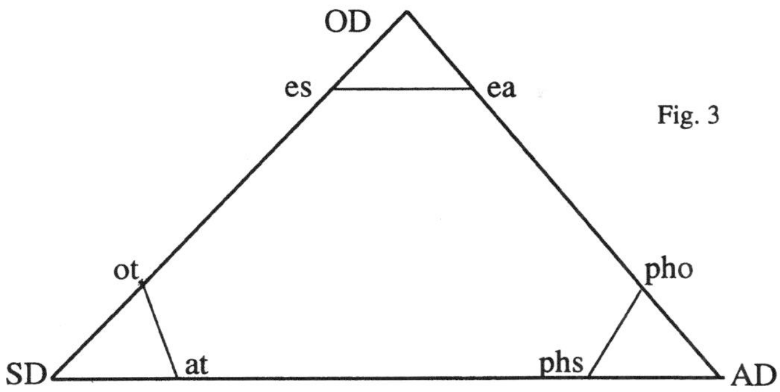

Fig. 3

From this peculiarity stems the key role played in aesthetic discourse by the infratext (the mental structure of the aesthetic object as an *eidos* of artistic wholeness). When the communicative function proper of the text is blocked the communicative event can take place only on one condition: the perceiver has the same mastery of its "referentially semantic content" as the author producing the text. The paradoxical nature of this condition, although it is wholly natural for the artistic paradigm of what Averintsev has called "reflective traditionalism" (Averintsev 1981, 11), is, I believe, what leads to deconstruction as a scientistic form of despair at the imagined impossibility of communication between the participants in a communicative event. Evidently only "I-in-the-world", or in other words *the architectonics of existence* (the second of our three constitutive moments), can be acknowledged as such a paradoxical content of aesthetic discourse, known to the addressee in advance. This object, which is on principle not susceptible to being made explicit, is implicitly present in any individual consciousness. It is directly given to me from within my "I" as a sense of my living presence in the world; realization of such an object (the self-realization of the subject) is the shared content of the various forms of the human individual's aesthetic relation to the world.[1]

The artistic text objectifies and generalizes the existential experience of self-realization, makes existence intellectually visible in the form of the hero, understood in a Bakhtinian way:

> *man* is the organizing form-and-content center of artistic vision, and, moreover, man as a *given human being* in his axiological present-on-hand existence in the world [i.e. not a generic being, but a represented "I" in its essential "otherness" in relation to the author and reader]. The world of artis-

> tic vision is a world which is organized, ordered, and consummated [...] *around* a given human being as *his* axiological surroundings [...] This axiological orientation and consolidation of the world *around* a given human being creates its aesthetic reality, which is distinct from its cognitional and ethical reality. (AH, 187)

> And it is this reality of the hero — the reality of another consciousness — that constitutes the *object* of aesthetic vision which imparts *aesthetic objectivity* to that vision. (AH, 199)

The heroic, tragic, comic, and so on architectonics of the specific reality of artistic vision ("the architectonic form of the whole") emerges, from the standpoint proposed by Bakhtin, as an intersubjective image/*eidos* of the given text, a counterweight to all its subjective phantom images which more or less fully, and with greater or lesser clarity, realize their aesthetic object.

Finally, the third constitutive peculiarity of aesthetic discourse lies in the receptive orientation towards a communicative event of *consensus*, towards a dialogue of *agreement* (see PT, 121, 125) between the author as the initiator of discourse and his addressee with regard to an aesthetic object which unites rather than divides them. "The basic feature of the aesthetic that sharply distinguishes it from cognition and performed action is its receptive, positively accepting character" (PCMF, 278).

Of course, there is nothing to stop the reader from entering into an argument, an ideological struggle of consciousnesses, with the author. But this would mean that the reader had moved outside aesthetic discourse as such and ascribed to the artistic text a cultural significance (political, religious, etc.) inappropriate to its nature. Such moves are not unusual in the practice of readers, but this does not cancel out the specifically aesthetic quality of the artistic text.

The communicative event of aesthetic discourse as a dialogue of agreement takes place only if both the artistic text (a semiotic cultural phenomenon) and its "world" of images (the work of art as a psychological phenomenon of consciousness) are two non-identifiable (creative and receptive) realizations of one and the same transtextual *eidos*, of a single paradigm of the artistic whole (the transtext), of an existential-architectonic "task" common to author and reader (PCMF, 316). Here we have "the inseparability [...], but also [the] not merging into one" (PCMF, 317) of the facets of the architectonics of discourse as an architectonics of *threefoldness*; this is a moment of enormously rich significance for the human spirit and all its most important cultural forms.

It is this "tripling" of the original aesthetic relation that in effect constitutes the autocommunicative mechanism of artistic creation. The intentional syncretism of the aesthetic object and aesthetic subject breaks down into a mental "task" (revealed to the author in the form of an "intention" (*zamysel*), but not reducible to an intention in his subjectivity), the creative realization of this task, and a receptive "examination", which shows itself in the author's editing of his own text as he verifies it against the *eidos* of his inspiration.

Something similar happens at the other pole of discourse, but in reverse order: the reader "edits" his own original artistic impression, moving along the path of "convergence" (see PT, 124) with the subject of the artistic utterance in relation to the aesthetic object. If the artistic text, by blocking the communicative function of speech activity, breaks the unity of subject and addressee immanent to authorial consciousness, thus producing the temptation of deconstruction, then the transtextuality of the "architectonic task" restores this unity. But it restores it between the sovereign consciousnesses of two or more participants in discourse, and in doing so accomplishes the great mission of true art, the mission of overcoming the isolation of human consciousness, of "strengthening through merging (but not identification)" (PT, 121), i.e. by means of *convergence*.

At this point it is essential to emphasize the obvious fact that Bakhtin's dialogism was born from the Christian idea of the collectivity (*sobornost'*) of souls, the convergence of individuals, and ultimately the dogma of the non-fused yet undivided character (*nesliannost'-nerazdel'nost'*) of the Holy Trinity. Bakhtin scholars today often lose sight of this, and consciously or unconsciously distort his conception of dialogue by reducing it to an opposition of consciousnesses colliding at the point of an object common to their purviews, but voiceless and inert. This is how the situation of aesthetic discourse is conceived in the particular instance of the avant-garde paradigm of artistic quality (neo-romantic pre-modernism, modernism, and postmodernism).

The conceptual complex of transtextuality as a counterbalance to the "Parnassian atheism"[2] of modern deconstructionist obsessions is an active presence in Bakhtin. However, it is for the most part not an overt presence, but a concealed intellectual potential awaiting its realization, its "festival of rebirth" (*prazdnik vozrozhdeniia*) (MHS, 170, translation modified). The elaboration of this conceptual complex as one of three hypostases of aesthetic discourse, and in particular the elaboration of the categories of "aesthetic object", "architectonic task" (supersubject) and "superaddressee", is a project of particular relevance for aesthetics today. In general, embedding the whole complex of problems associated with the theory of discourse deep into aesthetics is like an urgently needed blood transfusion: it is indispensable for the periodic rejuvenation of one of the oldest branches of the humanities. Bakhtin's intellectual enquiries in this field can be said to have set in train this resurrection and rejuvenation of aesthetics in the twentieth century. This process is not an end in itself. Its historical justification is that it partakes of the formation of a new cultural paradigm, that of the *salvation* of human culture.

NOTES

1. The content of the moral relation to the world, whose fundamental cultural form is religious discourse, is a realization of the "otherness" of the other and of me myself as other-for-others. The primary link of ethical (religious) discourse is the addressee, not the subject, as in aesthetic (artistic) discourse, and not the object, as in epistemological discourse.
2. "Parnasskii afeizm", Pushkin's throwaway characterization of romanticism in his lyric "K Rodzianke" (1825), which is perhaps the most profound ever given. Rejecting any and every classical "rule", the romantic ignores transtextuality completely, loses faith in the *eide* of creation, and takes flight into the subjective world of phantoms, which makes it necessary to remind him, perhaps rather too categorically: "You are wrong to imagine, artist | That you are creator of your creations" (A.K. Tolstoi). A more correct formulation would be "You are wrong to imagine, artist, that you alone are creator of your creations."

WORKS CITED

Averintsev, S.S. 1981. "Vvedenie: Drevnegrecheskaia poetika i mirovaia literatura", in Averintsev (ed.), *Poetika drevnegrecheskoi literatury* (Moscow: Nauka), 3–14.

Derrida, J. 1981 [1972]. *Dissemination*, tr. B. Johnson (London: Athlone Press).

Heisenberg, W. 1959. *Physics and Philosophy: The Revolution in Modern Science* (London: Allen and Unwin).

Holquist, M. 1986. "The Surd Heard: Bakhtin and Derrida", in G.S. Morson (ed.), *Literature and History: Theoretical Problems and Russian Case Studies* (Stanford: Stanford University Press), 137–156.

Kujundzic, D. 1990. "Laughter as Otherness in Bakhtin and Derrida", in R.F. Barsky and M. Holquist (eds.), *Bakhtin and Otherness* (*Discours social/Social Discourse* (Montreal), 3/1–2), 271–294.

Lotman, Iu.M. 1992 [1973]. "O dvukh modeliakh kommunikatsii v sisteme kul'tury", in *Izbrannye stat'i v trekh tomakh*, vol. 1 (*Stat'i po semiotike i tipologii kul'tury*) (Tallinn: Aleksandra), 76–89.

MacCannell, J.F. 1985. "The Temporality of Textuality: Bakhtin and Derrida", in *MLN* (*Modern Language Notes*), 100/5, 968–987.

Makhlin, V.L. 1990. "'Dialogizm' M.M. Bakhtina kak problema gumanitarnoi kul'tury XX veka", in D. Kujundzic and Makhlin (eds.), *Bakhtinskii sbornik* (Moscow), 1, 107–129.

van Dijk, T.A. 1988. "The Analysis of News as Discourse", in *News Analysis: Case Studies of International and National News in the Press* (Hillsdale, NJ: Lawrence Erlbaum Associates), 1–30.

BAKHTIN AND VALÉRY: TOWARDS A POETICS OF DIALOGISM

Angela Biancofiore, Université Paul Valéry, Montpellier

The path that has led me to compare Bakhtin's and Valéry's theories of literature passes through the fertile fields of dialogism. I would like to illustrate how, despite the many differences between Valéry's and Bakhtin's aesthetic theories, it is possible to identify a common ground: the role of dialogue in the process of literary production, and the notion of alterity in literary communication.

THE APPROPRIATION OF THE WORD

Reflections about inner dialogue and the dialogic nature of thought often occur in Valéry's *Notebooks*. In a passage entitled "Le Robinson pensif" ("Pensive Robinson") he underlines that "L'individu est un dialogue" ["the individual is a dialogue"], and gives a definition of the communication occurring between the self and him-/herself: "Le moi se dit *moi* ou *toi* ou *il*. Il y a les 3 personnes en moi. La Trinité. Celle qui tutoie le moi; celle qui le traite de *Lui*" ["The I says to him-/herself *I* or *you* or *he*. The three persons are in me. The Trinity. The person who addresses the I as you; the one who calls it *Him*"] (Valéry 1973–74, I, 440). Valéry perceives the basic role that the polarity of persons plays in discourse (cf. Benveniste 1966 [1958]). The self speaks with him-/herself through others:

> L'homme ne communique avec soi-même que dans la mesure où il sait *communiquer* avec ses semblables et par les mêmes moyens.
>
> Il a appris à *se* parler — par le détour de ce que j'appellerais l'*Autrui*. Entre *lui* et *lui*, l'intermédiaire est Autrui. (Valéry 1973–74, I, 456)
>
> [Man communicates with himself only to the extent that he knows how to *communicate* with those like him and by the same means.
>
> He learned to speak *to himself* via the detour of what I would call the *Other*. Between *him* and *him* the intermediary is the Other.]

Inner dialogue implies a divided speaking subject: this dialogue may create hypotheses which the subject cannot foresee at the outset; inner dialogue has a revealing and innovative character. According to Valéry, the one who speaks invents, experiments, or translates works on a "second level". "Cette voix (morbidement) peut devenir tout étrangère. L'existence de cette parole de soi à soi — est signe d'une *coupure*" ["This voice may (morbidly) become entirely foreign. The existence of this word from self to self is the sign of an *excision*"] (Valéry 1973–74, I, 407).

Bakhtin–Voloshinov focuses on the question of communication between the self and him-/herself in the essay "Literary Stylistics", particularly in the section entitled "The Construction of the Utterance". He foregrounds the role of the inner listener whose absence can bring the dissolution of the speaking subject's personality. Personality becomes alienated when the subject finds him-/herself ideologically "out" of his class environment, when s/he works within a language where meaning can no longer be recognized: s/he does not accept the new meanings growing within words, and no longer believes in the old meanings. Consciousness finds itself displaced with regard to the communicative exchange in everyday life, roaming undetermined grounds, at the limits between the old and the new linguistic-ideological world. As Bakhtin–Voloshinov states:

> When the personality falls out of the social sphere, when the usual system of values and attitudes is broken down, nothing is left in the ravaged consciousness that might become the authoritative and acknowledged expression of productive and ideologically valid social conduct. The world of new words and new verbal meanings, born in the "fiery furnace" of revolution, together with the new social being, remain beyond the threshold of his consciousness, do not enter his purview and have not become "his own". His old words, however, have lost their connection with reality, have ceased to function as signs or symbols for it, and the personality has been left alone with its own vague moods and experiences, which are already, for the most part, *beyond the bounds* of social expression in language. (LS, 120–121)

This case of linguistic alienation can be found in contemporary life, for example in the migration of a great number of people from the countryside to a large city or from one continent to another (what comes most readily to mind is the recent dramatic exodus of the Kurdish people after the war with Iraq, or the movement of 23,000 Albanian refugees towards the Adriatic coast of Italy which began in March 1991). The collision between two different linguistic worlds (in the same language or between two different languages) gives rise to linguistic alienation, which also relates to differences of class, race and gender (see Díaz-Diocaretz 1989 and Ponzio 1990).

The problem of the appropriation of the word is relevant in both Bakhtin's and Valéry's notes. In "Literary Stylistics" and "Discourse in the Novel" the speaking subject's alienation is considered originary, deeply connected with the start of the subject's appropriation of the word (*slovo*). The subject finds him-/herself in language as if s/he were in an alien body, like a child in the mother's womb. According to Bakhtin, "Just as the body is formed initially in the mother's womb (body), a person's consciousness awakens wrapped in another's consciousness. Only later does one begin to be subsumed by neutral words and categories, that is, one is defined as a person irrespective of I and other" (N70, 138). The Bakhtin Circle sets the problem of alienation and appropriation in the arena of class struggle (see *FCS*, *MPL*, LS), but also on the plane of literary creation (see DN). For Valéry, on the other hand, the main problem is self-awareness (the Valérian obsession *par excellence*). In the effort to conquer self-awareness, the subject discovers his/her own word as alienated. The Self is crowded with alien voices and ready-made thoughts:

> — Et quoi! vous êtes l'unique, ô Moi, et vous n'avez, jusqu'au plus intime de votre pensée que des voix statistiques. Vous vous éveillez, pensée, toute préformee par je ne sais qui ou quels! *Et dans mon sein je ne trouve que d'autres*! (Valéry 1957–61, XXII [1939–40], 249)
>
> [— So! You are the only one, oh I, and even in the most intimate depths of your thought you have only statistical voices. You awake, thought, entirely preformed by I know not who or which! *And in my breast I find only others*!]

As a first approach to creation Valéry proposes a "nettoyage de la situation verbale" (Valéry 1957c [1939], 1316) ("cleaning up [of] the verbal situation", Valéry 1958b [1939], 54), such as erasure of linguistic conventions belonging to the sphere of what he calls *Fiducia*. In an article entitled "Hypothèse" ("Hypothesis"), which appeared in 1929, Valéry defines *Fiducia* as society, language, laws, arts, custom and so forth; every effect unequal to its cause needs conventions by which a second reality is established, merging with the sensible world, covering it, dominating it. Sometimes, however, this second reality crumbles and what appears is the frightful simplicity of elementary life. When Valéry analyses the social aspects of *Fiducia*, he transposes the question of linguistic alienation to a specifically social level. In considering the artificial web of sign systems that we are enveloped in, Valéry says that

> Dans nos désirs, dans nos regrets, dans nos recherches, dans nos émotions et passions, et jusque dans l'effort que nous faisons pour nous connaître, nous sommes le jouet de choses absentes, — qui n'ont même pas besoin d'exister pour agir. (1960b [1929], 945)
>
> [In our desires, our regrets, our quests, in our emotions and passions, and even in our effort to know ourselves, we are the puppets of nonexistent things — things that need not even exist to affect us.] (Valéry 1964 [1929], 233)

From 1929 Valéry underlines the danger of the media's concealed power, so that he seems very close to our times, characterized as they are by rapidly consuming/producing codes.

A THREE-VOICED DIALOGUE

Bakhtin in his works of the 1930s and 1940s posits an insurmountable distance between the novel and lyric poetry as between a deeply dialogical expression and a monological one. Nevertheless, in his later article "The Problem of the Text" (1959–61) Bakhtin recognizes the specific dialogism of lyric poetry: "Self-objectification (in the lyric, in the confession, and so forth) as self-alienation and, to a certain degree, a surmounting of the self. By objectifying myself (i.e. by placing myself outside) I gain the opportunity to have an authentically dialogic relation with myself" (PT, 122). In this article a conception of a three-voiced dialogue emerges which pertains specifically to literary production, but also, more generally, to linguistic production: "The word is a drama in which three characters participate (it is not a duet but a trio). It is performed outside the author, and it cannot be introjected into the author" (PT, 122). The Bakhtinian triad of author–hero–listener corresponds to the three persons who in Valéry's theory form the machine of discourse activity always implied in every speech act: "Je–Tu–Il" ("I–Thou–He"), "*JE* dit à *Toi* que *IL*" ("I says to Thou that HE") (see Valéry 1973–74, I, 452, II, 1182–1183; see also Biancofiore 1991, 185).

The most interesting and striking connection between Bakhtin's philosophy of language and Valéry's *poétique du langage* lies in the notion of exotopy or outsideness (*vnenakhodimost'*). The distance between the author and the author's image constitutes the background of all Valéry's thoughts about literary criticism and poetic production. For Valéry, the author is, almost paradoxically, a *created creator*. S/he is the mask generating the artwork, in a certain way, s/he becomes the machine producing the literary text in which the main characteristic is impersonality. The author as the created creator is in some way the child of her/his own work because s/he conforms to the image of the one who made the work, as it springs from within the artwork. As Valéry says:

> Ecrire, c'est engendrer un homme factice, celui qui ne pense ni ne dit tout, qui n'émet que le meilleur, et par ce choix est pareil à un automate dont la période mécanique s'appelle style. A cette machine parfaite je donne mon nom et passe pour elle. (Valéry 1957–61, IV [1906–13], 190)
>
> [To write is to engender a factitious man, a man who does not think or say everything, who gives out only what is best, and by virtue of this choice is like an automaton whose mechanical rhythm is called style. To this perfect machine I give my name, and I pass for it.]

This common ground unifying Bakhtin and Valéry underlies the critical approach to the text and to its author as an objectified image. In 1910 Valéry developed his theory on authorship, noting "Il ne faut donc jamais conclure de l'oeuvre à un homme — mais de l'oeuvre à un masque — et du masque à la machine" (Valéry 1960a [1924], 581) ["One should thus never draw conclusions from a work about an individual, but rather go from the work to a mask, and from the mask to the machine"]. Bakhtin outlined his theory of the image of the author in "The Problem of the Text" (1959–61, published posthumously in 1976), and developed it in "From Notes Made in 1970–71", although he had been exploring the relationship between art and life since 1919, when he wrote the remarkable "Art and Answerability".

During the First World War Valéry wrote *The Young Fate* (*La Jeune Parque*, 1917), the product of a period of great tension that does not openly enter this poem; nevertheless, in a letter to Maurice Denis, the author admitted that

> J'ai là une sorte de poème qui ne veut s'achever, un monstre gonflé des loisirs de mon inutilité pendant la guerre. Sans "sujets", sans nom, sans âge certain, hydre infiniment extensible, qui se peut aussi couper en morceaux — dont je ne dis pas que ce seraient autant de morceaux vivants—; bref, c'est aussi un train d'alexandrins (plus "réguliers" que ce n'est la mode), un train qui, pour ma stupeur, est sorti de mon long tunnel, un serpent de *trucks*, disons-le, chargé de toutes les sottises que je n'ai pas écrites pendant vingt et quelques années d'abstension et abstinences sérieuses. (Valéry 1957a [1953], 1624)
>
> [What I have is a sort of poem which does not want to be completed, a bloated monster born of the leisure of my wartime uselessness. Without "subjects", without a name, of uncertain age, an infinitely extensible hydra which could also be chopped into pieces — and I do not necessarily mean living pieces—; in short, it is also a train of alexandrines (more "regular" than is the fashion), a train which, through my stupor, has emerged from my long tunnel, what we might call a snake of freight wagons loaded with all the stupid nonsense that I didn't write over twenty-odd years of abstention and serious abstinence.]

EXPLORING THE HUMAN VOICE...

Both Valéry and Bakhtin denounce the lack of attention paid by linguistics to the voice in communicative exchange. In a *Notebook* entry of 1944 the author of *The Graveyard by the Sea* (*Le Cimetière marin*) wrote:

> Avant de *signifier* quoi que ce soit toute émission de langage *signale* que *quelqu'un parle*.
>
> Ceci est capital — et non relevé — ni donc développé par les linguistes.
>
> La seule *voix* dit bien des choses, avant d'agir comme porteuse de messages particuliers. Elle dit: Homme. Homme, femme, enfant. Telle langue, connue ou non. Demande, prie, ordonne; telle intention. Etc. (Valéry 1973–74, I, 473)
>
> [Before *signifying* anything any linguistic utterance *signals* that *somebody is speaking*.
>
> This is fundamental — and not taken up or, therefore, developed, by linguists.
>
> The *voice* alone says many things before acting as bearer of specific messages. It says: Man. Man, woman, child. Such and such a language, known or not. Asks, begs, commands; such and such an intention. Etc.]

In Valery's poetics the idea of voice is slightly different from what Bakhtin means by the term *golos*. According to the French poet, the voice represents the acting energy of the body which penetrates the poem, it is the very material of poetry rather than a simple bearer of meaning. The texture of the human voice perceived as pre-significant reveals poetry. Remarkable passages on the human voice can be found in drafts of Valéry's drama *My Faust* (*Mon Faust*), in which there is no dialogue between the characters (Faust and Lust), and the female character embodies the pure voice:

LUST

Je veux vous parler. Mais ne voyez-vous pas que je vous parle?

FAUST

Vos yeux parlent, c'est vrai. Votre visage... Vos mains.

LUST

N'est-ce pas?

FAUST

Oui. Mais je ne sais ce qu'ils disent. Comme si j'entendais une voix sans distinguer les mots...

LUST

Les mots me manquent et doivent me manquer. Mais toute je vous parle. Voyez que tout mon être n'est qu'une voix.

FAUST

C'est vrai. Vous êtes comme un poème... Inachevé, peut-être.

LUST

Ceci devrait suffire... L'inachevé dit tout bien plus que tout.

(Valéry 1977, 60–61)

[LUST

I wish to speak to you. But do you not see that I am speaking to you?

FAUST

Your eyes speak, it is true. Your face... Your hands.

LUST

Don't they?

FAUST

Yes. But I do not know what they say. As if I could hear a voice without being able to make out the words.

LUST

I lack words and must lack them. But all of me speaks to you. See that the whole of my being is but a voice.

FAUST

It is true. You are like a poem... An unfinished one, perhaps.

LUST

That ought to suffice... That which is incomplete says everything much more than anything else.]

In Bakhtin's writings the notion of voice is considerably more complex. We are dealing here with the meaning of intonation in communicative exchange and in poetry :"An intimate kinship binds intonational metaphor with *metaphor of gesticulation* (and was not the word itself originally linguistic gesture, a component of a complex body gesture?)" (DLDP, 16). Intonation is placed at the boundaries between the verbal and the non-verbal, and is oriented towards the listener and towards the topic (the hero). The analysis of the voice, related to the notion of word (*slovo*), involves the question of who is speaking in the text, and plays a great role in literary studies (see DN). The question of authorship is rooted in the process of the appropriation of the word, considered as the very universe of alien voices.

A CO-CREATIVE UNDERSTANDING

In "The Problem of Speech Genres" Bakhtin focuses on the role of the listener participating in the construction of the utterance. For *others* "my thought becomes actual thought for the first time (and thus also for my own self as well)" (PSG, 94). The *addressivity* of the utterance, that is, its quality of being directed to someone, characterizes the literary word. Valéry refers to adressivity in different terms when he speaks of a "dépendance d'autrui" (Valéry 1957b [1937], 1466) ("dependence on others", Valery 1958a [1937], 102).

In the dialogic, co-creative perception of the artwork (see N70, 142) we find in Bakhtin's theory another triad: author–addressee–superaddressee.

Addressivity does not solely concern the contemporary perceiver of the artwork. The author conceives his/her own work in a time without him-/herself: what Bakhtin calls "the future without me" (MHS, 167). The superaddressee breaks and widens the narrow horizons of contemporaneity because s/he represents, alongside the second consciousness (addressee), the possibility of response. Valéry's article "La Liberté de l'esprit" ("The Freedom of the Spirit") foregrounds rapid change in the way of perceiving the artwork. According to dominant values, the artwork must be new, or at any rate absolutely surprising (Valéry 1960c [1939], 1077). The ideal addressee of literature seems to be lost for ever (see Pasolini 1972 on the disappearance of the demand for poetry). A new way of perceiving the artwork imposes itself. A new modality reigns more and more today: a careless, absent-minded perception. Through the continuous wave of messages enveloping us, the media quickly change our perceptive habits. Valéry foresaw the danger of media-cracy, providing us with the new as something which is already-felt (see Perniola 1991). Art itself runs the risk of self-reproduction, without comparing itself with reality, trapped in the vicious circle of self-reception. The artwork today seems to enclose or lock itself in the sphere of an absolute intertextuality, like a product from specialized magazines — take, for example, the new mannerists' obsession with quotation.

In an epoch of the hypertrophying of artistic creation, when art takes the place of ritual in contemporary society, art survives under the form of its disappearance, and poetry lives on the bounds of silence like the work of Jabès or of Munier, under the threat of being swallowed up by silence. At every moment the artwork must legitimate itself, imposing its new order or "disorder" on the listener or addressee, pushing its way through the field of a ready-made interpretation (see Calabrese 1991). The web cast by the media builds up an image of a flatter and flatter spectator. On the bounds with absolute homologization a river flows, an underground river, which does not emerge at the surface, but flows tenaciously. Poetry flourishes outside official circuits, far from the gossipping non-dialogue of talk-shows.

I wish to conclude with two significant quotations from contemporary poets: Roger Munier, to whom the *Nouvelle Revue Française* dedicated an issue in May 1991, and Marilena Cataldini, a woman writer from Southern Italy. In Munier's poetics literature gives a name to the Without-name, it speaks for that which is nameless: the literary work is ultimately anonymous, like Holy Writ:

> Dans une vue comme celle que j'ai esquissée, le scripteur compte peu, s'il est vrai qu'il répond à l'appel le plus anonyme qui soit, qu'il a pour tâche de donner nom au Sans-nom, lieu au Sans-lieu. Son propre effacement est de rigueur. A la limite, les écrits devraient être eux-mêmes anonymes, comme le deviennent avec le temps les grands livres fondateurs, qu'ils s'appellent Rig-Véda, Zend-Avesta, Popol Vuh, Tao ou Bible. Qu'ils soient signés n'est guère qu'une marque de fabrique, que l'usure des siècles lentement efface. (Munier 1991, 71)
>
> [In a view like that which I have sketched, the one who writes counts for little, if it is true that he responds to the most anonymous of appeals, that his task is to give a name to the Without-name, place to the Without-place. His own erasure is *de rigueur*. At the very limit writings themselves should be anonymous, as happens with time to the great founding texts, be they called Rigveda, Zend-Avesta, Popol Vuh, Tao or Bible. The fact that they may be signed is no more than a brand-mark which the attrition of the centuries slowly erases.]

In Marilena Cataldini, as in Bakhtin's theory of literature and as in Valéry's *poétique de l'autrui*, the word is in the vocative, in need of the other's response:

> I surrender
> if two and two
> wraps me
> in the circuit of sense
> and you keep silent almost appeased
> and from your silence
> take flight
> timid specks of colour
> [...]
> But if I surrender
> which light
> will filter alchemies
> for the dark of the soul
> and I shall not have seen
> what I heard and saw:
> that silent clamour
> which dissolves me in the sky
> and for a short time
> together with my nude dream
> shines
> And you
> from down here
> have you ever seen me?
>
> (Cataldini 1991, 67)

The interesting points of contact between Bakhtinian theory of literature and Valéry's poetics allow us to construct a new approach to the artwork, an approach which is particularly relevant in the light of the latest trends of literary production and contemporary aesthetic studies. In Bakhtin's terms, only the insertion of the two theorists into "great time" can ensure a full understanding of their contributions to a theory of dialogism, which is related to the present needs of analysing the phenomena associated with the interpretation, production and circulation of the artwork.

WORKS CITED

Benveniste, E. 1974 [1958]. "De la subjectivité dans le langage", in *Problèmes de linguistique générale*, vol. 1 (Paris: Gallimard), 258–266.

Biancofiore, A. 1991. *L'opera e il metodo. Da Baudelaire a Valéry* (Lecce: Milella).

Calabrese, O. 1991. *Caos e bellezza. Immagini del neobarocco* (Milan: Domus/ Academy).

Cataldini, M. 1991. "For Ep-art", in V. Mazzotta (ed.), *Ep-Art* (Exhibition Catalogue) (Lecce: n.p.), 67.

Díaz-Diocaretz, M. 1989. "Bakhtin, Discourse, and Feminist Theories", in Díaz-Diocaretz (ed.), *The Bakhtin Circle Today* (*Critical Studies* (Amsterdam and Atlanta), 1/2), 121–139.

Munier, R. 1991. "L'Exigence d'écrire", in *La Nouvelle Revue Française*, 460, 63–71.

Pasolini, P.P. 1972. *Empirismo eretico* (Milan: Garzanti).

Perniola, M. 1991. *Del sentire* (Turin: Einaudi).

Ponzio, A. 1990. "Bakhtinian Alterity and the Search for Identity in Europe Today", in R.F. Barsky and M. Holquist (eds.), *Bakhtin and Otherness* (*Discours social/ Social Discourse* (Montreal), 3/1–2), 217–227.

Valéry, P. 1957–60. *Oeuvres*, 2 vols., ed J. Hytier (Paris: Gallimard).

________. 1957–61. *Cahiers: Edition intégrale*, 29 vols. (Paris: CNRS).

________. 1957a [1953]. [Extract from letter to Maurice Denis], in Valéry 1957–60, I, 1615.

________. 1957b [1937]. "Fragments des mémoires d'un poème", in Valéry 1957–60, I, 1464–1491.

________. 1957c [1939]. "Poésie et pensée abstraite", in Valéry 1957–60, I, 1314–1339.

________. 1958a [1937]. "Memoirs of a Poem", in *The Collected Works of Paul Valéry*, vol. 7 (*The Art of Poetry*), tr. D. Folliot (New York: Pantheon Books Inc.), 100–132 (translation of 1957b [1937]).

________. 1958b [1939]. "Poetry and Abstract Thought", in *The Collected Works of Paul Valéry*, vol. 7 (*The Art of Poetry*), tr. D. Folliot (New York: Pantheon Books Inc.), 52–81 (translation of 1957c [1939]).

________. 1960a [1924]. "Cahier B 1910", in Valéry 1957–60, II, 571–594.

________. 1960b [1929]. "Hypothèse", in Valéry 1957–60, II, 942–945.

________. 1960c [1939]. "La Liberté de l'esprit", in Valéry 1957–60, II, 1076–1099.

________. 1964 [1929]. "Hypothesis", in *The Collected Works of Paul Valéry*, vol. 13 (*Aesthetics*), tr. R. Manheim (New York: Pantheon Books Inc.), 229–233 (translation of 1960b [1929]).

________. 1973–74. *Cahiers*, 2 vols., ed. J. Robinson (Paris: Gallimard).

________. 1977. *Mes théâtres* (Paris: Gallimard).

"We Are the Real": Bakhtin and Representation of Speech

Alastair Renfrew, University of Strathclyde

Tzvetan Todorov concludes his pursuit of the question of genre in Bakhtin with the perception that Bakhtin's various analyses of novelistic sub-genres must be considered under at least two separate headings: "those bearing on the representation of discourse, and those devoted to the representation of the world" (Todorov 1984, 91). This is in a sense the perfect "conclusion" to a section of what is essentially an introductory work: it is at once a codified résumé of certain elements of Todorov's reading of Bakhtin, and an indication (almost a challenge) as to the territory into which subsequent studies of genre must venture. It must be admitted, however, that such conclusive "perfection", appropriate as it is in its specifically limited context, is in another sense inevitably and seriously deficient. In order to be an adequate basis for the kind of subsequent study it implicitly promotes, Todorov's distinction between the representation of discourse and the representation of (the rest of) the world would require thorough examination in relation to Bakhtin's writings, both on genre and in general; we would require to de-code (and to question the validity of) the assumptions implied by the distinction. It is not, however, my intention to attempt such a broad approach to Bakhtin's work, re-excavating it in order to "test" the suitability of

Todorov's distinction as a basis from which to proceed. This is because there is inherent in *both* terms of that distinction an assumption which does not exclusively or even primarily relate to Bakhtin, an assumption so fundamental as to demand attention not only prior to a more detailed analysis of Bakhtin and genre, but prior also to an assessment of the role that same distinction might play in such an analysis. Todorov, above all else, assumes the centrality of mimetic representation in Bakhtin's theory of literary genre. He explicitly distinguishes categories of objects of representation, and if we are not already entitled to infer concomitant distinctions with respect to the "means" of representation (the "media" being the third of Aristotle's terms in this connection: see in particular *Poetics*, I.47a18–b29; II.48a1–18; III.48a19–25), the question of the relationship of object and means and of the overall "effect" of different kinds of representation cannot be deferred too long. That Bakhtin conceives of literary creation primarily in terms of the representation of an object is, however, never the subject of explicit or implicit doubt. This acceptance of a specifically representational frame, whether pragmatically motivated or not, represents the most fundamental assumption "encoded" in Todorov's initial formulation, and it is with Bakhtin's precise location with regard to perennial approaches to the question of representation that this article will be concerned. It is perhaps worth stressing at this point that this is not another in a long line of attempts to bring Bakhtin to bear on particularly "problematic" issues in critical theory, some of which have tended to overstate his utility as an "unexpected" and benign purveyor of resolution (and harmony?); it is on the contrary an attempt to bring general developments in a particular theoretical area to bear on Bakhtin, selecting the appropriate tool for a particular purpose (the further elucidation and "extension" of a particular aspect of Bakhtin's work, his location in a specific critical landscape), rather than applying a universal tool, Bakhtin himself, for any and every purpose.

I.

The fact that the whole question of representation has made such a vengeful comeback in recent times (partly, though not exclusively, through the debate on realism) should not obscure the fact that it has been around for as long as there has been theoretical writing devoted to what we now call literature. There has, however, been a tendency to assume that representation has somehow only become problematic in this century, and that the texts which founded the mimetic theory that has so dominated criticism of Western art and literature are themselves unsurpassably lucid and unambiguous, ideally representative, even, of a less problematic epoch.[1] Plato in fact offers two contradictory conceptions of mimesis in *The Republic*, the first of which, in Book III, is predicated on the idea that the poet or singer is guilty, quite literally, of *concealment* of his self in the speech of his characters. This, as Gerald Else has pointed out, primarily derives from one of the *three* meanings of the word mimesis current in Plato's time, namely the *imitation* or copying of "another person's actions or way of doing things, in general" (Else 1986, 26). It is notable that Plato also discusses this version of mimesis as it relates to behaviour in life (as opposed to poetry), labelling it, with certain qualifications, a moral ill. The other definitions of mimesis centre on *miming*, physically acting out a plot or character, and, finally, *copying* or "making a *replica* of something". This sense of miming is in fact a species of the physical imitation discussed immediately above, and the two taken together give us a full appreciation of the "impersonation" (the "nefarious concealment", as Else has it) which Plato is so anxious to decry in Book III. This sense of the "nefarious" has undoubtedly accompanied the reception of verbal art and art in general in all times, but constitutes little more than a side-show alongside the main event of the Platonic legacy to literary criticism. We might more accurately call it Aristotle's legacy, because the last of our three definitions, "the making of a replica", informs the sense of literary mimesis which is given in Book X of Plato's *Republic*, and which is developed by Aristotle in the *Poetics* into the systematic theory of representation with which any subsequent restatement of the question has been obliged to engage. Plato, in Book X, establishes the poet as an artificer of what is already, for Plato, artifice: he makes copies, in the verbal medium, of human action in its varying degrees of courage, beauty etc., and these properties are in turn merely imperfect manifestations of the eternal Ideas of Courage, Beauty, etc. We need only subtract what is specific to Plato and the Greeks (and which need not trouble us)[2] to be left with the core of mimetic representation: the poet constructs an image-in-words with reference to a specific object of representation. The "status" of that object (whether it is "high" or "low", or whether it is real or "imaginary", etc.) is not of pressing concern at this stage. The idea of the poet as a "maker" of replicas in the form of "verbal structures", then, is the "version" of mimesis which is subsequently differentiated by Aristotle as a *process*, in terms of its media, its methods or means, and (crucially with regard to Bakhtin) its *objects*, and forms not only the basis of the rest of Aristotle's poetic formulations, but the basis also of approaches to the question of representation in Western art.

The semantic instability out of which our conception of mimesis emerged is not, however, as potentially debilitating to our understanding as the ambiguity which inheres *in the concept itself.* Perhaps the first and most remarkable thing to note is not the perennially destabilizing effect this ambiguity has had on responses to Aristotle, because, it would seem, it has had little such effect. On the contrary, Aristotle's formulations have not only remained relevant all the way down to Bakhtin's own time, but have remained so in virtually unaltered form. Lubomir Doležel has attributed to Auerbach's *Mimesis* the restoration of "the status of mimetic criticism after the modernist onslaught" (Doležel 1988, 47). There is, however, a real sense in which the "modernist onslaught" can be argued, with reference to both the literary and critical works of some of the great modernists themselves, and indeed to Auerbach's treatment of them in *Mimesis*, to have been conducted against everything *but* mimetic theory. Auerbach's book reaches a kind of climax in his essay "The Brown Stocking", when he declares Woolf's project to be the representation of "a more real reality" (Auerbach 1953 [1946], 540). This may be taken as shorthand for the series of questions Auerbach raises regarding both the object of Woolf's representation and the means by which such a representation may be "successfully" achieved. At no stage, however, is there any doubt as to the fact that Woolf is engaged in the rendering of a perceived reality, and an implicitly superior rendering at that. We might, with Doležel, express no surprise at such a strategy on the part of the author of *Mimesis*, but it is important to stress that Auerbach's "strategy" is no mere critical construct, and is explicitly sanctioned by Woolf herself (see in particular Woolf 1994 [1925]). Auerbach in fact plays a somewhat disingenuous role: taking his cue from the disruptions of a supposedly straightforward representational process initiated by the development of "psychological realism", he catalogues the problems faced by the mimetic artist in the quintessentially "Modern" conditions of "decline" and "fragmentation", only to demonstrate how the "Modernist" writer has developed ways to surmount these problems. Woolf and co. "are guided by the consideration that it is a hopeless venture to try to be really complete within the total exterior continuum" and "hesitate to impose upon life, which is their subject, an order which it does not possess in itself" (Auerbach 1953 [1946], 548). Auerbach, and Woolf (and Lawrence and Joyce?), are concerned with another level of representation, a level upon which "consciousness" can be represented, and which demands some degree of homology between the form of the representation and its object. Bakhtin, of course, conceives of consciousness precisely as speech, a thread which will be taken up at a later stage. For the moment, we can conclude that Auerbach's critique may be viewed as a pragmatic attempt to preserve the idea of a mimetic verbal art, but the artistic strategies of Woolf and co. must be construed somewhat more forcefully as strategies for the further entrenchment of a mimetic approach; the former might be argued to be a response to an "onslaught", but only one in which the latter played no part.

Dupont-Roc and Lallot confront the problem of ambiguity head-on, offering what might be termed an antidote to Woolfian ambition: "Mimetic activity [...] establishes a complex relation between the two objects, model and copy: it implies both resemblance and difference, both identification and transformation, in one and the same operation" (Dupont-Roc and Lallot 1980, 157). Mieke Bal, paying particular heed to the idea of transformation in the process of representation, notes that Dupont-Roc and Lallot's formulation "does not prevent the possibility of realism in the sense of an equivalence of model and copy", but that such an equivalence must be extremely rare, if not practically impossible (Bal 1982, 174). Bal develops this into the suggestion that differing degrees of equivalence between model and copy are best understood in terms of differing degrees of "changes within the sign" itself, or differing degrees of transformation of model into copy. In other words, representation, semiotically speaking, is a "staggered" process.

These issues, and also the issue of the relationship between mimetic theory and modernism, are touched upon by Roland Barthes in "The Reality Effect" (Barthes 1982). Although Doležel, again, has pointed out the dangers of simply identifying the question of mimesis and the question of realism, it is clearly possible to approach the latter as a component of the former, and Barthes is only one of a clamour of voices who have spoken on this "component" (see for example Levine 1974, Stern 1973, Mackay 1964, 940–973 and Riffaterre 1990, especially Introduction). Rather than chart the many and varied rejoinders in the so-called "debate on realism", I want, provisionally, to take one of the most influential "conclusions" of that debate at face value, a conclusion which is perhaps expressed best of all in the words of, once again, Tzvetan Todorov in his editorial introduction to the reprint of Barthes's article. Todorov considers Barthes to have offered the clearest statement of the principle that "a text is not determined by those things which it evokes" (Todorov 1982, 4). Barthes is specifically concerned with the function of apparently "superfluous" descriptive material, and he concludes that this function is determined by specifically conventional imperatives, rather than solely by the imperatives of verisimilitude. Flaubert's description of Rouen, for example, "has a meaning, but that meaning is given by its conformity, not to the object of description, but to the cultural rules governing representation" (Barthes 1982, 14).[3] And these "cultural rules", Barthes argues, are derived as much from aesthetic as from referential considerations: "realism" ("any discourse which accepts statements whose only justification is their referent") depends absolutely on what Barthes terms a "referential illusion", the illusion of "*direct collusion of referent and signifier*" (16, emphasis added). That Barthes considers the resultant "reality effect" the origin of "the aesthetic of all the standard works of modernity" now appears, specifically in its relation to our earlier discussion of Woolf, purely incidental, although we must at least acknowledge the mitigating effect of the lower case initial in his "modernity".

Barthes is as significant a moment as any in the seemingly irrevocable fusion of the terms "realism" and "naive", a fusion which is achieved through the instálment as orthodoxy of a Saussurean semiotic. The "naivety" of realism, as Bruce Robbins (with the benefit of a slightly longer view) has argued, functioned for a time as a grounding certainty which "a given author, text, period, or genre can be shown to rise sophisticatedly and self-consciously above" (Robbins 1993, 227). Robbins attempts to explain what is, for him, an almost pathological tendency in "professional" literery studies to adhere to this article of faith, and argues that such approaches are not founded upon any kind of inherent necessity, but are rather "ritualistic reiterations of what the discipline of literary criticism takes to be its founding postulates, re-enactments of its creation myth. Realism is not any old subject for criticism; it's what we have told ourselves we exist by not being" (Robbins 1993, 227). The task facing literary studies, in this analysis, is to find a more dependable guarantee of its own existence, a task which will necessarily involve a renewal of the liturgy of representation.

II.

Bakhtin's own varied writings on the novel, in line with Todorov's initial assumption (but seemingly in contradiction to the same commentator's gloss on Barthes), are marked by an overwhelming concern for, precisely, that which the text evokes. That concern is initially expressed in his attention to the nature of the object of representation, but this approach is rarely undertaken in isolation from examination of, to return to Aristotle's terminology, the means or methods by which the representation of different categories of object is achieved. It is this relationship between the nature of a given object and the means of its representation which comes to dominate; Bakhtin is ultimately concerned (if the limits of his concern can be identified simply with the limits of literature) with what various literary "means" are *able* to evoke.

Bakhtin's pursuit of his own essential object is the common element of a number of individual works which are, nonetheless, diverse in approach (and in their conclusions): various works seek to define the object of representation in various specific ways, and end up dealing with what are essentially different categories of object, but all proceed from definition of the nature of the object to the implications of that nature for various means of representation. It is possible by this principle to organize certain of Bakhtin's works into a kind of spectrum, delimited at one extreme by an almost "pure" concern with language as the principal object of representation ("Discourse in the Novel"), and at the other by a less specific concern with physical reality and the image of man in relation to it ("Forms of Time and of the Chronotope in the Novel"). The surviving material from "The *Bildungsroman* and its Significance in the History of Realism" would gravitate towards the latter of these two extremes, but the work which bears strong affinities to both ends of the spectrum, and which could be said to occupy its centre, is *Problems of Dostoevsky's Poetics*. This, again, accords with Todorov's distinction between representation of discourse and representation of "the world", and I intend to justify privileging the former of these two by arguing that the relationship between the object and means of representation is at its most complex when the object is primarily conceived in terms of language.[4] This will involve considering the movement from the centre of our spectrum to the extreme inhabited by language, that is, examining the development of Bakhtin's conception of the object of representation (and the demands that conception makes upon literary means) from *Problems of Dostoevsky's Poetics* to "Discourse in the Novel".

At no stage in *Dostoevsky*, either explicitly or implicitly, does Bakhtin undermine the fundamental idea that the work of literature is a representation in the verbal medium of some element of the external world, "an *artistic* vision of the world" (*PDP*, 11/15). What he immediately and consistently calls into question is the nature of the object of representation and, consequently, the nature of the relationship of authorial voice, character voice, and "objective" reality. The object of representation in Dostoevsky turns out not to be an object at all, or at least not the type of object conceived in other fictions. Bakhtin in fact defines the object in Dostoevsky (and hence his own ideal of the object) in two sets of related terms: we shall take first his contention that the character in Dostoevsky is virtually the living embodiment of a particular *idea*, which "becomes the *object of artistic representation*" (*PDP*, 85/141). The function, and hence the definition, of the idea in Dostoevsky must be distinguished from its function in the monologic work, where it is ultimately identified with a unified authorial point of view.[5] In Dostoevsky, provisionally at least, the idea is an entity not of the individual consciousness, but rather of the dialogic relations between consciousnesses; the implication is of course that these properties pertain to the immanent condition of the idea beyond the closed literary world of Dostoevsky, which point is made explicit in Bakhtin's contention that Dostoevsky, quite simply, understood "the dialogical nature of human thought, the dialogical nature of the idea" (*PDP*, 87/146). It requires no particular emphasis that this is an argument less about Dostoevsky than about his substantive "knowledge" of the condition of things; its place in a nominally literary analysis is owed to the simple fact that we and Bakhtin have access to its conclusion only through the literary work. The "dialogical nature of human thought" and literature (of the kind produced by Dostoevsky) are in this sense absolutely dependent one upon the other, locked in a symbiotic relationship where each is a component of the definition of the other. Returning to more literally practical matters, the conventional literary "combination" of the "abstract" idea and the "concrete" living person must, as we have begun to see, result in the misrepresentation of both, founded as it is upon a *misapprehension* of both: either the work or character is reducible to a series of ideological propositions, or the human referent of the story is denied any ideological content whatsoever.[6] Their absolute identification, on the other hand, intensifies the life of both.

Bakhtin's epistemological conclusion (or point of embarkation) with regard to a particular class of object has direct implications not only for our understanding of that class in itself, but also for the actual means of its representation in the literary text. It is precisely these implications that generate the second set of terms in which Bakhtin defines the object and its relation to the means of its representation. An understanding of the inherent nature of human thought is transposed in Dostoevsky into an image of a living person, and this identification functions as a kind of guarantee: it ensures that the character remains "unfinalized and inexhaustible" (*PDP*, 86/143), permitting it to remain open and susceptible to development in

Bakhtin's process of dialogic interaction. Much has been made of the apparently total "freedom" this implies for the character, even to the extent that Bakhtin's formulations have been understood as a contribution to the problem of authorial absence. Without submitting to the temptation to dwell for too long on a precise description of what Bakhtin may or may not have intended in this connection, a question which demands an entire bibliography all of its own, it is necessary for my purposes to stress Bakhtin's fundamental caution:

> It would be absurd to think that authorial consciousness is in no way expressed in Dostoevsky's novels. The consciousness of the creator of a polyphonic novel is always and everywhere present in the novel, and is active in it to the highest degree. But the function of this consciousness and the forms of its activity are different than in the monologic novel. (*PDP*, 67–68/116)

What is of paramount importance is not the thematic function of finalization, nor, in technical terms, the "horizontal" relations between the various open-ended character voices, but rather the "vertical" relations between those voices, the authorial voice which organizes them, and, crucially, the referent in the real world towards which both are directed. In describing the function of the authorial voice in the specifically dialogic novel in terms of the creation of characters who are *capable of authoring* their "own fully-weighted ideological conceptions" (*PDP*, 5/6), whose interaction leads to the destruction of a single, unified ("monological") plane, and ultimately transcends any expectation of "a so-called objective description of the external world" (*PDP*, 23/39, quoting Engel′gardt), Bakhtin is not simply offering a superficial statement of relativism; he is offering instead *a description of the complex mechanics of representation.* Bakhtin conceives of the process of representation as inevitably staggered, but in a quite different sense from that discussed earlier in relation to Mieke Bal's description of the semiotic structure of representation. Both offer versions of the manner in which the apprehension of an object by a subject is disrupted, each of which is constructed around the idea that the process of representation can never consist in a single, simple operation. But where Bal finds a solution in the dynamics of the sign, preferring to concentrate once again on abstract means of signification, Bakhtin, consistent with his definition of the units of language as the real instantiations of actual speakers, finds his solution in the dynamics of voices and their relation to the objects of their discourse. The Dostoevskian character's voice, to return to the particular example under discussion,

> is constructed in the same way as is the author's in the usual type of novel. The character's discourse about himself and about the world is weighted as fully as the ordinary authorial word; it is not subordinated to the objectified image of the character, [merely] as one of his characteristics, nor does it serve as the mouth-piece of the authorial voice.

Further,

> That portion [of the novel] which is concerned with the relation of the story, with the construction of representation, and with the provision of information, must be re-orientated in relation to this new world — a world not of objects, but of fully autonomous *subjects*. (*PDP*, 7/8–9, emphasis added)

Bakhtin detects in Dostoevsky the intercession of another speaking subject between the author and the object of his discourse; in other words, that which is possessed of a voice is brought out in relief from the background of a unified and objectified reality which previously stood in apposition to a single subject, the author. That voice is at once represented by the author, and itself participates in the act of representation; the major characters in Dostoevsky are principally represented in their own words about themselves, and the world external to them is represented by means of the particular form of speech of each particular character. It is possible to proceed from the analogy of the spectrum in the description of Bakhtin's writings themselves to the analogy of the prism in description of the function of character speech in dialogical fiction; external reality is represented by means of its refraction through the speech of a given character, and ultimately through the many "languages" organized in a given novel. The "pure" object can only be attained, or constructed, through the speaking subject.

III.

Discourse itself, then, as both a very particular "object" of representation and as a secondary control in the processing of other objects, takes on a significance in Bakhtin's nominally literary project which cannot be over-emphasized. Already in *Problems of Dostoevsky's Poetics*, searching for an analogy which might convey the nuance of his conception of human thought, Bakhtin offers the following:

> The idea is in this respect like discourse, with which it is dialectically one. Like discourse, the idea wants to be heard, understood and "answered" by other voices from other positions. Like discourse, the idea is by nature dialogic, monologue being nothing but a contingent compositional form of its expression, which has arisen on the basis of the ideological monologism of the modern era. (*PDP*, 88/147)

The grounds of this analogy, or rather the specific grounds upon which it is constructed in the thought of Bakhtin (and/or Voloshinov), are both complex and various (see *MPL*, chapter one, and DLDP), but we need concentrate only on the sense in which they are the markers of an essential *continuity*. The fact that Bakhtin's terminology develops from the "person/idea" of *Dostoevsky* to the "living word" of "Discourse in the Novel", that the "consciousness" of the earlier work is replaced by language or "discourse" in the later, might suggest a concomitant "development" in the focus of those works. I wish to suggest, however, that such developments represent only a refinement of the terms in which Bakhtin is attempting to define an essentially constant object; the term "object" is here used in a particularly concentrated sense, because, as we have already seen, it is with the nature of different types of object of literary representation, and the different means by which that representation is achieved, that Bakhtin is concerned. If the object of representation in Dostoevsky turns out not to be an object at all, but rather another speaking *subject*, Bakhtin turns in "Discourse in the Novel" to the exploration of the nature of that subject through an examination of the language(s) in which it speaks, and of the means by which this diversity of speech can be rendered.

Bakhtin's paramount concern in "Discourse in the Novel" remains, however, unaltered: he continues to pursue the question of what the novel is *able to evoke*. But the referent in this process of evocation/representation is defined in new, if related, terms. It is slightly misleading, even, to speak of "new" terms, because Bakhtin in fact conflates both sets of terms with which we are familiar from *Dostoevsky*: consistent with the conception of consciousness in terms of speech, Bakhtin's earlier description predicated on the identification of the character and the idea, and the merging in the character of discourse about self and about the external world, is "replaced" in "Discourse in the Novel" by a description predicated upon the nature of language itself. The core of that description consists in Bakhtin's insistence that the conception of language as abstract and unified ("monolithic") is patently unsustainable; rather, to rely on a perhaps over-used quotation,

> At any given moment in its evolution, language is stratified not only into linguistic dialects [...] but also, and for us this is the essential point, into socio-ideological languages: the languages of social groupings, "professional" languages, "generic" languages, the languages of different generations, etc. From this point of view, literary language is itself just one of these languages of heteroglossia, and is in its turn stratified into [various] languages (generic, the languages of various tendencies, etc.). (DN, 271–272/85)

This fundamentally heteroglot condition of language is in itself sufficient to lend it a certain degree of complexity as an object of literary representation, but the bare matter of diverse and disembodied styles or idioms in language, or their superficial admixture in certain types of literary work, is merely a component, albeit an extremely important one, of the problem. Of greater importance are the conditions in which heteroglossia develops and is made manifest, and the ways in which the diverse languages of heteroglossia interact; it is here that we confront the full complexity of language as an object of representation. Bakhtin's insistence in *Dostoevsky* upon the interdependence of the "abstract" idea and the "concrete" living person is mirrored by his insistence in "Discourse in the Novel" upon the significance of the utterance as the point at which the demands of both "a normative-centralizing system of a unitary language" and "living heteroglossia" (DN, 272/85) are met, and hence of the significance of each individual utterance in the process of linguistic stratification. Bakhtin not only reasserts his concern with the *condition* of things in the later work's pursuit of language, he reasserts also that the condition of things is accessible only in the particular, in this case in the actualized speech acts of living people, or in the literary work, which is both an actualized speech act in itself, but is also an organized system of representations of diverse "types" of speech act.

I have termed Bakhtin's replacement of the earlier "thought" or "consciousness" with the new category "language" a "refinement", but it might be slightly less presumptuous simply to say that, in respect of the present discussion, such a substitution proves immensely facilitating, allowing as it does not simply a restatement of the process described in *Dostoevsky*, but a restatement which allows the very *mechanics* of that process to become even more explicit. The unique object in *Dostoevsky*, that is, the object conceived as a "fully competent subject", the "prism" through which external reality is refracted, suggested a model from which we could infer a crucial intercession between author and object; the agent of that intercession was described in terms, broadly, of consciousness, terms which required to be supplemented from other areas of Bakhtin's work, but which nonetheless made clear that a simple, unidirectional authorial representation in fact rendered little of the essence of the object. The reorientation of this question purely in the light of language, as it is conceived by Bakhtin, literally demonstrates why this should be so. The refinement of Bakhtin's "other" subject into a specifically (exclusively) *speaking* subject lays bare the relationship of the elements of the process of "refraction" described in *Dostoevsky*: the *voice* of the character is constructed by the author, and enters into the whole of the work in the capacity of a represented object, but is at the same time an active participant in the representation of itself and of other objects in the work as a whole, it is at once represented, and representing.

This new and explicit status of the speech of characters in certain types of literary work (whether or not it is formally marked off as "dialogue", in the conventional sense of that term) has a single and overwhelming consequence for the question of representation, which might nonetheless be examined in two related contexts. The first is Bakhtin's opposition of the "novelistic" to the "poetic", which is among many other things the perfect means of approach to this question. The object of representation defined in terms of language itself will by its very nature make demands on the means by which the representation is achieved which differ from those made by other classes of object: the diverse, heteroglot nature of language makes an obvious but significant challenge to the capacity of any formal means devised to reflect it, and that challenge is intensified in the face of Bakhtin's conception of the way speech types interact and develop through an endless series of individual instantiations, a conception which culminates in the need for formal literary means to confront the problem of another speaking subject, the represented and representing. The "novelistic" in this sense need bear no relation to what we have conventionally termed "the Novel", just as the "poetic" need bear no relation to "poetry": the novelistic is simply that which responds to the imperatives of the at once represented and representing "object", which, in Bakhtin's terms, represents the character as something capable also of being the agent of representation, and proceeds by means of the creation of a series of interacting "images of language". In "pure" poetic genres, on the other hand, any heteroglot element

> is essentially displayed as a *thing*, it does not lie on the *same* plane as the actual language of the work: it is the represented gesture of a character, and not a representing word. Elements of heteroglossia enter here [...] in the capacity of a represented thing. [...] The poet speaks even of the other in his own language. (DN, 287/100)

This is not, as has been supposed, a polemic aimed at poetry as such, but is rather a response to what Bakhtin saw as the formal imperatives concomitant to his conception of language, a response which he, not unnaturally, sought to construct from the set of literary definitions which came most readily to hand. In any case, it is on the basis of how well equipped various formal devices are to respond to the dual status of language that Bakhtin conducts his "inventory" of characteristically "novelistic" techniques in chapter three of "Discourse in the Novel". It is worth noting at this point that Mieke Bal concludes the article cited above with the suggestion that a generic inventory might be constructed on the basis of the varying degrees of transformation of model into copy, ranging from a purely hypothetical zero transformation to a perhaps similarly hypothetical total transformation (Bal 1982, 174). Once again, although proceeding from a substantively different basis, the shape of Bal's aspirations allows us to focus on parallel aspirations in Bakhtin, particularly on the aspiration to construct a fundamentally different principle of generic differentiation, a principle derived from the mechanics of diverse schemes of representation.

The second context will allow us to pursue to their logical conclusions some of the implications arising from the first, and will allow us also to return to explicit consideration of those Aristotelian formulations which form the background to much of our discussion of both *Problems of Dostoevsky's Poetics* and "Discourse in the Novel". Bakhtin's opposition of poetic and novelistic discourses has been interpreted as a proposition of the necessity of a degree of homology between, roughly, form and content in the literary work: Morson and Emerson, for example, argue that the novel is in Bakhtin's terms "the most accurate conception of human experience ever developed". This is predicated on the idea, which they also attribute to Bakhtin, that "genres are really forms of thinking" (Morson and Emerson 1990, 280; for the background to this, see *FM*, chapter 7). It is not my intention to question the precise terms in which Morson and Emerson respond to this aspect of Bakhtin; the difficulties thrown up by the definition of a loose literary form in terms of *conception* (even those produced by the fact that a homology between the formal, organizational properties of a literary work and that which it seeks to represent must always be, at the very least, a figure of thought) are not as important, in the present context, as the recognition that Morson and Emerson's interpretation is a meaningful and defensible response to a particularly original aspect of Bakhtin's hypothesis. What I do wish to suggest is that these difficulties are effectively avoided if we dispense with the tool of homology, enlisted for a very particular description of the affinity of the categories of form and content, and find a way to describe instead the relationship of the categories upon which we have insisted throughout, means and object. Aristotle's original classificatory system consisted of three progressive levels, the second and third of which proposed differentiation of the process of representation in terms of, respectively, its object and its means. The relationship between these levels was basically sequential, the system being analytic rather than prescriptive, appropriate for, precisely, the classification of extant literary practices.[7] In Bakhtin's hands, however, the means of representation, as we have seen in our discussion of *Problems of Dostoevsky's Poetics*, become increasingly dependent on the terms in which their object is conceived. When the entire category "object of representation" is conceived as language, which point has been the main thrust of our discussion of "Discourse in the Novel", the increasingly affective relationship between object and means develops into something else again: Aristotle's categories "object" and "means" are *conflated*, their relationship ultimately becoming one of identification. Gerald Else purposely retains the hyperbaton "human beings doing" (Else 1986, 80) in his translation of Plato; Bakhtin's conflation essentially consists in the replacement of this formula for the object of representation with a formulation appropriated from a quite different context, "human beings speaking" (Mackay 1964, 7), a seemingly perfect formulation for the *representing* object, which has escaped categorization merely as object.

The consequences for literary studies of such a momentous conflation are potentially limitless (some have become manifest quite independently of Bakhtin), but one issue, which has quietly dominated this article, must immediately appear in a quite different aspect. Barthes's particular concentration on the semiotic implications of "naive realism", his seemingly absolute statement of the principle that "a text is not determined by those things which it evokes" (Todorov 1982, 4), is clearly antithetical to Bakhtin's theorization of representation, which from the first moment of its availability in French or English has stood on the wrong side of the orthodoxy of which Barthes is so persuasive a proponent. Bruce Robbins, in characterizing more recent responses to questions of realism and representation in terms of a "displacement" from the epistemological to the social (Robbins 1993, 225), indicates a way out of what has become a genuine impasse, and in terms which are particularly, though not of course exclusively, appropriate to Bakhtin. Whereas Barthes neglects to engage with (we cannot say "denies") the social aspect of representation, Bakhtin employs epistemological analysis specifically in the service of a socially grounded project. Bakhtin implicitly denies, in his very practice throughout the avowedly "literary" works, what is explicitly denied in the "philosophical" works of the early 1920s, namely the necessity of a disjuncture between the epistemological and the social. This unity allows him to insist on the essential secondariness of the text, implying therefore its relationship to whatever he holds to be "primary", but without accepting the terms in which that relationship has been portrayed as straightforward. We might even be permitted to conjecture that Bakhtin's response to Barthes's bravura ventriloquization of the inanimate, "we are the real", would simply have been "on the contrary, *we are*".

NOTES

1. This is not, of course, to ignore the flood of material provoked by Derrida's dismantling of Plato's *Phaedrus*, much of which has repercussions for the present question, but which is principally concerned with the implications of Plato's (surreptitious) insistence on origin: see Derrida 1981 [1972]. Else (1986) deals at length with the inconsistencies of both *The Republic* and *The Poetics*, and is moved to the explicit statement that Plato was neither absolutely coherent, nor infallible. Dupont-Roc and Lallot (1980) deal with inconsistency at another, more interpretive level.
2. Although this lies at the core of what has troubled Derrida and those who have responded to him.
3. Barthes goes on to ask the question implicit in Dupont-Roc and Lallot: where could any representation with pretensions to absolute verisimilitude conceivably "end" (Barthes 1982, 14)?
4. An examination of Bakhtin's orientation with regard to "the representation of the world" would be considerably more straightforward. The title of the dissertation from which *Rabelais* derives is "François Rabelais in the History of Realism", and in the final published version of the book Bakhtin defends his expression "grotesque realism", for example, in the following terms: "Those particularities, which so sharply distinguish the medieval and Renaissance grotesque from the romantic and modern version [...] can be defined most adequately as *realistic*" (*RW*, 52/61). The surviving fragment on the *Bildungsroman* is also explicitly situated in the "history of realism", and is closely related to Bakhtin's key work in this connection, "Forms of Time and of the Chronotope in the Novel". It is in these works that we find the detail to support the assertion (specifically limited to this context) that Bakhtin, like Dostoevsky, is a realist "of the highest order".

5. Bakhtin distinguishes three common variants of the function of the idea in the single-voiced work: the idea as the principle of authorial point of view; the idea as the outcome or conclusion to which the novel leads; and the idea, although identified with the author, as directly expressed by word or deed of the main character (these are not mutually exclusive, and indeed all three might be present in varying degree in a single work). (*PDP*, 82–85/137–141). Bakhtin's preface to this discussion makes it clear that it is only artificially limited to literature, and properly forms only a part of a broader examination of the "belief in the self-sufficiency of a single consciousness in all spheres of ideological life", which "is a deep structural feature of ideological creation in modern times" (82/137).
6. Ideas are not, so to speak, "the same" within and outwith the novel (or the "kind" of literary work of which Bakhtin is speaking); see also the discussion of Dostoevsky's "personal ideology" (*PDP*, 92–97/155–163).
7. The point at which the prescriptive gives way to, or becomes indistinguishable from, the descriptive is not at issue in the present context, although it must be admitted that such a "confusion" must accompany the development of some form of affective relationship between various objects and the means of their representation.

WORKS CITED

Auerbach, E. 1953 [1946]. *Mimesis: The Representation of Reality in Western Literature*, tr. W.R. Trask (Princeton: Princeton University Press).

Bal, M. 1982. "Mimesis and Genre Theory in Aristotle's *Poetics*", in *Poetics Today*, 3/1, 171–180.

Barthes, R. 1982. "The Reality Effect", in T. Todorov (ed.), *French Literary Theory Today*, tr. R. Carter (Cambridge: Cambridge University Press; Maison des sciences de l'homme), 11–17.

Derrida, J. 1981 [1972]. "Plato's Pharmacy", in *Dissemination*, tr. B. Johnson (London: Athlone Press), 61–171.

Doležel, L. 1988. "Mimesis and Possible Worlds", in *Poetics Today*, 9/3, 475–496.

Dupont-Roc, R., and J. Lallot 1980. "Introduction" and "Notes", in *Aristote: La Poétique* (Paris: Seuil).

Else, G.F. 1986. *Plato and Aristotle on Poetry* (Chapel Hill and London: University of North Carolina Press).

Levine, G. 1974. "Realism Reconsidered", in J. Halperin (ed.), *The Theory of the Novel* (Oxford: Oxford University Press), 233–256.

Mackay, A. 1964. *Ficciones* (Long Beach: Ballantrae, 1964).

Morson, G.S., and C. Emerson 1990. *Mikhail Bakhtin: Creation of a Prosaics* (Stanford: Stanford University Press).

Riffaterre, M. 1990. *Fictional Truth* (Baltimore and London: Johns Hopkins University Press).

Robbins, B. 1993. "Modernism and Literary Realism: Response", in G. Levine (ed.), *Realism and Representation: Essays on the Problem of Realism in Relation to Science, Literature, and Culture* (Madison and London: University of Wisconsin Press, 1993), 225–231.

Stern, J.P. 1973. *Realism* (London and New York: Routledge).

Todorov, T. 1982. "French Poetics Today", in Todorov (ed.), *French Literary Theory Today*, tr. R. Carter (Cambridge: Cambridge University Press; Maison des sciences de l'homme), 1–7.

________. 1984. *Mikhail Bakhtin: The Dialogical Principle*, tr. W. Godzich (Manchester and Minneapolis: Manchester University Press; University of Minnesota Press).

Woolf, V. 1994 [1925]. "Modern Fiction", in *The Essays of Virginia Woolf*, vol. 4 (London: Hogarth), 157–164.

A Time and
a Place

BAKHTIN'S CONCEPT OF "CHRONOTOPE": THE KANTIAN CONNECTION

Bernhard F. Scholz, Groningen University

INTRODUCTION: BAKHTIN'S USE OF TERMS

Apart from having greatly enriched our understanding of the development of narrative literature, Bakhtin has added a remarkable number of neologisms to the terminological repertoire of literary scholarship. "Dialogicity", "carnivalization", "polyglossia", "heteroglossia", "chronotope" and "novelistic discourse" immediately come to mind. Characteristically, all of these neologisms have retained a strongly Bakhtinian flavour: to use any one of them is to be thought of as "working with Bakhtin". However, some of these coinages ("dialogicity", "novelistic discourse", perhaps also "carnivalization") appear to be well on their way to becoming elements of the "nomenclature" of literary scholarship, i.e. to serving as common names for certain phenomena while no longer immediately evoking the specific connotations of the original context. Others, like "chronotope", "polyglossia" and "heteroglossia", so far appear to have retained more of their original character as terms introduced in a specific theoretical context. In their case more of that original context needs to be known if their use is to be understood properly.[1]

That terms stubbornly retain traces of their contexts of introduction into the terminological repertoire is not at all uncommon in literary scholarship; in a discipline which appears to be ineradicably paradigm-bound this is no more than one would expect. But there is a problem with certain terms coined by Bakhtin: with many, if not all, of Bakhtin's terms, it appears, it is extremely difficult to reconstruct the context of introduction. A glance at a number of recent studies of Bakhtin in fact indicates that even his most devoted followers are at times puzzled by a certain fuzziness in his use of terms, by a shortcoming which they would undoubtedly be hard put to accept from a lesser figure. Bakhtin's language, as one critic has put it tersely, "moves between alternative and contradictory formulations in a single essay and thus produces a set of concepts whose explanatory importance is matched by an unnerving tendency to slide from one formulation to the next with disturbing ease" (Hirschkop 1986, 73). "Bakhtin", another critic has felt compelled to state, "is often careless in his use of terms, including those of his own coinage" (Morson 1986, 81). Bakhtin's terms, in other words, frequently do not satisfy the standards of explicitness and context-freeness which terms are normally expected to meet.

Criticisms such as these are frequently followed by attempts to explain away the shortcomings. There were, we are told, good reasons for Bakhtin's peculiar handling of terms. Bakhtin's work "reads like 'inner speech' (speech in which it is unnecessary to spell out those things one already knows and others are not intended to hear)" and in this way conforms to an "almost instinctive desire not to be too explicit in writing for a Soviet audience" (Morson 1986, 81). At first glance an explanation such as this sounds plausible enough: avoidance of terminological rigour might conceivably serve the twofold communicative end of obstructing exoteric communication with the many, and of putting esoteric communication with the few in its place. But trying to imagine Bakhtin bent on producing a type of "inner speech" which involves vague, even contradictory terms, for the sole purpose of being understood by some readers and not by others, is another matter. Only a somewhat inept Inspector Clouseau, one suspects, would credibly be thrown off Bakhtin's scent by an intentionally careless use of terms like "heteroglossia", "chronotope" or "dialogue".

But even if this were a plausible explanation of Bakhtin's linguistic behaviour, what would still argue against it would be the fact that it is ultimately an explanation along the lines of the hermetic principle of *ignotum per ignotius*. It contains no hint as to what is meant by "inner speech", or as to how the select few whom that "inner speech" was meant to reach could be sure that they had indeed understood Bakhtin as he wished to be understood, assuming, naturally, that, as a user of "inner speech", he wished to be understood at all.

No doubt Bakhtinian usage frequently lacks the kind of explicitness and context-freeness which we have been taught to expect of the terms we encounter in scholarly texts. More often than not his terms are introduced in the wake of a number of concrete examples rather than by means of explicit definitions, and their meanings only gradually unfold as the argument progresses and the examples accumulate. Bakhtin's terms, in other words, are frequently encountered "in use", without explicit statement of the rules governing such use, and the hapless commentator wishing to make those terms teachable and learnable can at times do little more than offer well-intended paraphrases which s/he hopes will cover as much as possible of the terrain covered by Bakhtin himself.

The following entry under "chronotope" in the glossary appended to *The Dialogic Imagination* is a telling case in point:

> CHRONOTOPE [*xronotop*]
> Literally, "time-space". A unit of analysis for studying texts according to the ratio and nature of the temporal and spatial categories represented. The distinctiveness of this concept as opposed to most other uses of time and space in literary analysis lies in the fact that neither category is privileged; they are utterly interdependent. The chronotope is an optic for reading texts as x-rays of the forces at work in the culture system from which they spring. (Emerson and Holquist 1981, 425–426)[2]

This rather elaborate paraphrase employs a number of concepts which, the authors apparently thought, would be more familiar to their readers than the term itself, and hence capable of clarifying its meaning and use. However, on closer inspection it appears that the concepts of time and space as referred to in this gloss are located indiscriminately both on the meta-level ("unit of analysis", "optic") and on the object level ("temporal and spatial categories represented", "texts as x-rays"). In addition, thanks to the ambiguous formulation "categories represented", time and space as categories amenable to representation by means of narrative texts are somehow or other also to be found outside the text. The matter is further complicated by the assertion that the chronotope should be understood as an "optic" (i.e. as a tool of analysis) for reading texts which in their turn are to be understood as "x-rays" (i.e. also as analytical instruments) of certain, presumably extra-textual, cultural forces. The question raised by such sadly failed attempts at clarification is this: is Bakhtin's usage indeed incurably vague, or do we simply lack the proper tools for analyzing it?

Bakhtin's own explanation for his seemingly imprecise usage of the term "chronotope" in "Forms of Time and of the Chronotope in the Novel", which the commentators appear to have overlooked, is admittedly less intriguing than the conspiracy hypothesis referred to above. But it has the merit of pointing a way towards a hermeneutic of Bakhtinian texts:

> We do not pretend to completeness or precision in our theoretical formulations and definitions. *Here and abroad, serious work on the study of space and time in art and literature has only just begun. Such work will in its further development eventually supplement, and perhaps substantially correct,* the characteristics of novelistic chronotopes offered by us here. (FTC, 85; emphasis added)

Bakhtin, this passage suggests, did not himself attribute any finality either to his theoretical formulations or to his definitions. Instead he saw his own work (and, we are entitled to add, he wished his work to be seen) in relation to work carried out by a number of contemporaries who were embarked on projects similar to his own. Add to this the fact that, as the subtitle of "Forms of Time" suggests, he wished his book-length essay to be viewed as "*Notes toward* a Historical Poetics", rather than as a closing statement, and we may find ourselves in possession of an important clue as to how to read Bakhtin's texts. Rather than trying to read them as self-contained monological treatises, we should perhaps try to read them as at times rather tentative contributions to an ongoing debate. Perhaps we should even allow for the possibility that their final meaning is not necessarily to be found in what Bakhtin's texts appear to be saying in and by themselves, but in the subject matter which Bakhtin shared with the other participants of that debate, i.e. in the shared problems, and in the solutions to them which he, among others, suggested.

Such an approach, it seems to me, is validated by Bakhtin's own reflections on the possibility of literary scholarship which can be found in a brief essay first published in 1975, but apparently written between 1940 and 1970. Bakhtin there insists on a fundamental difference between the knowledge of things and the knowledge of persons, and he identifies the domain of the humanities as that of "*expressive* and *speaking* being" as opposed to that of "things" (Bakhtin 1975, 205). To this distinction corresponds a gnoseological one between "the activity of the person who cognizes a voiceless thing" and "the activity of the person who cognizes another subject, i.e. the *dialogical* activity of the cognizing person, which encounters the dialogical activity of the cognized subject" (206). Since the object of the humanities is, according to Bakhtin, "speaking being", the activity of producing knowledge here must take on the form of a dialogical activity. Applied to the understanding of texts this leads to the insight that:

> Every word (every sign) of a text leads beyond its boundaries. It is [therefore] inadmissible to limit the analysis (of knowledge and understanding) exclusively to the text under consideration. Any understanding is an act of relating the text under consideration with other texts, and of reinterpreting it in the new context (my own, the present one, the future one). [...] The stages of this dialogical movement of understanding are: point of departure — the given text; movement backwards — past contexts; movement forward — anticipation (and beginning) of the future context. (206–207)

Any clarification of Bakhtin's use of a term like "chronotope", this passage suggests, must go beyond paraphrasing the context in which that term occurs. It must involve an attempt at reconstructing as much as possible of the dialogical movement which originally brought it into the debate on literature. What follows below therefore is not intended simply as an attempt to identify certain Kantian echoes and influences in Bakhtin's discussions of the chronotopes of literature. Rather, it aims to trace the extent of Bakhtin's dialogue with Kant which was to result in highly original conception of the space–time relations of (narrative) texts.

REFERENCES TO KANT AND OTHERS

In the introductory section of "Forms of Time" Bakhtin offers his readers an all too brief account of the provenance of the term "chronotope", which he will use to refer to "the intrinsic connectedness of temporal and spatial relationships that are artistically expressed in literature". He points out that "this term [space-time] is employed in mathematics, and was introduced as part of Einstein's Theory of Relativity", only to suggest immediately afterwards that "the special meaning it has in relativity theory is not important for our purposes" and that he is "borrowing it for literary criticism almost as a metaphor (almost, but not entirely)." Then follows Bakhtin's principal reason for importing the term into literary criticism: "it expresses the inseparability of space and time (time as the fourth dimension of space)", and then a formulation with a strongly Kantian ring, which indicates the class of entities to which the chronotope belongs: "we understand the chronotope as a *formally constitutive category* of literature" (FTC, 84; emphasis added).

Bakhtin, it appears, takes it for granted that his readers are familiar with the concept of a formally constitutive category of a particular realm of objects, and with the possibility of analyzing literature in terms of its formally constitutive categories. A footnote of an autobiographical nature follows: "In the summer of 1925, the author of these lines attended a lecture by A.A. Uxtomskij on the chronotope in biology; in the lecture questions of aesthetics were also touched upon" (FTC, 84). Since the link between this note and the sentence in the body of the text to which it is added is tenuous indeed, we must assume that it is meant to be read as an addition to the whole paragraph. But what exactly does it add apart from autobiographical anecdote? The analogy to "chronotope in literature" would have been "chronotope in life", while that of "chronotope in biology" would have been "chronotope in criticism". Was Bakhtin simply confounding a discipline studying a realm of objects with the realm of objects studied by that discipline?

The third and last reference in this introductory section to an authority in a field other than literary criticism is to an early part of Kant's *Critique of Pure Reason* which bears the title "Transcendental Aesthetics", and consists of two sections entitled "About Space" and "About Time" respectively. Kant's analysis of space and time does not, however, address itself explicitly to the "intrinsic connectedness of temporal and spatial relationships" in which Bakhtin is primarily interested, and which prompted the importation of the term "chronotope" from the discourses of mathematics, physics and biology in the first place. As in the case of the reference to Ukhtomskii, the reference to Kant is contained in a footnote: "In his 'Transcendental Aesthetics'", Bakhtin observes,

> Kant defines space and time as indispensable forms of any cognition, beginning with elementary perceptions and representations. Here we employ the Kantian evaluation of the importance of these forms in the cognitive process, but differ from Kant in taking them not as "transcendental" but as forms of the most immediate reality. We shall attempt to show the role these forms play in the process of concrete artistic cognition (artistic visualization) under conditions obtaining in the genre of the novel. (FTC, 85)

The passage in the body of Bakhtin's text to which this footnote is appended reads as follows: "The chronotope as a formally constitutive category determines to a significant degree the image of man in literature as well. The image of man is always intrinsically chronotopic" (FTC, 85).

The claim that a chronotope is a "formally constitutive category of literature" is thus put forward twice, first accompanied by a reference to the discourses of mathematics, physics and biology, then by a reference to

Kantian transcendental philosophy. But now there is the additional claim that the chronotope as a formally constitutive category of literature has anthropological implications: it determines the image of man in literature.

We are left to wonder what all of this information amounts to. What can as astute a theorist as Bakhtin have meant when he claimed that he was borrowing a term from the discourse of physics and using it "almost as a metaphor (almost, but not entirely)"? Surely, unlike being blind or being excited, being a metaphor is an either/or issue rather than an issue which would admit gradation. A term can be used either literally or metaphorically and thus non-literally; there does not seem to be a possibility of using a term almost as a metaphor, but not entirely.[3] And what are we to make of those all-too-brief references to mathematics, Einsteinian physics and Ukhtomskian biology in the context of a paragraph which in addition contains what looks like a pointer to Kant, a suspicion subsequently borne out by the footnote devoted to the German philosopher?

There have been a number of attempts at unravelling this knot of cryptic references, most notably Michael Holquist's informed discussion of Bakhtin's interest in Ukhtomskii (see Holquist 1986, 67–70), and Gary Saul Morson and Caryl Emerson's analysis of the reference to Einstein (see Morson and Emerson 1990, 367–369). The Kantian connection has not fared nearly so well, as can be gleaned from the following remarks by Morson and Emerson:

> Kant, of course, argued long ago that time and space are indispensable forms of cognition and Bakhtin explicitly endorses this view. But he differs from Kant by stressing that in chronotopic analysis, time and space are regarded "not as 'transcendental' but as forms of the most immediate reality". Bakhtin's crucial point is that time and space vary in *qualities*; different social activities and representations of those activities presume different kinds of time and space. (Morson and Emerson 1990, 367)

True, one wishes to say, Kant did indeed consider time and space as *a priori* forms of perception (*Anschauung*). But he expressly did not list time and space in his table of categories. The reason for this is that for Kant, as for Aristotle, the categories had to do with thought rather than perception, and time and space were for Kant forms of perception rather than of thought. How, then, can Bakhtin speak of the chronotope as a "formally constitutive category of literature", and of the "image of man in literature", and support this claim with a reference to a passage in Kant which deals with forms of perception rather than with categories of thought? The phrase "not as 'transcendental' but as forms of the most immediate reality", which, as we shall see later on, stands most in need of commentary, is quoted by Morson and Emerson as if its meaning were obvious, and while it is undoubtedly correct to maintain that the various chronotopes identified by Bakhtin differ with respect to their qualities (how else should they differ?), it is not at all clear why that fact should have suggested to Bakhtin that he should take time and space as "forms of the most immediate reality" rather than, in Kantian fashion, as *a priori* conditions of the possibility of perceiving reality, and that he should freely alternate the phrase "constitutive category of" with "forms of". Is all this due to the fact that "Bakhtin's work has no philosophical rigor", as has recently been claimed by a reviewer (Kelly 1992, 46)?

Michael Holquist has addressed the problem of Bakhtin's qualified use of Kant's analysis of time and space in a number of places (Holquist and Clark 1984; Clark and Holquist 1984, 39, 43, 59 and *passim*),[4] but most recently in his introduction to the English translation of Bakhtin's early philosophical essays. Bakhtin, Holquist suggests, wished to distance himself from what he calls the "transcendentalized Kant" (Holquist 1990, xxii) of the Marburg Neo-Kantians, especially that of Hermann Cohen, by distinguishing "between *all* cognitive levels of awareness and the kind of *situated* awareness individual human beings experience in the unique sites they occupy in the world at a particular time and in a particular place" (Holquist 1990, xxii).[5] Holquist quotes Bakhtin: "'The discovery of an a priori, transcendental element in our understanding did not open an exit from the interior of our understanding...' Kant's transcendental subject is the positing merely of 'a gnoseological subject', because 'epistemological reflection has nothing to do with the individual form of experiencing an object ... it has to do with the transcendent forms of the object (and not of the experience)...'" (xxi–xxii). Is it possible that Bakhtin who, Holquist tells us, was drawn "back again and again to the three great *Critiques*, especially *The Critique of Pure Reason* and *The Critique of Practical Judgment* [*sic*!]" (xxi) could have confused transcendental issues with psychological ones in as crude a manner as is here imputed to him?[6]

If the Kantian concepts of space and time have any justified meaning, this meaning must indeed be invariant to all situational transformations due to the individual forms of perceiving objects. That Kantian epistemological reflection concerns the transcendental (not transcendent!) forms of the object but does not address itself to the contingent individual form of experiencing an object can in fact be taken as a rough and ready statement of the Kantian programme, with its distinction between transcendental and psychological, i.e. empirical questions. As such, however, it is hardly suitable as a basis for an attack on Kant. Could it be that Bakhtin was considering the possibility of talking about varying forms of experiencing an object *within the context of the conceptual framework of (Neo-)Kantian transcendental analysis*, rather than rejecting transcendental analysis, and contemplating a non-transcendental alternative? Only the latter possibility, it seems to me, is suggested by Holquist's use of quotation.

Bakhtin, we should keep in mind, was not primarily concerned with establishing his intellectual genealogy by means of his reference to Kant. Rather, having introduced a neologism ("chronotope"), and having said something about its semantics (it is meant as a name/term for "the intrinsic connectedness of temporal and spatial relationships that are artistically expressed in literature"), Bakhtin wished to say something about the *type* of concept to which the chronotope belonged, and he did so by means of the (Neo-)Kantian conceptual framework which dominated German philosophy prior to the ascendancy of Husserlian Phenomenology and Neo-Positivism. That framework, one might say, provided him with the conceptual means for articulating an insight into the role of space–time relations which, under different circumstances, he might conceivably have articulated in a different framework. The terms of that framework, we may assume, he thought to be immediately "projectable" in the sense of not requiring additional clarification: as far as its conceptual type is concerned, a chronotope is a "formally constitutive category of literature" which as such "determines to a significant degree the image of man in literature". And in the context of this attempt at clarifying the conceptual status of the concept of chronotope Bakhtin apparently saw a need to refer to Kant's "Transcendental Aesthetics". The focus of Bakhtin's own argument, then, is literature rather than intellectual autobiography, and we must here ask what the footnote reference to the "Transcendental Aesthetics" means in terms of Bakhtin's use of "chronotope" as a term for a category of literature, rather than in terms of his own relationship to Kant and Cohen.[7]

A CLOSER LOOK AT THE KANTIAN CONNECTION

Let us assume for the time being that Bakhtin borrowed the term "chronotope" from the discourses of mathematics, physics and biology because he found attractive the idea that space and time should not be viewed independently of each other but as somehow welded together in a space–time continuum.[8] Let us further assume that the placing of the reference to Kant's

"Transcendental Aesthetics" in a footnote supporting the claim that the image of man [in literature] is intrinsically chronotopic, odd as it may look at first sight, was deliberate. And let us finally assume that the identification of the chronotope as a "formally constitutive category [of literature]" is not just a manner of speaking which could, without serious loss of meaning, be replaced by formulations such as "a constitutive element of literature", "a dimension of literature", or even "an essential element of literature".[9]

In the light of these assumptions, let us look once again at the key lines of that footnote reference to Kant:

> Kant defines space and time as indispensable forms of any cognition, beginning with elementary perceptions and representations. Here we employ the Kantian evaluation of the importance of these forms in the cognitive process, but differ from Kant in taking them not as "transcendental" but as forms of the most immediate reality. We shall attempt to show the role these forms play in the process of concrete artistic cognition [...] (FTC, 85)

Kant, we may take it, would have agreed with Bakhtin's attribution of the claim that time and space should be considered as forms of cognition, although he would undoubtedly have preferred the term perception (*Anschauung*) in order to be able to arrive at a more clear-cut distinction between this and understanding (*Verstand*). But he probably would have found it problematic, if not impossible, to follow Bakhtin and place representations on a par with perceptions, if by representations are meant perceptions and/or thoughts encoded by means of one or another symbolic system. Representation as an encoding of perceptions and thoughts was not a topic of Kant's philosophizing.[10]

Was Bakhtin perhaps moving in the direction of distinguishing between perceptions of objects pure and simple and represented perceptions of objects when he placed cognitions and representations side by side? He was, after all, interested in studying the role of the chronotope as a formally constitutive category of *literature* and not, like Kant, in analysing the concepts of space and time in relation to *consciousness* (*Bewußtsein*).

From a Kantian point of view it is also rather difficult to see how space and time could retain the role granted to them by Bakhtin "in the cognitive process", i.e. as *a priori* conditions of the possibility of perceiving objects, but at the same time were to be taken "not as 'transcendental' but as forms of the most immediate reality", only to be restored, in the sentence immediately following, to a role with a definitely transcendental ring, namely one in the cognitive process of "artistic cognition (artistic visualization)". Was Bakhtin perhaps trying at this point — not very successfully, to be sure — to distinguish between a most immediate reality informed or constituted by a particular chronotope, and a *representation* (in the sense of an "encoding") of that reality in a literary work? Such a move, for which Kant clearly saw no need, would have been a very plausible one indeed for someone studying a *textual* universe, rather than the universe of *physical* objects and their transcendental constitution, which was the domain of objects of Newtonian physics as studied by Kant. Such a possibility is suggested by Bakhtin's passing remark about a "process of assimilating an actual historical chronotope in literature", which is said to be "complicated and erratic", and which, presumably because of its erratic nature, frequently assimilates only "certain isolated aspects of the chronotope". There are, it seems, chronotopes to be found prior to being assimilated by literature and thus outside of literature as well as in literature, and of those outside literature "only certain specific forms of an actual chronotope were reflected in art" (FTC, 85). Bakhtin, with characteristic nonchalance, did not pursue this highly interesting issue of "actual" chronotopes as opposed to chronotopes "reflected in art" any further, nor did he apparently see any need to clarify what he meant by "assimilating" and "reflecting" in this context.[11]

But the problem with which Bakhtin may have been wrestling at this point, and the reason for adding this footnote in the first place, may also have been a more fundamental one. The focus of Kantian transcendental analysis was, it hardly needs restating, consciousness. It is to be assumed, as he puts it in the famous "Vorrede" to the second edition of his *Critique of Pure Reason*,

> that reason only perceives that which it produces after its own design; that it must not be content to follow, as it were, in the leading-strings of nature, but must proceed in advance with principles of judgment according to unvarying laws, and compel nature to reply to its questions. (Kant 1956 [1787], 10)

Kant sets out to determine the precise character of that activity of designing and constructing nature on the basis of experience, and to identify the principles which are used in coercing nature to answer.[12] Kant, one might say, had before him Newtonian natural science as an open-ended designing and coercing activity, and he found time and space among the principles which play a role in that activity.[13] In the *Critique of Pure Reason* Kant invariably uses "transcendental" to refer to a manner of knowing objects rather than to any properties which those objects might possess. Thus he states in the programmatic "Einleitung" to his first *Critique*: "I apply the term *transcendental* to all knowledge which is not so much occupied with objects as with the mode of our cognition of these objects [mit unserer Erkenntnisart von Gegenständen], so far as this mode of cognition is possible *a priori*" (Kant 1956 [1787], 38). In keeping with this use of the term "transcendental", Kant offers, in his "Transcendental Aesthetics", a "transcendental" analysis of space and time, i.e. an analysis which is meant to reveal the role which both play in ordering the manifold of appearances in terms of definite relationships, namely those of sequence (time) and apposition (space). The point of the Kantian analyses of space and time was thus to ward off the idea that we could somehow think of space and time as things, and of objects inserted, as it were, in space and time. Space and time were to be regarded not as things, but as sources of knowledge, as conditions of the possibility of experience, and objects were to be understood as constituted under those conditions. Space and time, as Ernst Cassirer put it in a contrastive study of the concepts of space of time in Kantian Critical Philosophy and Einsteinian Theory of Relativity, "signify only a fixed law of the mind, a schema of connection by which what is sensuously perceived is set in certain relations of coexistence and sequence. Thus the two have, in spite of their 'transcendental ideality,' 'empirical reality'" (Cassirer 1953 [1921/1923], 412). As *forms* of possible experience, one might say, they can be "read off" the experiences formed by them, read off, that is, the temporally sequentialized and spatially juxtaposed objects. But they will not be found as elements of the *contents* of those experiences. It is difficult indeed to imagine a Bakhtin who was not fully aware of this conception of the role of space and time in the shaping of the contents of sense perception.

But Kant was interested in the conditions of the possibility of ordering in general, rather than in any specific historically manifest forms which that ordering activity may have taken in the course of human history. So in the section on "Transcendental Aesthetics" he did not explicitly deal with the possibility that both the sequential and the appositional ordering of the manifold of appearances might proceed along a number of widely divergent lines. It would, however, be wrong to maintain that Kant's position with regard to space and time as forms of cognition did not, in principle, allow for such varieties of sequential and appositional ordering. What he was exclusively concerned with was to demonstrate that there were factors involved in the process of cognition which were not derived from experience and which, therefore, had to be assumed to have their origin in the mind, prior to, and independent of, experience.

Bakhtin, we have just noted, was studying the highly variegated textual universe of literature, rather than the uniform nature of Newtonian physics. Furthermore, he was not so much interested in the *general capacity* of designing and coercing by means of transcendental forms, but in the *historical evidence* of such activity. And even though he spoke of the "process of concrete artistic cognition (artistic visualization)", it was *cognition achieved* and *visualization achieved*, that is, the historical evidence of such cognition and vision, that occupied him in his historical studies of literature. Natural science, if I may extend the Kantian image, is the act of designing and coercing nature; literature, as a corpus of texts, presents versions of nature designed and coerced in conformity to certain principles. Literature, as a historical phenomenon, is — like older stages of science — the repository of sedimented designs, of answers given to the coercing questions of reason.

Bakhtin therefore, faced with a multifarious body of literature ranging over many centuries and over a great variety of cultures, and displaying a great number of vastly divergent organizing principles, could and did take what he called the "Kantian evaluation of the importance of these forms in the cognitive process" for granted. But he was less interested in Kant's "transcendental" question about the forms "which make that the manifold of appearance *can* be arranged under certain relations" ["welches macht, daß das Mannigfaltige der Erscheinung in gewissen Verhältnissen geordnet werden *kann*"] (Kant 1956 [1787], 41; translation modified) but in analyzing certain historically manifest ordered manifolds, some of then still productive, others obsolete.[14] Less abstractly: while Kant was interested in determining the subjective factors involved in viewing and designing the world, Bakhtin, we might put it for the sake of contrast, was interested in the many different structures of "worlds viewed". Hence, I would submit, his insistence on paying attention to "the most immediate reality"; hence also the decision not to "take" space and time "as 'transcendental'", i.e. as analysed in the "Transcendental Aesthetics" as forms of perception, but to show instead "the role these forms play in the process of concrete artistic cognition", with the evidence of artistic cognition supplied by the corpus of narrative texts which Bakhtin had before him. Bakhtin's decision to treat space and time not as "transcendental", but as forms of "immediate reality", must therefore not be understood as a decision against, nor even as a modification of, the Kantian project. Instead, it was a shift of focus *within* that project which, not surprisingly perhaps, bears a striking similarity to the Husserlian shift of focus between *noetic* and *noematic* analyses:[15] just as a proper analysis of the Husserlian *noema* requires recourse to the *noetic acts* which produced it, a proper analysis of "most immediate reality" in the sense in which Bakhtin uses that expression requires recourse to the *transcendental forms* of space and time, which are responsible for the sequential and appositional ordering of that reality.

That the formulation "not as ... but as ..." can easily be misunderstood as implying a rejection of the Kantian point of departure is due, I believe, to a certain carelessness on Bakhtin's part. Bakhtin, it would seem, his attention focused on the corpus of literary texts, did not distinguish clearly enough between space and time as forms of immediate reality and as forms of *represented* immediate reality. Kant, one might argue, made it his task to analyse only the former. Writing before the aegis of what has been termed the "linguistic turn" of philosophy, he nowhere addressed himself to the problem of language or, as Bakhtin was to do, to the (narrative) texts of a culture as a repository of manifolds of appearances ordered by means of space and time. Bakhtin, on the other hand, appears to have focused so exclusively on those texts that he tends to neglect the fact that the ordering of manifolds of appearances in literary texts involved the additional step of encoding those orderings in accordance with the rules of a primary and a secondary modelling system (see Lotman 1977 [1964]).

On this reading, then, Bakhtin's statement that he will take time and space "not as 'transcendental' but as forms of the most immediate reality" will no longer have to be understood, as was the case in Holquist's reading, as involving a confusion of transcendental and empirical analyses. The footnote devoted to the "Transcendental Aesthetics" now will have to be read as an attempt not to jettison transcendental analysis altogether, but to hint at a different focus for transcendental analysis: not (only) the acts of perception and understanding are to be studied from a transcendental point of view, but the results, the products of those acts; not (only) artistic cognition and visualization, but (also) the artistically perceived and visualized object as "embodied" in the literary and artistic monuments of a culture.

EXTERNAL AND INTERNAL PERSPECTIVES ON THE CHRONOTOPE OF A NARRATIVE

Our interpretation of the footnote devoted to Kant will also shed some light, I believe, on Bakhtin's cryptic claim in the conclusion to "Forms of Time" that "the relationships themselves that exist *among* chronotopes cannot enter into any of the relationships contained *within* chronotopes" (FTC, 252). Bakhtin, it will be recalled, views a chronotope as "a formally constitutive category of literature"; but in the footnote accompanying the second instance of this formulation he suggests that he will "attempt to show the role these forms [i.e. of space and time as "forms of the most immediate reality"] play in the process of concrete artistic cognition (artistic visualization)" (FTC,

85). Is Bakhtin here using the terms "category" and "form" interchangeably, i.e. are space and time as formally constitutive categories of literature identical with forms of artistic cognition/visualization?[16]

There is, however, a good reason for not treating both expressions as interchangeable, and for assuming that Bakhtin actually wished to retain that difference. Speaking of the "adventure" chronotope of the Greek novel, Bakhtin, it will be recalled, stresses the fact that there is absolutely no change visible in the characters or in their love, despite all the adventures they undergo, and that Greek romance-time "does not have even an elementary biological or maturational duration." Bakhtin concludes this discussion by stating: "Such is adventure-time as an entity. But what is it like on the inside?" (FTC, 90, 91). A moment's consideration will reveal that this seemingly innocent alternative — adventure-time "as an entity" or as viewed from "the inside" — in fact articulates an important heuristic alternative for the student of (historical) chronotopes: s/he can focus on the manner in which the sequential and the appositional ordering of the manifold of appearances of a particular chronotope appears to the personages populating the world ordered by that chronotope, or s/he can focus on the manner in which that ordering appears "as an entity", i.e. looked at from the outside. Bakhtin raises the question "but what is it like on the inside?" only with regard to the adventure chronotope of the Greek novel. But it is obviously possible to distinguish, for *any* chronotope, between the way in which the sequential and appositional ordering of the manifold of appearances is perceived from within the world ordered by the chronotope and the way in which that ordering appears to the reader looking at that world from the outside. With the "adventure" chronotope of the Greek novel this difference is particularly striking. Looked at from the inside, all appears to be governed by chance through and through: Bakhtin speaks of a "veritable downpour of 'suddenlys' and 'at just that moments'" (FTC, 95). However, looked at from the outside, i.e. from the perspective of the reader, sameness and unchangingness reign supreme, and the eventual "happy ending" is never in doubt. Thus the inside and the outside perspectives on the world ordered by one and the same chronotope may offer totally different perceptions of one and the same sequence of events: while the inside perspective, i.e. the perspective of the personage "in the story", is dominated by the question of *whether* things will ever come to a good end, the outside perspective of the reader is dominated by the question of *how* the good end which is never really in doubt will eventually come about.

It can be argued that the possibility of distinguishing between an inside and an outside view of a series of events ordered sequentially and appositionally by means of a chronotope is already implied in the distinction between the chronotope as a formally constitutive category of literature and as a form of artistic cognition/visualization which Bakhtin employed in the introductory section of "Forms of Time". As *forms of (artistic) cognition/visualization* chronotopes are part and parcel of every perception, every awareness of a series of events; discussing space and time and their interrelatedness as forms of artistic cognition/visualization will therefore provide an answer to the question "But what is it like on the inside?" As *constitutive categories of literature* chronotopes are best seen as constructs of the ensemble of rules which achieve the sequential and appositional ordering of the manifold. It is the external perspective on chronotopes (understanding them as constituent categories of literature), rather than the internal perspective (understanding them as forms of cognition) that Bakhtin appears to have in mind when he calls them "the organizing centers for the fundamental narrative events of the novel", and speaks of their "plot-generating" potential (FTC, 250, 251). The participant in the events of a world ordered by means of a particular chronotope clearly need not have a conceptual awareness of that chronotope as an organizing center of the events or as a constituent category of literature, just as he need not have a conceptual awareness of the precise manner in which her/his life is "emplotted". But s/he may, as a participant, have an awareness of fate, of chance, of providence, of necessity, of fortune and accident, of curses, demons, and witches governing life, all of them culture- and life-world-specific ways of accounting for necessity and order in life, and all of them amenable to reconstruction by means of the concept of chronotope. Medvedev, a member of the "Kantian seminar" which met in Leningrad in the mid-1920s, had written in 1928: "*literature in its 'content' reflects and refracts the reflections and refractions of other ideological spheres* (ethics, cognition, political doctrines, religion, etc.), i.e. *literature reflects in its 'content' that ideological purview as a whole, of which it is itself a part*" (IT, 75). The Bakhtinian chronotope, as a literary device for sequentially and appositionally ordering manifolds, reflects and refracts the orderings which are characteristic of other ideological spheres, and which are known by the participants of those spheres from an internal point of view as curses, providence, fate etc., but these are reflections and refractions in terms of chronotopes, i.e. from an external perspective.

Assuming that this reconstruction of the distinction between a chronotope as a form of artistic cognition and as a constituent category of literature in terms of an inside and an outside perspective is valid, Bakhtin's claim in the "Concluding Remarks" that "the relationships [...] that exist *among* chronotopes cannot enter into any of the relationships contained *within* chronotopes" (FTC, 252) takes on a new significance. "Relationships existing *among* chronotopes" would have to be understood as relationships among concepts governing the sequential and appositional ordering of a manifold of appearances, concepts generating plots, while "relationships contained *within* chronotopes" would have to be understood as relationships among the elements of the manifold ordered by means of a chronotope, i.e. relationships holding in a world generated by means of a specific chronotope. Studying "relationships existing *among* chronotopes" and studying "relationships contained within chronotopes" would have to be viewed as two clearly distinct activities.

Bakhtin, as has been said, deals with the question of the difference between the inside and the outside perspective on the events shaped by a chronotope only with regard to the "adventure" chronotope, and he does so only in a rather cursory fashion. But it is a question which could profitably be raised about any other chronotope. Very likely the outcome of such an investigation would be that in the case of some chronotopes a difference in awareness on the part of the *agent in the story* and the *reader of the story* is a defining feature of the chronotope itself, while in others that is not the case. In either event, an observer is positioned in a chronotope-specific relation to the sequentially and appositionally ordered manifold of events. It is the stance of that chronotope-specific observer vis-à-vis the events narrated which will have to be adopted by the reader if s/he is to perceive the represented sequence of events as intended. In other words, the image of the "implied reader" of literature, may, on closer inspection, turn out to be as "intrinsically chronotopic" as the "image of man in literature" studied by Bakhtin.

The distinction between an inside and an outside view of a world ordered by a particular chronotope, with its implications for the positioning of the implied reader, must not be confused with the problem of the author's (and reader's) own chronotope, which Bakhtin discusses in passing in the last sections of the "Concluding Remarks". Bakhtin here raises the possibility of identifying a chronotope characterizing the author as the "creator of the work", and marking out the latter's actions as a "distinctive form of [...] activity." It is the author as author who "segments the work into parts (songs, chapters and so on) that assume [...] a kind of external expression — without however directly reflecting the represented chronotopes." Bakhtin views as the observational basis for this claim about a specific author's chronotope the fact that "we can with relative clarity sense in the segmentation of ancient epic songs the chronotope of the singer and his audience, or the chronotope of storytelling in traditional tales" (FTC, 254). Besides the chronotopes governing the represented world, there are the chronotopes of the governing communicative situations in which those represented worlds are narrated. And just as the chronotopes of the represented world can be read off the sequentially and appositionally ordered manifolds of represented events, those of the communicative situation can be read off the segmentation, i.e. the sequentially and appositionally ordered manifold of the parts of the work. Bakhtin formulates this insight as follows:

> every work has a beginning and an *end*, the event represented in it likewise has a beginning and an end, but these beginnings and ends lie in different worlds, in different chronotopes [*sic*!] that can never fuse with each other or be identical to each other but that are, at the same time, interrelated and indissolubly tied up with each other. We might put it as follows: before us are two events — the event that is narrated in the work and the event of narration itself (we ourselves participate in the latter, as listeners or readers); these events take place in different times [...] and in different places, but at the same time these two events are indissolubly united in a single but complex event that we might call the work in the totality of all its events [...] (FTC, 255)

Read in conjunction with his detailed analyses of a number of chronotopes, and with his brief remarks on the inside and the outside view of a represented world ordered by a chronotope, these observations on the author's chronotope suggest that the concept of chronotope may be capable of making systematic sense of a number of features of narrative texts for which neither Formalist nor Structuralist narrative theory has managed to provide a unified account. As Bakhtin's own analyses amply demonstrate, it provides the conceptual basis for a theory of fable/story capable of accounting for variability in the ordering of events. But Bakhtin's own brief hints about inside and outside views of a represented world ordered by a particular chronotope suggest that the chronotope also promises to offer a conceptual basis for dealing with at least some of the features which are usually dealt with by a theory of focalization. Only now the systematic account of those features would constitute an integral part of the theory of fable/story, rather than being added on to that theory, and involving as problematic an hypostasis as that of the "focalizer" (see Bal 1990). And, judging by what Bakhtin has to say — again, all too briefly and cryptically — about the difference between the event narrated in the work and the event of narration in relation to the chronotopes of the represented world and of the author/reader, it may even offer the possibility of conceptually linking the theory of plot (*siuzhet*) with the theory of story (*fabula*) in such a way that the Formalist inheritance of treating plot as an end in itself, and story as material, might finally be left behind.[17]

CHRONOTOPE AND THE STRUCTURALIST THEORY OF STORY

Literary theory has suffered badly from the fact that new concepts and theories are contantly being introduced into the debate, retained for a while for their novelty value, and then dropped in favour of even newer concepts. A question which is rarely asked in connection with this march of most-favoured concepts is whether and how a new concept which is being proposed might be viewed as a successor concept to an older one, and whether the adoption of that new concept will represent a conceptual advance beyond the position reached with the aid of the concept which is being replaced. This question, it seems to me, needs to be asked every time a new concept is proposed if literary theory is to become cumulative and move beyond sectarianism.

As far as Bakhtin's chronotope is concerned, this question would have to be raised first with an eye on the situation of continental, in particular Slavic, literary scholarship as practised in the mid- and late 1930s when Bakhtin introduced the concept for the first time (see Scholz forthcoming), and then again with an eye on the situation of scholarship during the mid-1970s and early 1980s when Bakhtin's works were beginning to receive attention in the West.

Current interest in Bakhtin's work, needless to say, has little to do with the situation of literary scholarship during the 1930s. Its beginnings coincide with the waning of Structuralist poetics which had dominated the 1970s, and it could be argued that to the extent that literary theorists have not turned towards post-Saussurean schools for answers to problems left unresolved by Structuralism, they have turned to Bakhtinian poetics as a more radical alternative point of departure for solving those problems.

Since both the introduction of the concept of chronotope into literary theory, and the identification of a number of concrete manifestations of chronotopes in the history of Western literature, were intended by Bakhtin to shed new light on what he thought was a "formally constitutive category" of literature, it may be worth raising the question of whether Bakhtin's position does indeed represent an advance over the Structuralist treatment of time and space, or whether what Bakhtin has to offer is also offered by what is without doubt a much more carefully elaborated and a much more comprehensive conceptual framework. Bakhtin's concept of the chronotope, I shall argue, can indeed be seen to fill a serious gap in Structuralist poetics, namely that of a theory of "story" which will be sensitive to historical change, and which will allow us to talk about "story" not just as a functional re-construal which needs to be undertaken so that the importance of *récit* as essentially a reordering and restructuring of *histoire* can be understood, but as a construal in its own right which will allow us better to understand some of the most fundamental characteristics of narrative.

A chronotope, we have seen, is a principle of sequentially and appositionally ordering a manifold of events. It orders these events into what are generally known as "plots". A chronotope must therefore not be thought of as somehow being present *in* the literary work as one of its elements. Rather, using more familiar terminology, it must be thought of as a principle of generating the plots of narratives. "Actual chronotopes", as opposed to chronotopes "assimilated" by or "reflected" in art, as Bakhtin refers to them in a momentary lapse into realist epistemology, must therefore not be thought of as different types of chronotopes, certainly not different in the sense of "primary" as opposed to "secondary" ones. Rather, "actual" chronotopes must be viewed as culturally sanctioned principles of sequentially and appositionally ordering which are capable of generating the plots of historical as well as fictional narrative. They retain this capability as long as their sanctioning remains intact. As Bakhtin's own analyses of a number of historically manifest chronotopes suggest, the plots of particular types of narrative can only be reconstructed adequately if we succeed in reconstructing the concomitant chronotope, just as the particular chronotope of a type of narrative can only be ascertained if we succeed in reconstructing the stories it generated. What Bakhtin actually does in all of his analyses of historically manifest chronotopes, sometimes more, sometimes less systematically, is to reconstruct chronotopes and plots as corollaries of each other. Extending the study of chronotopes beyond those identified by Bakhtin himself will therefore have to involve paying particular attention to this correlation: a striking specification of time and space, no matter how pregnant with cultural meanings, which does not generate a recognizably different plot-structure, will not qualify as a chronotope in its own right, and two plots which can be understood as having been generated by one and the same chronotope will have to be viewed as possessing the same plot-structure.

There are, then, four levels to be considered in a Bakhtinian analysis of narrative: the level of the concrete narrative text; that of the plot of that text; that of the concomitant plot-structure; and, finally, that of the concomitant chronotope. In accordance with this interpretation of the Bakhtinian theory of chronotope, two seemingly different plots may, on closer inspection, turn out to be indistinguishable and therefore identical with regard to a particular plot-structure, just as two seemingly different plot-structures may turn out, on closer interpretation, to be indistinguishable and therefore identical with regard to a particular chronotope. The conception of the relation of plot, plot-structure and chronotope, which, I would submit, is implicit in Bakhtin's theory of the chronotope, thus involves the principle of the identity of indiscernibles[18] on two levels, that of plot in relation to plot-structure, and that of plot-structure in relation to chronotope. In this four-tier structure the chronotope represents the most abstract level, but significantly, even at this most abstract level the Bakhtinian reflection of narrative does not aim to disentangle itself from historical contingency: rather than positing a variable series of *timeless abstract oppositions* as the ultimate generating principle of a particular plot,[19] it identifies those principles as *assimilated actual historical chronotopes* (FTC, 85). It thereby manages to avoid having to sever the ties which link a particular plot, a particular plot-structure or a particular literary chronotope to the life-world in the context of which it was produced. Stronger yet, Bakhtinian analysis of narrative offers a means of conceptualizing that link without having to resort, as, for example, Lucien Goldmann was forced to do, to postulating spurious homologies between social structures and plot-structures (see Goldmann 1975), or, worse, having to take refuge in an aesthetics of mirroring. Therein, I would like to submit, lies the principal significance for narrative theory of Bakhtin's decision to historicize the Kantian *a priori* and to substitute for the latter's "one" time and "one" space a series of historically manifest chronotopes.

Distinguishing between narrative texts, plots, plot-structures and chronotopes, and their relations, admittedly involves a certain amount of "structuralizing" of Bakhtin's theory of the chronotope.[20] What this "structuralizing" of Bakhtin's theory of the chronotope suggests is that where Structuralist narrative theory usually distinguishes between *histoire* (story) and *récit* (narrative),[21] Bakhtin effectively splits the concept of story in two: into the concept of chronotope for referring to the generative principle of plot, and the concept of plot-structure for referring to the chronotope-typical sequence of events ordered in accordance with that principle.

The significance of this difference between a Structuralist and a Bakhtinian analysis of narrative becomes clear if we consider a standard Structuralist definition of "story" from a Bakhtinian perspective: "'Story' designates the narrated events, abstracted from their disposition in the text and *reconstructed in their chronological order*, together with the participants in these events" (Rimmon-Kenan 1983, 3). "Story" is thus viewed as a product of a twofold process of decomposition and recomposition. It is assembled in accordance with the ordering principle of chronology from events which first had to be extracted from their place in the textual continuum. Note the formulation "reconstructed in *their* chronological order". The disposition of the events in the textual continuum is thereby implicitly understood to represent a deviation from an order which itself is not the result of a human ordering activity. The elements of that ordering, i.e. the narrated events, are first abstracted from their place in the text then subsequently reconstituted in their chronological order. What is concealed by the formulation "reconstructed in their chronological order" is the fact that this is a reconstruction in terms of a particular ordering principle, namely that of chronology. The question to ask from the standpoint of Bakhtinian narrative theory must clearly be: "why settle on chronological order as a principle for reconstructing story?" And, recalling the plurality of chronotopes as principles of sequential and appositional ordering of a manifold of events: "why settle on chronological order exclusively?" The standard Structuralist answer, as the quotation from Rimmon-Kenan suggests, would undoubtedly be that we are indeed in possession of the "story" of a narrative once we have managed to re-arrange the narrated events in their chronological order. Rimmon-Kenan's justification for this procedure is most telling: "Strict linear chronology [...] is neither natural nor an actual characteristic of most stories. It is a conventional norm which has become so widespread as to replace the actual multilinear temporality and acquire a pseudo-natural status" (Rimmon-Kenan 1983, 17).

Strict linear chronology, the principle of Structuralist reconstruction of story, despite the fact that it is correctly understood not to constitute a "natural" or an "actual" characteristic of most stories, is nevertheless put to use as a principle of reconstruction because of its "pseudo-natural" status. The justification for settling on linear chronology as a principle of reconstruction emerges if we consider what is presented as indeed the "actual" characteristic of most stories: multilinearity, an ordering of events, that is, can be understood by adding and interlacing several strictly linear orderings, and thus an ordering which does not fundamentally depart from chronological ordering. Strict linear chronology, used as an analytical tool, will indeed serve at times to "straighten out", as it were, the entangled actual multilinear temporality of stories. But in so doing it removes from sight just how multilinear temporality, as a feature of the represented lived world of such a story, is experienced by the inhabitants of that world. Bakhtinian chronotopes, we saw earlier on, invite us to investigate the inside as well as the outside view of a chronotope. Treating linear chronology as yet another chronotope, and investigating it in this manner, we shall soon discover that it has only an outside, and that no inside view corresponds to it.

Taking our stand with the Bakhtinian distinction between reconstructed story and principle of reconstruction, Structuralist narrative theory, then, can be seen to admit one, and only one, chronotope, namely that of linear chronological order.[22] Significantly, Bakhtin does not explicitly deal with this chronotope: it is, after all, "neither natural nor an actual characteristic of most stories". Undoubtedly linear chronological sequences could be reconstructed for every single narrative for which Bakhtin tried to reconstruct the appropriate chronotope. But the concept of linear chronological time is clearly not suitable for reconstructing the sequential and appositional ordering of events which is "actually" to be found in stories. The reason for this failure would appear to be that the chronotope of Structuralist narrative theory, which sequentially orders the manifold of events in terms of linear chronology and causality, locates the characters of a story on points of a temporal continuum which is itself an abstraction from "lived time", and, in so doing, dislocates them from the sequence of events in which we, as readers, see them and they see themselves as agents. What moves in time, Niklas Luhmann has suggested, is "past/present/future *together*, is, in other words, the present *together* with the past and the future as its temporal horizons" (Luhmann 1975, 114). The chronotope of linear chronology abstracts from those temporal horizons in which the agents of stories hope, fear, remember, love, expect, anticipate and hate. The concept of linear chronology as put to use in Structuralist narrative theory thus makes it impossible to understand why and how, as Bakhtin puts it, "the image of man is always intrinsically chronotopic" (FTC, 85), and to come to grips with the reflection and refraction of ideological reality which, Medvedev had suggested, characterizes literature. The chronotope of linear chronology and causality, one might say, is the chronotope of natural science, i.e. the chronotope which allows one to reconstruct the sequential and appositional ordering characterizing the experiments of natural science. But it does not allow one to map the sense of time passing, which, for example, informs the actions of the characters of Virginia Woolf's *To the Lighthouse*, or the awareness of the fulfilment of time in St Paul's *Letter to the Galatians* (St Paul, 4,4: "But when the fullness of time came, God sent forth his son, born of a woman, born under the law"), or, to mention but two of Bakhtin's own examples, the sense of time which characterizes the chronotopes of Greek Romance (FTC, 86–110) or of the Idyll (FTC, 224–242). That is to say, it does not allow a modelling of the "actual" chronotopes of literature, chronotopes in the sense of formally constitutive categories of literature.[23]

Bakhtinian chronotopes, if we approach them from the point of view of producing narratives, can be said to generate stories: they are qualitative principles of sequentially and appositionally ordering manifolds of intuitions into stories. The producer of a narrative, it is clear, need not be aware of these principles as principles; he simply utilizes certain ways of ordering which are sanctioned by his culture. He may not even be aware of an activity of ordering. The plausible stories of a culture are, in a sense, found, not made. The situation is different for the reader of stories generated by one or another chronotope, who is trying to ascertain which one it is: if the chronotope is still productive, the story in question will make sense immediately, and again the informing chronotope may remain invisible. Only if a chronotope is no longer productive, only if, as Bakhtin puts it, the chronotope in question has "lost any meaning that was productive in actuality or adequate to later historical situations" (FTC, 85), or if it is not yet an established chronotope, will it become visible as the form of the story which cannot be reconstructed on the basis of currently productive chronotopes. Chronotopes, we might put it, if they impinge on our awareness at all, do so only in the temporal modes which St Augustin in Book XI of the *Confessions* identified as those of *praesens de praeteritis* and *praesens de futuris*. The Structuralist chronotope of linear chronology, with its insistence that there is, if not a natural, then at least a pseudo-natural, order to all stories tends to obliterate this fundamentally hermeneutic dimension of the search for chronotopes.

CONCLUDING REMARKS: THE CHRONOTOPE OF BAKHTIN'S STUDY OF CHRONOTOPES

Will it be thought unnecessarily mannered to ask in conclusion whether Bakhtin's concept of chronotope, understood as a qualitative principle of sequentially and appositionally ordering manifolds, can be applied to chronotope research itself? Both chronotope research in the Bakhtinian vein and Structuralist reconstructions of stories by means of the chronotope of linear chronology, understood as meta-level activities, involve an ordering of ordered manifolds. In the case of Bakhtinian chronotope research this is a predominantly sequential ordering which aims, as the subtitle of "Forms of Time" suggests, at an historical poetics. The chronotope which informs the Structuralist reconstruction of story, by contrast, achieves a predominantly appositional ordering: literature as a simultaneous present, literature as system. The goal of Structuralism was indeed a systematic rather than an historical poetics. What, we may ask, was the fundamental conceptual decision which brought about that difference? In the case of Bakhtinian chronotope theory it was the decision to treat the chronotopes of literature as assimilated or reflected "actual" chronotopes, thereby supplying each of them with an historical index, and identifying for each of them a "Sitz im Leben". In the case of Structuralist chronotope research — if we may call it that — it was the decision to relate the events of story to an abstract chronological continuum which would order those events in terms of an "and then ... and then ... and then", but, unlike the Bakhtinian approach, would not relate this ordering to the temporal horizons of the agents in the story or to those of the readers of stories.[24]

NOTES

1. On the structure of the terminological repertoire of literary scholarship, especially the difference between its "nomenclature" and its "terminology proper", see Slawinski 1975.
2. In a later study, the x-ray imagery recurs in a slightly modified version: "He looks at genres not just in their narrow literary context but as icons that fix the world view of the ages from which they spring. Genre is to him an x-ray of a specific world view, a crystallization of the concepts particular to a given time and to a given social stratum in a specific society. A genre, therefore, embodies a historically specific idea of what it means to be human" (Clark and Holquist 1984, 275). Thus a genre is alternately an icon (Rublev's or Peirce's?) of a world-view, an x-ray of a world-view, a crystallization of certain concepts, and, finally, an embodiment of an idea of what it means to be human. Needless to say, the meaning and use of the term "chronotope" is not clarified by garnishing it with fanciful metaphors and vague concepts.
3. The suggestion put forward by Gary Saul Morson and Caryl Emerson that "Bakhtin appears to mean that the relation of 'chronotope' to Einsteinian 'time–space' is something weaker than identity, but stronger than mere metaphor or analogy", a suggestion supported with a reference to general systems theory, is not very helpful, since it is based on a confusion of the object-level (cultural, economic, psychological, hydraulic and other systems) and the meta-level (terminologies introduced in order to be able to refer to those systems and their elements) (see Morson and Emerson 1990, 307, 488 n. 1).
4. Holquist and Clark 1984 contains a brief hint at the programme of Ernst Cassirer's *Philosophy of Symbolic Forms* to "broaden the scope of categorical operations into the mind's use of symbols" and at the significance of that

programme for Bakhtin. Unfortunately Holquist and Clark leave it at that hint and waste time on rather abstruse speculations about Hermann Cohen's much later interest in the Talmud. The article teems with inaccuracies, ranging from references to "such universities as Baden [sic!] and Freiburg" (302) to the unsustainable claim that "the Marburg philosophers believed that ethics, the doctrine of man [sic!], should be the centre of philosophy" (304). Their quotation (306) from Wilhelm Windelband's *History of Philosophy* is truncated to serve their thesis about the place of ethics in Neo-Kantianism. Windelband insists that "Philosophy can live only as a science of values which are universally valid", and he directs this claim against the destructive relativism he diagnoses in Nietzsche: "The revolt of boundless individualism culminates in the claim that all values are relative" (Windelband 1958 [1901], 680). Holquist and Clark leave out the relative clause without indicating that they have done so, and treat the remaining statement that "Philosophy can live only as a science of values" as proof of Windelband's (and other Neo-Kantians') insistence on the centrality of ethics.

5. For a detailed, up-to-date discussion of Neo-Kantianism in relation to Kant, see Köhnke 1993; on Cohen's version of Neo-Kantianism, see 273–301. To speak, as Holquist does, of the "transcendentalized Kant" of the Marburg Neo-Kantians is rather misleading.
6. Kant himself distinguishes clearly between a transcendental and a physiological analysis in his discussion of the difference between his own and Edmund Burke's exposition of the Sublime in *Critique of Judgement* (Kant 1914 [1790], 147–150).
7. Around 1937–38, when the bulk of "Forms of Time" was written, talk of "constituent categories" could also have evoked a Husserlian phenomenological framework. By that time the first volume of Husserl's *Ideas Pertaining to a Pure Phenomenology*, with its detailed discussions of categories, "Ding-Konstitution", time and space, had gone through three editions (1913, 1922, and 1928). So the reference to Kant, despite the fact that it may seem to diverge from Kantian positions, must be understood as suggesting the Kantian rather than the Husserlian transcendental framework as a context for the concept of a "constituent category of literature".
8. The physicists' concept of a space–time continuum had actually been recognized by the leading members of the Marburg School as a major challenge to philosophy. Thus Hermann Cohen devotes a whole paragraph of his *Logic of Pure Knowledge* to the "Relativitätsproblem" ("problem of relativity") (Cohen 1914 [1902], 198–199), and in a paragraph on Albert Einstein he credits the latter with having contributed to the solution of certain problems of Critical Idealism (296–299). Paul Natorp, Hermann Cohen's pupil, in a speech to the Kant-Gesellschaft commemorating the death of Cohen, contemplates the possibility of an "idealistische Deutung der wohl größten wissenschaftlichen Entdeckung unsrer Tage, der gänzlichen Relativierung aller zeiträumlichen

Bestimmung, der Invarianz aber der Naturgesetzlichkeit dieser Relativität gegenüber" ("an Idealist interpretation of perhaps the greatest scientific discovery of the age, namely the total relativization of all temporal-spatial determinations, and, at the same time, the invariability of natural laws in the face of relativity") (Natorp 1918, 18). And, last but not least, Ernst Cassirer in 1921 published an essay of about 100 pages with the title "Zur Einstein'schen Relativitätstheorie" ("On Einsteinian Relativity Theory"). It contains twenty pages of detailed analyses of the concepts of space and time as explicated by Critical Idealism and in the context of the Theory of Relativity. According to Cassirer, "when Einstein characterizes as a fundamental feature of the theory of relativity that it takes from space and time 'the last remainder of *physical objectivity*', it is clear that the theory only accomplishes the most definite application and carrying through of the standpoint of critical idealism within empirical science itself" (Cassirer 1953 [1921/1923], 412, my translation). Thus, with his interest in time and space, Bakhtin did not stand alone among the (Neo-)Kantians. The issue was in fact something of a common concern of scientists and philosophers of all stripes during the first third of the century.

9. The distinction between the term "chronotope" and its referent, the concept of chronotope, will allow us to later raise the question whether other terms have been used to refer to the same or a closely related concept.

10. Equating "representation" with "encoding" may actually involve a misreading both of Kant and of Bakhtin: if "representation" here stands for the Kantian *Darstellung*, it would have to be understood as saying that the objects perceived and constituted in the act of cognition "represent", as appearances, the transcendental forms thanks to which they can appear to us. Cf. Paul Natorp's concise statement "Anschauung, Gegebenheit ist für Kant unmittelbar 'Darstellung' des Gegenstands" ("According to Kant, perception and givenness amounts to the 'representation' of the object") (Natorp 1918, 17). The study of alternative ways of ordering experience, and of "encoding" those alternatives, only became a topic of philosophizing in the Kantian tradition in Ernst Cassirer's *Philosophy of Symbolic Forms*, the three volumes of which were first published in 1923, 1924 and 1929 (Cassirer 1964 [1923–29]).

11. It would undoubtedly be important to have this point clarified in order to be able to determine the extent to which Bakhtin, despite his avowed affinity with (Neo-)Kantian epistemology, subscribed to a (socialist) realist theory of art mirroring a reality which exists outside art.

12. It should be pointed out that Kant, in the section of the *Critique of Pure Reason* entitled "Transcendental Aesthetic", does not deal with aesthetic issues in the modern sense of that term. His reasons for adopting the term "aesthetic" in a work which was intended to lay the epistemological foundations of Newtonian physics deserve quoting in full: "The Germans are the only people who at present [i.e. around 1781] use this word to indicate what others call the critique of taste. At the foundation of this term lies the disappointed hope, which the

eminent analyst, Baumgarten, conceived, of subjecting the criticism of the beautiful to principles of reason, and so of elevating its rules into a science. But his endeavours were vain. For the said rules or criteria are, in respect to their chief sources, merely empirical, consequently never can serve as determinate laws *a priori*, by which our judgment in matters of taste is to be directed. It is rather our judgment which forms the proper test as to the correctness of the principles. On this account it is advisable to give up the use of the term as designating the critique of taste, and to apply it solely to that doctrine which is true science — the science of the laws of sensibility — and thus come nearer to the language and the sense of the ancients in their well-known division of the objects of cognition into αισθητα και νοητα or to share it with speculative philosophy, and employ it partly in a transcendental, partly in a psychological signification" (Kant 1956 [1787], 42, n. 1).

13. On Kant's explication of the concepts of space and time in relation to mathematics and physics see, e.g., Körner 1955, ch. 1. Köhnke has recently suggested that at the basis of Hermann Cohen's reception of Kant is the illicit transfer of Kant's ideas on construction and of the analyses of time and space from the area of mathematics to that of empirical science (Köhnke 1993, 273–301).
14. That may be the thrust of Bakhtin's observation that certain generic forms reflecting an actual chronotope, "at first productive, were then reinforced by tradition; in their subsequent development they continued stubbornly to exist, up to and beyond the point at which they had lost any meaning that was productive in actuality or adequate to later historical situations" (FTC, 85). There are, in other words, both productive and obsolete ways of designing and coercing nature.
15. See Husserl's claim in *Ideas Pertaining to a Pure Phenomenology* that "wie wir in der Noese die pure Hyle haben in eins mit ihrer Auffassung, so im Noema das, was sozusagen 'Leistung' der Auffassung der Hyle oder 'Leistung' des Bewußtseins ist, und diese Leistung enthält eine Komponente, die von der Hyle herstammt, und eine die von den noetischen Momenten herstammt" ["just as in the act of noesis we have the pure hyle together with its apperception, we have in the noema what we might call the 'product/result' of the apperception of the hyle, or the 'product/result' of consciousness. This product contains a component derived from the hyle, and another which has its origins in the noetic aspects"] (Husserl 1950, 412) (Beilage XXIV: the English translation by F. Kersten (Husserl 1982) does not offer translations of the "Beilagen" of the 1950 German edition). For a discussion of this Husserlian distinction see, e.g., Diemer 1965, 61–89.
16. A decision to posit such an identity could perhaps be understood to be in line with Hermann Cohen's refusal to give space and time a different status from that of the categories (see Cohen 1918 [1871], 275ff.). Cohen later articulated his doubts about the Kantian distinction between "forms" and "categories" in greater detail his *Logic of Pure Knowledge* (Cohen 1914 [1902], 150ff.).

17. With these possibilities, it will be noted, we are back at a point in Bakhtin's own development prior to the beginning of work on the concept of chronotope (c. 1937–38). In *The Formal Method in Literary Scholarship*, first published in Russian in 1928 under Medvedev's name, but now assumed to be a joint work of Medvedev and Bakhtin, one comes across an extended critique of the Formalist preference of plot (*siuzhet*) over story (*fabula*), and their reductive treatment of story as "material only". According to Medvedev/Bakhtin, what the Formalists overlooked was the fact that story, as "the event which underlies plot, an event from life, ethics, politics, history", has a "definite ideological and practical significance" in its own right. Story, it is argued, must not only be seen to provide the motivation of the constructive device of plot; it must be understood as a constructive principle in its own right (see *FM*, 106–118 (106)). It could be argued that this call for an adequate theory of *fabula* which might supplement the theory of plot developed by the Formalists was taken up by Bakhtin himself ten years later when he began work on the chronotope. But while the criticism of Formalism offered in the *Formal Method* proceeded from a broadly Marxist position, the solution offered a decade later was, as we have seen, (Neo-)Kantian. (I am grateful to Brian McHale, Tel Aviv, for drawing my attention to *The Formal Method*.)
18. "Eadem seu coincidentia sunt, quorum alterutrum ubilicet potest alteri substitui salva veritate": see the entry "Indiscernibilien" in Ritter and Gründer (eds.), 1976, 283–286.
19. This, I take it, was a strategy frequently employed by Structuralist narrative theory: see, e.g., the discussion of "handlungsstrukturkonstitutive [*sic*!] Oppositionen" ("oppositions which constitute the structures of actions") in Link 1979, 268 ff.
20. Bakhtin, who, it is well known, was not overly sympathetic to Structuralism, would probably not have chosen to describe the analytical strategy of "Forms of Time" in this manner. His analyses are devoted to identifying a number of chronotopes, not to meta-level reflections on the methodological steps involved in making those identifications. Setting out Bakhtin's approach in this manner must therefore be viewed as an heuristic device only, one which will facilitate a contrastive analysis of a Structuralist and a Bakhtinian approach to narrative.
21. Going beyond the original opposition of *histoire* and *récit*, Karlheinz Stierle has suggested a triadic division into *Geschehen*, *Geschichte* and *Text der Geschichte*, with *Geschehen* in contrast to *Geschichte* as yet devoid of meaning (Stierle 1975). The problem is obviously how to conceptualize such a meaningless *Geschehen*. Triadic schemes have also been suggested by Gérard Genette and Mieke Bal.
22. A rare exception to this general tendency is Pfister 1977. Pfister considers Aristotle's notion of *mythos* (plot) with its insistence on "Ganzheit, Einheitlichkeit und kausaler Geschlossenheit" as an instance of ordering events not only in terms of chronology but also of "sinnstiftende Relationierungen"

(266ff.) But he does not go beyond listing the familiar modern departures from Aristotle's ordering principle. Bakhtin, one might claim, is the first theorist to identify alternative orderings.

23. This failure of the chronotope of Structuralist narrative theory to allow for an adequate reconstruction of the "actual" ordering of the events of "story" is epitomized by Roland Barthes' suggestion that there are stories based on an implicit application of the logical error of "post hoc, ergo propter hoc" (see Barthes 1977 [1966]). Undoubtedly a chronotope such as that of medieval typological or figural thought can be described in this manner. But such a description, because it involves an inadequate principle of temporal ordering, namely a chronological one, amounts to a misdescription. "Post hoc, ergo propter hoc" may amount to a logical error if considered in logical terms; it amounts to a constituent principle of a type of story if considered in theological terms. On figural thought see Auerbach 1967.

24. With thanks to Ruud Teeuwen (Utrecht) for comments on an earlier version, to David Shepherd for help with Bakhtin's usage, and to Meir Sternberg (Tel Aviv) for a critical reading. An early conference version of this article appeared in Spanish under the title "El concepto de cronotopo en Bajtín: notas sobre la conexión kantiana", in R. Alvarado and L. Zavala (eds.), *Diálogos y Fronteras. El pensamiento de Bajtín en el mundo contemporáneo* (Mexico City: Nueva Imagen, 1993), 283–311.

WORKS CITED

Auerbach, E. 1967. "Figura", in *Gesammelte Aufsätze zur romanischen Philologie* (Berne and Munich: Francke), 55–92.

Bakhtin, M.M. 1975. "K metodologii literaturovedeniia", in *Kontekst 1974* (Moscow: Nauka), 203–212.

Bal, M. 1990. *De theorie van vertellen en verhalen: inleiding in de narratologie*, 5th ed. (Muiderberg: Coutinjo).

Barthes, R. 1977 [1966]. "Introduction to the Structural Analysis of Narratives", in *Image—Music—Text*, tr. S. Heath (London: Fontana, 1977), 79–124.

Cassirer, E. 1953 [1921/1923]. *Substance and Function and Einstein's Theory of Relativity*, tr. W.C. and M.C. Swabey (New York: Dover Publications).

________. 1964 [1923–29]. *Philosophie der Symbolischen Formen*, 3 vols. (Darmstadt: Wissenschaftliche Buchgesellschaft).

Clark, K., and M. Holquist 1984. *Mikhail Bakhtin* (Cambridge, MA and London: Harvard University Press).

Cohen, H. 1914 [1902]. *Logik der reinen Erkenntnis*, 2nd ed. (Berlin: Bruno Cassirer).

________. 1918 [1871]. *Kants Theorie der Erfahrung*, 3rd ed. (Berlin: Bruno Cassirer).

Diemer, A. 1965. *Edmund Husserl* (Monographien zur Philosophischen Forschung, vol. 15) (Meisenheim and Glan: Anton Hain).

Emerson, C., and M. Holquist 1981. "Glossary", in *The Dialogic Imagination: Four Essays by M.M. Bakhtin*, ed. Holquist, tr. Holquist and Emerson (Austin: University of Texas Press), 423–434.

Goldmann, L. 1975. *Towards a Sociology of the Novel*, tr. A. Sheridan (London: Tavistock).

Hirschkop, K. 1986. "A Response to the Forum on Mikhail Bakhtin", in G.S. Morson (ed.), *Bakhtin: Essays and Dialogues on His Work* (Chicago and London: University of Chicago Press), 73–79.

Holquist, J.M., and K. Clark 1984. "The Influence of Kant in the Early Works of M.M. Bakhtin", in J.P. Strelka (ed.), *Literary Theory and Criticism: Festschrift for René Wellek* (Berne and Frankfurt-am-Main: Peter Lang), 299–313.

Holquist, M. 1986. "Answering as Authoring: Mikhail Bakhtin's Trans-Linguistics", in G.S. Morson (ed.), *Bakhtin: Essays and Dialogues on His Work* (Chicago and London: University of Chicago Press), 59–71.

________. 1990. "Introduction: The Architectonics of Answerability", in *Art and Answerability: Early Philosophical Essays by M.M. Bakhtin*, ed. Holquist and V. Liapunov, tr. Liapunov and K. Brostrom (Austin: University of Texas Press), ix–xlix.

Husserl, E. 1950. *Ideen zu einer reinen Phänomenologie und phänomenologischen Philosophie. Buch I: Allgemeine Einführung in die reine Phänomenologie*, ed. W. Biemel (The Hague: Martinus Nijhoff).

________. 1982. *Ideas Pertaining to a Pure Phenomenology and to a Phenomenological Philosophy*, tr. F. Kersten (The Hague: Martinus Nijhoff).

Kant, I. 1914 [1790]. *Critique of Judgement*, tr. and ed. J.H. Bernard (London: Macmillan and Co.).

________. 1956 [1787]. *Critique of Pure Reason*, tr. J.M.D. Meiklejohn (London: J.M. Dent & Sons Ltd.; New York: E.P. Dutton & Co. Inc.).

Kelly, A. 1992. "Revealing Bakhtin", in *The New York Review of Books*, 39/15 (24 September), 44–48.

Köhnke, K.C. 1993. *Entstehung und Aufstieg des Neukantianismus. Die deutsche Universitätsphilosophie zwischen Idealismus und Positivismus* (Frankfurt-am-Main: Suhrkamp).

Körner, S. 1955. *Kant* (Harmondsworth: Penguin).

Link, J. 1979. *Literaturwissenschaftliche Grundbegriffe* (Munich: Fink).

Lotman, Iu.M. 1977 [1964]. *The Structure of the Artistic Text*, tr. R. Vroon (Ann Arbor: University of Michigan).

Luhmann, N. 1975. "Weltzeit und Systemgeschichte. Über Beziehungen zwischen Zeithorizonten und sozialen Strukturen gesellschaftlicher Systeme", in *Soziologische Aufklärung 2. Aufsätze zur Theorie der Gesellschaft* (Opladen: Westdeutscher Verlag), 103–133.

Morson, G.S. 1986. "Dialogue, Monologue and the Social: A Reply to Ken Hirschkop", in Morson (ed.), *Bakhtin: Essays and Dialogues on His Work* (Chicago and London: University of Chicago Press), 81–88.

_________, and C. Emerson 1990. *Mikhail Bakhtin: Creation of a Prosaics* (Stanford: Stanford University Press).

Natorp, P. 1918. "Hermann Cohens philosophische Leistung unter dem Gesichtspunkte des Systems", in A. Liebert (ed.), *Philosophische Vorträge veröffentlicht von der Kant-Gesellschaft*, 21 (Berlin: Reuther & Reichard).

Pfister, M. 1977. *Das Drama. Theorie und Analyse* (Munich: Fink, 1977).

Rimmon-Kenan, S. 1983. *Narrative Fiction: Contemporary Poetics* (London and New York: Methuen).

Ritter, J., and K. Gründer (eds.) 1976. *Historisches Wörterbuch der Philosophie*, vol. 4 (Basel: Schwabe).

Scholz, B. forthcoming. "'Totum ponere': The German Context of Bakhtin's Concept of Chronotope".

Slawinski, J. 1975. "Probleme der literaturwissenschaftlichen Terminologie", in *Literatur als System und Prozeß. Strukturalistische Aufsätze zur semantischen, kommunikativen, sozialen und historischen Dimension der Literatur*, tr. R. Figuth (Munich: Nymphenburger), 65–80.

Stierle, K. 1974 [1971]. "Geschehen, Geschichte, Text der Geschichte", in *Text als Handlung* (Munich: Fink), 49–55.

Windelband, W. 1958 [1901]. *A History of Philosophy II: Renaissance, Enlightenment, Modern*, tr. J.H. Tufts (New York: Harper and Brothers).

MODERNITY AND CHRONOTOPICITY IN BAKHTIN

Graham Pechey, University of Hertfordshire

One way of naming and making sense of the project Bakhtin had in mind in his work of the late 1930s and early 1940s is by means of a somewhat leaden and uninspiring phrase that occurs in the title of the *Bildungsroman* fragment and again in the title of his thesis on Rabelais. The "history of realism" is, it seems, what all these texts are variously trying to write. I want to suggest in this article that there is far more at stake here than an academic literary historiography reconciling a key slogan of Stalinist aesthetics with what some commentators would argue is Bakhtin's implicit preference for the novelistic canon of the nineteenth century. This notion of Bakhtin as narrating the prehistory of an achieved and finished and exemplary form of writing puts him in company he most assuredly would not want to keep. In the course of a complex "hidden polemic" with identifiable antagonists, Bakhtin subtly turns a whole currency of unsubtle slogans against their own official uses, and the upshot is a reading (in a very specific and critical historical moment) of the whole project of European modernity, a reading which speaks directly to the debates of *our* time.

"Forms of Time and of the Chronotope in the Novel" is the essay I wish most to focus on. This piece dating from 1937 (with a postscript of 1973) seems at first simply to function as a complement to "Discourse in the Novel" of a few years earlier, matching that essay's study of the textuality of novelistic language with a study of the referentiality of novelistic narrative, a stylistics of the novel with a compatible semantics, an anti-poetics of the *siuzhet* with an anti-poetics of the *fabula*. All of these distinctions rest on an opposition between reference and self-reference that the earlier essay has already undone; both essays are in fact characterized by a certain emphasis upon reflexivity. The novel as dialogue, in Bakhtin's strong sense, is the name for discourse as autocritique, in its critically self-signifying mode. The novel as narrative is discourse thematizing its own ineluctable situation in space and time. To tell a story is to dramatize the spatial difference and temporal deferral thanks to which telling is possible in the first place. Chronotopic analysis insists that the story's particulars only signify insofar as they have always already established in the most general way the spatio-temporal worldliness of the world. Far from being opposed, then, referentiality and reflexivity dissolve into each other: that is what these two great essays, taken together, suggest.[1] To see the Soviet Writers' Congress of 1934 as prompting in Bakhtin an impulse to correct the potential or residual "formalism" of "Discourse in the Novel" with the "realism" seemingly underwritten by "Forms of Time" is to miss the way the latter answers a reflexivity at the level of the speech-act with a reflexivity at the level of the spoken-about. It is also not to see how this later essay is a strategic move enabling Bakhtin to engage on common ground with the strongest body of Marxist writing on the novel then available — that which bears the signature of Georg Lukács.

Bakhtin counters Lukács's conception of the novel as most wholly itself when it is most "epic" not only by leaving that oldest among genres out of the novel's stock of chronotopic prototypes, but also by insisting that the novel is nothing if not always chronotopically diverse. The temporality of epic is monochronic, in the sense that it doesn't "know" another time besides its own. Chronotopicity being inseparable conceptually from the empirical multiplicity of chronotopes, and from the actuality of choice between them, an epic chronotope would be an historical contradiction in terms, a conceptual anachronism. When Bakhtin writes, then, about the novel's "generic heterogeneity" (FTC, 85), that phrase has a specific polemical resonance which could only come to be heard when his antagonist was no longer able to answer. We scarcely need to enforce the parallel with Bertolt Brecht's claims for the "range and variety of realist modes of writing" in his famous essays "against Lukács" (Brecht 1977 [1967], 68–85):[2] if the date had not been 1938 the Hungarian exile living in Moscow might just have learnt of these objections that were being formulated at almost the same time in Svendborg and Savelovo.

Bakhtin would no doubt never have polemicized in this way if his interests had not coincided with what Fredric Jameson describes as Lukács's "lifelong meditation on narrative, on its basic structures, its relationship to the reality it expresses, and its epistemological value when compared with other, more abstract and philosophical modes of understanding" (Jameson 1971, 163). The chronotope is the concept by means of which Bakhtin poses narrativity against conceptuality itself, while contesting the monopoly of Lukácsian "epic" narrativity. Lukács was at this time arguing that the proletarian novel of the future would reinvent the heroic narrative of the past (see Lukács 1936, 73–74): Bakhtin's later response (in 1941) was to stress the novel's constitutive relation to the present of unresolved contemporaneity. In 1936–38 he moves to undermine (the by then Marxist) Lukács by realizing some strongly antithetical motifs from *The Theory of the Novel.* That text may well start with the epic; its whole tendency nonetheless is to project the novel as a perpetual reinvention not of the epic but of itself. Unlike other genres "whose existence resides within the finished form", the novel "appears as something in the process of becoming" (Lukács 1971 [1920], 72–73). It thematizes its own reflexivity insofar as it mirrors its search for meaning in the quest of its problematic hero, its ceaseless becoming in the latter's striving. Its truth to life lies in its irony; only in the "self-abolition" (74) of its necessary subjectivity is the contingency of its world transcended and that immanence of meaning in life which is true concreteness fleetingly revealed. Finding its essence only in its constant self-reinvention, connoting the real only in its constant introversion, the novel combines a formalist textuality with an existentialist ethics and ontology.

It is from this dimension of the early Lukács — where there is no nostalgia for a lost totality and no hope of epic's dialectical return — that Bakhtin's whole work on the novel flows. Reviving some scandalously modernist themes under the sober rubric of "realism" (Brecht, we recall, used a similar code), and doing so with a breadth of historical scholarship Lukács himself could hardly have matched, Bakhtin in effect writes in 1936–41 the "series of concrete historical monographs" which in Jameson's view are implied by the schematic typology of *The Theory of the Novel* (Jameson 1971, 180). Lukács's last short paragraph on Dostoevsky was the cue for Bakhtin's first monograph; his other major works display the logic of a working back from that point through the Renaissance and Middle Ages to a classical antiquity far more concretely specified than that celebrated in Lukács's rhapsodic first paragraph, which begins "Happy are those ages when the starry sky is the map of all possible paths — ages whose paths are illuminated by the light of the stars" (Lukács 1971 [1920], 29).

If there is no comparable privileging of epic fullness in Bakhtin, that is partly because of the perspectives he sets up: antiquity is considered only in a backward glance from its end in the Hellenistic period, whilst modernity is considered only in intermittent glances forward from a history beginning then and ending in the Renaissance. Beyond this, he discusses from antiquity only those genres — the ancient "biographical forms" (FTC, 130) — that prefigure the novel's later construction of time as the dimension of historical becoming. "Biographical time" has its being wholly in the *agora*, the public square which is coextensive with the public sphere itself, where "all the most elevated categories [...] were realized concretely and fully incarnated, made visible and given a face" (FTC, 132). While classical Greece is then (to be sure) for both Bakhtin and Lukács the name for a state in which interiority and exteriority are not known apart from each other, it is clear nonetheless that Bakhtin not only invests less in this story but that he thinks of his version as overcoming the derealized abstraction he finds in Lukács. As he puts it, in a barely recalled but still pointed quotation from Lukács himself, "this utter exteriority of the individual did not exist in empty space ('under a starry sky, on the bare earth') but rather in an organic human collective, 'in the folk'" (FTC, 135).

This motif of "the folk" is one which runs through all the work of 1936–41. With this concept we hear the echoes of another dialogue running alongside the one with Lukács which we have already tuned into. Populist motifs derived from Maxim Gorky's speech to the 1934 Congress are tactically used against the valorization in Lukács of a high-bourgeois "critical realism". At the same time Bakhtin "destalinizes" the Gorkian stress on folklore as the common source of literary realism and philosophical materialism. If in Gorky the gigantism of popular mythology serves the hyperbole of Stalinist rhetoric and iconography — and if in that same context it glorifies the linear progress of technology, productivity, and of "mastery" over nature — in Bakhtin that same "grotesque realism" is ludic, parodic, directed against orthodoxy and austerity. If for Gorky the "immortal" people's unremitting labour is the great "creator of all ideas" (Gorky 1977 [1934], 53), for Bakhtin that function is equally fulfilled by their resounding anti-official *laughter*. Folklore conceived not as the residue of an originary fullness and wholeness but as an ongoing process of "exteriorization" frees Bakhtin from Lukács's classicizing fixation upon an ancient genre and a superseded polity.

The work of 1936–41 now falls into place as a detailed historical study of an order of narrativity which can undo the binaries of "abstract thought" without needing to look over one shoulder at its prelapsarian innocence in the epic. Bakhtin tells a story about stories which treats all categories in an almost Nietzschean way not as the fatal effects of a single Fall from immanence but as the ever-repeated effects of the "abstract" or the "conceptual" produced by ever-repeated fictions. Interiority, the private person, historical time: these great and deeply related (indeed inseparably connected) epistemological discoveries of modernity are traced back to the polymorphously perverse childhood of Western narrative. Bakhtin hypothesizes an alternative and plural infancy for the novel, which he then sees not only as carrying this heterogeneity into the future but as safeguarding the historical gains it has made possible. He returns to ancient kinds of storytelling which are not epic, examining them from the standpoint of that which they do not yet individually deliver but which they may be seen as enabling in combination; from the standpoint, that is, of a future in the Renaissance which is now along with antiquity itself part of our own past.

These uneven and staggered advances, these uncertain early steps of Western narrative, can only be baldly summarized here. Greek romance invents the private person at the cost of dematerializing space in a general alienness and time in a static reversibility; ancient biography conversely dynamizes time at the cost of submission to a teleology in which time is only the time of actualization of a potential that was always there in the first place; it is only in the "adventure novel of everyday life" (FTC, 127), dominated by the motif of metamorphosis, that a time at once irreversible and non-teleological is invented. Metamorphosis not only provides the prototype of an open-ended becoming that will later be extended beyond the protagonist to the world itself; it also offers the perspective of a third party privy to others' secrets which will shift from a peripheral to a central position in the modern novel. In Apuleius's ass we have the forerunner of that epistemological privilege of the socially underprivileged outsider that will re-emerge first as the intimate publicity of the memoir and the epistolary novel, modulating later into the (in the Formalist sense) "unmotivated" authorial anonym of the nineteenth and twentieth centuries.

Modern narrative's immediate forbear gets rather less space in Bakhtin's story. That is to say, medieval romance is treated neither in terms of its ruling-class origins — "a creation of the feudal nobility" was Gorky's description (1977 [1934], 36) — nor as a genre whose destiny it was to be demystified in novelistic parody, but is valued rather for its status as a latter-day epic of the quotidian marvellous, an early forerunner of the surreal in the dreamlike elasticity of its space and time. Sharing with epic the "glorified hero", it departs from epic insofar as it draws on a "storehouse of images" (FTC, 153) which crosses all national borders. We can only speculate how far this is directed polemically against the chauvinism of "socialist realism" or against the rise of fascism in Europe — or indeed against their political complicity, soon to be sealed in the Molotov–Ribbentrop pact. What is certain is that it encodes an endorsement of the internationalist tendency of high modernist art, against the Stalinist attacks on "rootless cosmopolitanism" so common at this time. All in all, chivalric romance is given a strong populist and future-oriented cast, assimilated to "folklore and fairy tales" from the "pre-class" past and to a Rabelaisian "grotesque realism" still to come (FTC, 155). When Bakhtin goes on to discuss *The Divine Comedy* as a "special" work "on the boundary line *between* two epochs"; when he follows Erich Auerbach in emphasizing the "extraordinary tension" (FTC, 158)[3] in that text between the otherwordly vertical of eternity and the horizontal of history straining ever forward; and when he concludes by assimilating Dante's work to Dostoevsky's — there can be no mistaking the analogy between two historical moments of transition. The relationship between Dante and his successors, including Rabelais, is the relationship of free and open participation in the same global project that Bakhtin would like to see between late-feudal Russia's great proto-modernist and the new writing of the (putatively) "socialist" order.

The Rabelaisian chronotope represents for Bakhtin the move that decisively brings modernity to birth. In this chronotope the elemental chronotopicity of folklore becomes conscious and militant, and the tense historical tangents of Dante break free of the extra-temporal synchrony of eternity. Taking his cue from Gorky this time, Bakhtin uses the name of Rabelais as a shorthand for the ceaseless incarnation of meanings and values along a spatio-temporal horizontal, a direct proportionality of worth to size in the worldly here and now. Chronotopicity militant wrenches apart what feudal discourse brings together, brings together what it sundered: ordinary contexts evaporate in a potentially infinite context portended by these extraordinary meetings. The spatio-temporality of the world and the corporeality of the body signify each other in their interpenetration; meaning is generated in a logic of the concrete, in simultaneities and coextensions. Bakhtin uses Rabelais to think a world of existential parataxis, where the human body signifies universally by drawing all signifiers to itself. It is almost as if he were trying singlehandedly to make good the absence in Russian history of a "Renaissance" or "Rabelaisian" moment, and to supply the goods of an epochal shift that his own national culture had never had in practice or had had only vicariously, in versions imported from those classicizing cultures by means of which the rising classes of Europe had sought to consolidate their power. It is easy to see the hyperbole of Bakhtin's case as an infection caught from the very Stalinist discourse he opposed. It can also be seen as a symptom of the strain of the task of epochal redemption he here takes on, a task beyond the power of any individual to carry out, let along anyone as obscure as he then was, in the least auspicious of all places and times.

Two propositions would seem to sum up the thrust of this article so far: that Bakhtin's cultural preferences might be described as modernist rather than realist, or at least as rendering that distinction less than absolute, a matter of tact and of context; and that Bakhtin is repoliticizing and declassicizing the story of modernity, emphasizing its birth crisis and the early unity of its now-separated discoveries — in short, narrating its history from below. These two threads of Bakhtin's textual fabric are not in fact separable: give the case made for Rabelais as European modernity's midwife a slight twist, and you have a defence of the whole contemporary practice of European modernism. A "socialist realism" which modelled itself upon Rabelais rather than Homer could hardly define itself so absolutely against (say) James Joyce; indeed anyone taking Bakhtin's account of *Gargantua and Pantagruel* truly to heart could not consistently baulk at *Ulysses* or at the Joycean "Work in Progress" that was just then coming to an end. The other side of Joyce's Rabelaisian materialization of language is a semanticization of the body that is no less Rabelaisian in its inventorial thoroughness. Bakhtin helps us to read the Joycean text in the spirit of those alternative readings which were coming through a few years ago, and which stress the "politics" of Joyce's "style". In the long view that Bakhtin offers us, a text like *Ulysses* appears less as innovation than as a revival of the early assertiveness of the "low" genres raised by Rabelais into a concrete universalism: its celebrated "textuality" is inseparable from a chronotopicity at once global and radical.

This submission of all categories to a logic of the spatio-temporal had been not so much lost as reduced or made invisible, first with the novel's subordination under classicism, and then (in the nineteenth century) within an ideology of "literature" which canonized the novel at the cost of binding it the more firmly to the abstract universalism of the unsituated and purely thinking modern subject. Although this now canonical "realism" shares with its "grotesque" (Bakhtin) or "fantastic" (Gorky) forerunner in Rabelais an affirmation of the body and its world against an alienating social order — and this is after all what justifies Lukács and other Marxists in calling such "bourgeois" writing "critical" — neither of these two constituents of Bakhtin's hypothetical "ancient complex" is able to signify in its own right, in a mutual overstepping of boundaries. Bakhtin nowhere (in works currently available in English) mentions Joyce, but his case here provides the terms for a strong defence of the latter's work. If to break as Joyce very patently does with the moralized spatio-temporality of the "idyllic" chronotope and to re-establish thereby a revitalized chronotopicity is to be "modernist", then modernism is no longer to be denounced for its anti-"realism", and the Stalinist aesthetic is shown up in all its narrowness and historical shortsightedness. And so it is that when we read Samuel Beckett writing in 1929 that Joyce reduces "various expressive media to their primitive economic directness" and fuses "these primal essences into an assimilated medium for the exteriorization of thought" (Beckett et al. 1929, 16), we could be forgiven for thinking that these words were Bakhtin's on Rabelais. Bakhtin's unique feat is (without knowing it, and however bizarre this may sound) to have reconciled the terms used by Gorky on an occasion notorious for its anathematization of modernism with those used by Beckett in the volume he co-wrote under the self-parodic title *Our Exagmination round his Factification for Incamination of "Work in Progress"* just five years before.

Against the whole Aristotelian and Cartesian tradition in which time is thought apart from space and both apart from value, Bakhtin poses "the single great event that is life" (FTC, 211). Like Beckett himself on Vico in the volume cited, he seeks the rejoining of conceptuality and metaphoricity in a radical chronotopicity. The modern project is as it were re-imagined in its most combative and popular-utopian moments, along a line that largely elevates artists over philosophers.[4] If the Renaissance *is* Rabelais, the Enlightenment is epitomized in a Goethe for whom the world was always an emerging *event*, who could "*see time*" in "the spatial whole of the world" (BSHR, 25 and *passim*). We would not expect the modernism of Bakhtin's thinking in the 1930s to have gone along with open polemical support for contemporary aesthetic practice (as that of the Formalists had been bound to Futurism, or as Ernst Bloch was then backing the Expressionists). And it is no loss that it did not do so: Bakhtin's modernist critique of modernity — every bit as radical as that of Max Horkheimer and Theodor Adorno — is achieved by the simple and yet astonishingly creative gesture of projecting the story of the European avant-garde back into the continent's past. What Peter Bürger has seen as that movement's doomed will to sublate art in life is imagined as having happened: carnival is the name Bakhtin gives to this perpetual possibility.[5]

By 1940 we find Bakhtin offering secularized modernity an alternative icon: the closed classical body was then serving the iconography not of emancipation but of the century's colluding authoritarianisms; only in the grotesque body open to the world could progress still hope to think itself as human freedom. Read with the other late writings, the "Concluding Remarks" added in 1973 to the chronotope essay help us to see the Rabelais book as the last heroic throw of the modernist Bakhtin. The Bakhtin who breaks his silence after the war and the death of Stalin is a Bakhtin who has soberly recognized the *hubris* of the "carnival sense of the world" in the face of carnage on a world scale. Instead of reading the modern as a matter of revolutionary breaks and acts of forgetting of the past — "one ridicules in order to forget" (EN, 23), he had once said — Bakhtin emphasizes in the concept of "great time" the long memory of genres and the immortality of all meanings. Now more concerned with the threat of a dogma of relativism than with exposing the relativity in dogmatism, he reinflects his earlier themes of "responsibility" and "outsideness".[6] The story he had once told of modernity as permanent revolution, a story in which first the novel and then carnival were the heroes, is not cancelled. It simply becomes one of the many stories we might tell from the absolute position/positional absolute of our unique place in the present, our own global chronotope.

NOTES

1. For another view of the realism–reflexivity opposition which uses Bakhtin as the agent of its deconstruction, see Jefferson 1986.
2. The phrase quoted is my translation of the title of another essay, not yet (to my knowledge) translated into English: see Brecht 1971.
3. See also Auerbach 1953 [1946], 174–202, and in particular his claim that Dante's "beyond" is "changeless and of all time and yet full of history" (197). The likeness between Bakhtin's reading of Dante and Auerbach's may have to do with their common relationship to the tradition of German philology (their readings of Rabelais are also extraordinarily alike, even in phraseology); Bakhtin might also have read Auerbach's *Dante als Dichter der irdischen Welt*, first published in 1929.
4. Bakhtin's insistence on treating literature as a form of knowledge is an emphasis whose moment has now clearly come (it is only the obverse of that corresponding move which treats philosophy as a form of narrative), and it will be welcome to those who see Jürgen Habermas's reconstructive critique of modernity as too narrowly founded upon a critique of reason. There is another and more complex and contradictory history of modernity to be written which is not fixated upon its "philosophical discourse" alone: see Cascardi 1992, *passim*, for an eloquent version of this case.

5. See Bürger 1984, 49: "The avantgardistes proposed the sublation of art — sublation in the Hegelian sense of the term: art was not to be simply destroyed, but transferred to the praxis of life where it would be preserved, albeit in a changed form."
6. I have discussed Bakhtin's concept of "great time" at some length in an essay which seeks to place three of his later writings (PT, N70 and MHS) in the context of twentieth-century philosophical hermeneutics: see Pechey 1993.

WORKS CITED

Auerbach, E. 1953 [1946]. *Mimesis: The Representation of Reality in Western Literature* (Princeton: Princeton University Press).

Beckett, S., et al. 1929. *Our Exagmination round his Factification for Incamination of "Work in Progress"* (London: Faber and Faber).

Brecht, B. 1971. "Weite und Vielfalt der realistischen Schreibweise", in *Über Realismus* (Frankfurt am Main: Suhrkamp Verlag), 88–97.

________. 1977 [1967]. "Against Georg Lukács", in *Aesthetics and Politics: Debates between Bloch, Lukács, Brecht, Benjamin, Adorno* (London: Verso), 68–85.

Bürger, P. 1984. *The Theory of the Avant-Garde* (Manchester: Manchester University Press).

Cascardi, A. 1992. *The Subject of Modernity* (Cambridge: Cambridge University Press).

Gorky, M. 1977 [1934]. "Soviet Literature", in *Soviet Writers' Congress 1934: The Debate on Socialist Realism and Modernism in the Soviet Union* (London: Lawrence and Wishart), 25–69.

Jameson, F. 1971. *Marxism and Form: Twentieth-Century Dialectical Theories of Literature* (Princeton: Princeton University Press).

Jefferson, A. 1986. "Realism Reconsidered: Bakhtin's Dialogism and the 'Will to Reference'", in *Australian Journal of French Studies*, 23/2, 169–184.

Lukács, G. 1936. "Essay on the Novel", in *International Literature*, 5, 68–74.

________. 1971 [1920], *The Theory of the Novel* (London: Merlin Press).

Pechey, G. 1993. "Eternity and Modernity: Bakhtin and the Epistemological Sublime", in *Theoria*, 81–82, 61–85.

IS DIALOGISM FOR REAL?

Ken Hirschkop, University of Manchester

Is dialogism for real? In one sense, absolutely. How could one doubt it when discussion of this concept and of its best known theorist, Mikhail Bakhtin, has given rise to such a torrent of articles, books, conferences and commentary? It's for real at least in the sense that, say, the 1986 Mets or rap turned out to be "for real", its phenomenal success as a theoretical concept indicating it was an idea whose time had come. But even rap and the Mets, however dynastic their ambitions may have been, never claimed to have been there all along; the concept of dialogism, on the other hand, claims to identify a feature of language which was waiting to be discovered, something we hadn't noticed about the texts we worked with, but which, once acknowledged, would bring us at least as much pleasure as victory in the World Series or an evening with Bill Bev Devoe. When Bakhtin told us that those works we knew as "novels" were really dialogues in disguise, and that their stylistic techniques — irony, parody, free indirect discourse, and so forth — were really the indices of some fundamental dialogical quality of language, he provided not only analytical tools but cause for celebration. Dialogue — we always knew what that was, and for a long time we've known it was good — but to learn that it was a force active even in something as unspontaneous as a novel: this was a pleasant, and only initially surprising discovery, now well on its way to becoming common sense.

Just why such a discovery would be welcomed is obvious enough. Dialogue is so powerful a value in a liberal democratic political culture, so evident a political virtue, that the invitation to find it in literary works may prove impossible to refuse. So, let me warn you in advance, my argument is bound to appear somewhat churlish and mean-spirited. Much of what currently passes for Bakhtinian analysis would have us believe that novels are for all intents and purposes dialogues, despite the rather obvious fact that a single person composes them. What I wish to do in this article is to remind myself, as well as my readers, of the difference between a dialogue and a novel, and thus of the difference between dialogue and what we call dialogism. We need to remind ourselves of this so that we are forced to consider what is at stake when Bakhtin attempts to apply the idea of dialogue to formally finished works, like novels, works which, whatever their linguistic complexity, are composed by historical individuals, often with the luxury of great care and conscious reflection and without the spontaneous dangers of actual linguistic exchange. As you will see, my argument will not be that this application represents a regrettable error on Bakhtin's part: I do not wish to act like a schoolmaster, certainly not in relation to someone obviously more clever than myself and to whose work many of us have devoted far too many of the best years of our lives. Instead I will try to show that the confusion or overlapping between dialogue and dialogism is what makes Bakhtin's work interesting and provocative. In what follows I will argue that we will do ourselves, and dialogue, a favour by keeping it separate from dialogism, and from finished texts. We will do ourselves a favour by, well, not kidding ourselves that one person can speak on behalf of two; we will do dialogue a favour by showing that what Bakhtin calls novels are necessary, precisely because they do things which we cannot rightfully expect of dialogue. In short, I hope that my discussion of dialogism will reveal the limits of dialogue, limits which need airing in liberal democratic regimes such as ours, which overload dialogue with expectations and responsibilities.

What sort of expectations? In American public political life dialogue signifies the resolution of conflicts by verbal means, implying the acceptance of certain liberal political tenets: an understanding of the necessity to find compromise solutions between opposing positions, an acknowledgement of the importance of discussion and debate, recognition of the private nature of many social interests. To have or start a dialogue between individuals or between political or social actors (Washington and Baghdad, let us remind ourselves, are capable of having dialogues, unlikely and strange as this may seem) is to put oneself into a scene of compromise and negotiation, of ideological give-and-take, and to agree that language rather than physical violence is the preferable means of ending a dispute. This political charge is perhaps what distinguishes modern dialogue from its private cousins, the conversation and the chat. Of course, our conversations are often also dialogues, strictly speaking, but for significant reasons we don't choose to label them so, reserving that honour not for gossip with the grocer or repartee with the cabby but for occasions of a more formal sort.

Yet the political value of dialogue doesn't depend on this formality alone; it is not merely a question of the arena in which a discourse takes place. So, for example, it turns out that many exchanges between social actors aren't really dialogues, although they resemble them at first glance. Both speakers come to the table, they talk, one utters, the other responds, there is give-and-take, yet in the end it doesn't quite work. It's this that distinguishes, in current parlance, the "meaningful dialogue" from the mere going-through-the-motions version. For true dialogue to take place one has to exchange not only statements or sentences but something else — ideas, positions — and one has to do so with a willingness to take on board those proffered by one's interlocutor.

It's this more abstract consideration which opens the door for Bakhtin. For he will argue that such an exchange or interaction of positions is possible even in the absence of the formal written or verbal structure of dialogue, that the single work and even the single utterance may embody such an exchange by being, as he says, "double-voiced" or "double-directed". By this Bakhtin means that a single utterance or statement may contain two in principle separable meanings: "two socio-linguistic consciousnesses", as he puts it "come together and fight it out on the territory of the utterance" (DN, 360/172; here and subsequently the translation of Bakhtin is my own). Parody, the representation of oral speech, the critical representation of social dialects, stylization: all these literary phenomena may be thrown together by virtue of the fact that they seem to combine the intentions or semantic position typical of a speech form with a second accent, added, so to speak, by the author, who orchestrates the target language in line with his or her own aesthetic purposes.

It is in the first work published under Bakhtin's name (canny distinction that!), *Problems of Dostoevsky's Art*, published in 1929 and reworked into the now better known *Problems of Dostoevsky's Poetics* in 1961–62, that Bakhtin first proposed to invest so much significance in novelistic style. In fact, he argues that Dostoevsky can create dialogue within the confines of the novel precisely to the extent that he can "make present" the heroes of his work: "everything [in the novel] must touch the hero's raw nerve, it must provoke him, interrogate him, polemicize with and taunt him if necessary, everything must be addressed to the hero, must face him, it should be experienced as *discourse about someone present*" (Bakhtin 1929, 70). Put like this, the case appears somewhat ridiculous: how can you call this a dialogue when the hero can't actually answer back? The answer lies in the distinctions drawn above: if dialogue isn't merely the formal alternation of speech acts, and is only truly realized when actually different interests or values face off against each other, then arguably one can take the next step and do without the formal alternation of positions, the actual two-sidedness of dialogue, altogether.

In fact, Bakhtin does not so much step as leap to this conclusion, literally bounding across the practical difficulties. For Bakhtin argues that dialogical interaction is built into the very structure of language itself, so that any statement actually involves debate with alternative value positions. Thus: "Every concrete discourse or utterance finds the object at which it is directed always, so to speak, already qualified, argued over, evaluated, enveloped by the obscuring fog or, if you like, the light of other, already spoken discourses about it" (DN, 276/89–90). Since reading these words of Bakhtin's, many a literary critic has slept easier in his or her bed, happy in the knowledge that even most isolated statement encounters, or "makes present" if you like, partners in dialogue, who are somehow buried in the language itself. What I want to draw your attention to, however, is Bakhtin's need to describe dialogism in the language of encounter, for it indicates some recognition of the fact that the good stuff one gets from dialogue, the political and social payoff, depends upon the "presence" of multiple speakers. Hence that rather bizarre sense that by opening your mouth or lifting your pen (two, I realize, antiquated forms of expression) you are magically transported to something resembling the House of Commons or a family squabble. "A living utterance", Bakhtin claims, "cannot avoid becoming an active participant in social dialogue" (DN, 276/90): one cannot speak without getting into an argument.

That Bakhtin should be compelled to describe dialogism in terms of encounter and making present the other is no accident, for the virtues of dialogism are too closely bound up with the actual situation of dialogue to admit any distinction. The great things achieved by the novel depend on its ability to summon up "other persons", as the following makes clear: "To the fully embodied consciousness of the hero, the author can only juxtapose one kind of objective world: a world of other consciousnesses having equal rights" (Bakhtin 1929, 57). One finds here the not so surreptitious introduction of a central *political* concept, that of equal rights, into a description of linguistic style. It is a concept essential to Bakhtin's idea of dialogism, and yet it is not really a linguistic concept at all. Equal rights are characteristic of liberal political orders, they exist by virtue of formal constitutions and legal institutions to protect them, and while their existence has a central bearing on language, one can't distinguish as a matter of *style* voices with rights from voices without them. Dostoevsky's dialogism is presented as discourse which simply reveals possibilities latent within language itself, but further scrutiny reveals an unstated reliance on the project of Western liberalism.

It could not, I would like to argue, be otherwise. Bakhtin needs to borrow such concepts, for he is asking language to bear some additional weight, to carry ethico-political baggage which it can't generate from its own resources. Analyse language as much as you please: you cannot really derive the social and political values bound up in the idea of dialogism. *Pace* Bakhtin and others as well (like Habermas), the structure of speech itself seems to me too neutral to be made the basis of a moral or political philosophy. It's not that I'm against communication; it's just that speech seems too various in its uses and forms, too willing an accomplice of every sort of social relation, friendly or exploitative, empowering or oppressive, to provide by itself standards for our social life. There is no such thing as speech by itself, in a void, without people, bodies, social relations and a natural world, and it is only from speech in collusion with all of that that we may extract some well-founded guidance for politics and social value.

Bakhtin, however, would appear to think he can do without a more inclusive account of the human and social world. Of course he is practically legend for his insistence on the situatedness, the context-boundness of language, but he rarely if ever discusses the structure of that world or that context; he consistently attempts to derive his criteria for dialogue from language itself. It's this feature of his argument which lends dialogism its flexibility: dialogism is not language given such and such a social world, it's language *per se*, and so dialogism of the novelistic sort justifies itself as language which does what language gotta do.

Close inspection reveals, however, that to endow language with some kind of inner political impetus Bakhtin is forced to smuggle into it social and political attributes which really don't belong there, or which can't be assumed to follow from the mere act of speech. The characterization of language as a scene of encounters, as in essence "social dialogue", effectively introduces social and political values of two kinds. In the first place, by endowing linguistic units with the attribute of personhood, it renders them eligible for the protections afforded by Kantian ethics. Consider just what Dostoevsky's dialogism consists of — a refusal to reduce heroes to instruments of an authorial plan, the granting to personal discourse of a certain measure of autonomy, the treatment of language as deserving of respect merely because it is the language of other human beings — and you realize that its principal features come, not from a theory of language or discourse, but from Kantian ethics, a link made explicit when Bakhtin at the end of his days described discourse itself as the "kingdom of ends" (N70, 135/339). In the second place, the making present of others by means of linguistic derring-do allows Dostoevsky, according to Bakhtin, to create a kind of miniature *Gemeinschaft* within the space of the novel, a Buberian religious community in which the presence of others in the guise of the purely human makes possible a radically new form of personal relation. I have no particular argument with either of these projects, but they represent precisely that: projects with an interesting and chequered political history, not realizations of ontological attributes of language.

The celebrated essay "Discourse in the Novel" is another exercise in community-making, only in this case the act of discourse plunges you not into a religious *Gemeinschaft* but into the rather more heterogeneous world of the public square. The "novel", whatever Bakhtin means by that, summons up not persons but entire social groups:

> The necessary prerequisite of the novel as a genre is the internal stratification of a national language into social dialects, group habits, professional jargons, generic languages, the languages of generations and age-groups, the languages of authorities, of movements, of circles and passing fashions, the languages of socio-political days and even hours [...] The novel orchestrates all its themes by means of this social heteroglossia [...] (DN, 262–263/76)

What appeared to be a novel is in fact something between a bazaar and a political meeting, and it can be so because the novelist is able to double-voice his or her language, to make it serve both the aesthetic intentions of the novel itself and those embedded in the social speech-types or languages of society. Surely at this point one is entitled to believe that dialogism recreates a kind of linguistic interchange, that it embodies language as "social life" — interaction, linguistic exchange, verbal to and fro — in opposition to the isolation of the individual. After all, the very opening of the essay reminds us of the novel's contact with "the social life of discourse, outside the artist's study, in the open spaces of public squares and streets", in contrast to the "the cloistered artist" offered as an embodiment of the traditional poet (DN, 259/73). And surely it is no less true that the novelistic genres, in this text lauded as dialogism in its purest form, are therefore literary embodiments of dialogue, for they offer to summon up not actual persons, but points of view. Indeed, as we are all aware, something close to an entire critical industry has grown up around this basic premise: that the novelistic form, as defined by Bakhtin, incarnates that openness to exchange, that interest in diversity of points of view, which we consider intrinsic to dialogue in its social and political sense.

And yet ... Again one runs into the fundamental problem, that in fact novels, even when we include in that definition as disparate a range of works as Bakhtin would have us do, are not spontaneous acts of conversation or political meetings, and that the author, for better or worse, must represent the language of these various social, historical and temporal groups. Whatever the values made flesh in the novel, the openness and spontaneity we deem essential to dialogue aren't found there. It is as if George Bush and Dick Cheney proposed a dialogue with, say, their Iraqi antagonists, in which the latter did not actually show up, but were, by dint of the speech tact of George Bush and company, represented linguistically. We would rightly regard such a dialogue as a sham, and we could do so even if we had absolute faith in the literary abilities and moral sincerity of our own national leaders. To the extent that dialogue is seen as a legitimating social and political good, it requires the participation of actually different individuals or what we would call "accredited representatives" of the relevant social groups. Dialogism can't claim this legitimacy for its own speech acts, for there is no real dialogue there, but an interesting kind of complexity, itself the consequence of the novelist's peculiar task in relation to the language which surrounds him or her.

However, as I mentioned at the beginning, my aim is not to wag a theoretical finger at those who believe reading Dickens is like taking the floor of the House of Commons. On the contrary, the point I am most concerned to make is that the difference between dialogism and dialogue is what renders the former relevant to our social and political life, that in fact "dialogism" as a distinctive kind of discourse calls attention to fundamental features of our social and political life too often obscured by our obsession with dialogue. In brief, my claim will be that dialogism describes the work of those "secondary genres" whose job it is to cite and represent the languages generated in so-called primary genres (everyday speech, etc.), and that this citation and representation is an ineluctable feature of the socio-political life of the modern nation-state. In the case of such genres, dialogue is neither possible nor appropriate, and it provides no standard or critical ideal.

A careful examination of the text of "Discourse in the Novel" reveals two quite different socio-political justifications for dialogism: it is valued not only for reproducing the spontaneity of dialogue, but also as a literary form which puts us in touch with a vital, popular, "public-square" world of struggling historical discourses. The novel, Bakhtin argues, infuses its language with an "intentional feeling for the historical and social concreteness and relativity of living discourse, for its participation in historical becoming and social struggle" (DN, 331/144), bringing us closer to the ground of some putatively real, popular, actually living discourse.

So while the rhetoric of dialogue continues from Bakhtin's Dostoevsky book, "Discourse in the Novel" in fact inaugurates a sharp populist turn away from Kantian ethics and its interest in autonomous self-regulating individuals. It's not that the conversation of the public square, now idolized, isn't composed of dialogues, it's just that it is valued not for the equal rights embodied within it, but for its quasi-Nietzschean "liveliness", its earthiness and vulgarity, its imbrication with interests and struggles. That one can continue to call this dialogism isn't, on reflection, that surprising, for in both the earlier and later works what's at stake isn't dialogue itself, which is in any case out of the question, but some broader social project.

In the case of the essay on the novel, the field of extra-linguistic value which provides the novel with a purpose is a vision of the life of "the people". Of course, like every kind of populism, Bakhtin's entails the projection onto popular life of values which are the product of intellectual meditation on the life of "the people". So while the dialogism of the novel endows discourse with a vigour and liveliness associated with the popular, this liveliness itself is only made visible by the novelist him or herself. It depends on the novelist's being able to see, beneath the surface details of popular social life, the fundamental drama of heteroglossia played out within it: "Behind every utterance in a genuine novel one senses the elemental force of social languages with their inner logic and inner necessity. The image reveals not just the actuality, but also the possibilities of a given language, its, so to speak, ideal limits, and its total integral meaning" (DN, 356/168).

By making "formal markers of languages, manners and styles into symbols for social points of view" (DN, 357/169), the novelist infuses the mundane stylistic marker with the force of popular life, and it is precisely this process, referred to throughout "Discourse in the Novel" as the making of "images of languages", which defines the distinctive phenomenon called dialogism. The key to novelistic dialogism, then, is not an immersion in the authentic plebeian sociability of the public square, but the novelist's ability to endow so-called popular or everyday language with an historical or social significance it lacks in its everyday context. Such a transformation or refraction of everyday language is not really a dialogue at all: it lacks the most elementary features of actual political dialogue, and could not possibly claim legitimacy on that basis. It should be described in quite different terms: as representation or, if you like, "citation" and "reaccentuation", the aesthetic processing of the language of others for specific ends. What the novelist does to so-called everyday language or heteroglossia is distinctive and important on its own terms. In actual dialogues we don't necessarily ponder the historical significance of word choice, pronunciation, or syntax: but in the novel, as theorized by Bakhtin, the most intimate and throwaway stylistic feature becomes the index of a grand historical drama, the simple conversation an arena for sociological conflict.

If novelistic dialogism appears nevertheless to be confused with some other kind of dialogue, this is an almost inevitable consequence of populism itself. For "the people", as a rhetorical category, has the advantage of designating both a separate group within society, opposed to the official or to the lordly or both, and a form of society in its own right, a form which can be valued as somehow more real or authentic than the pretentious world of self-regarding individuals which opposes it. It's possible to contrast the popular *ersatz* peasant community with the intellectual one, arguing that the former is more social, more dialogical if you like. Such a vision, however, represses the fact that the novel has its own formal properties: it doesn't just take the languages of the public square into itself, it changes the way we see them, endowing them with a depth of social meaning they lack in everyday intercourse. In doing so, it doesn't so much violate the norms of dialogue as draw our attention to the fact that dialogue cannot achieve everything, that the difference between a novel and the public square is not only inevitable, but productive, valuable, essential to our social life. For the novel does things to heteroglossia that heteroglossia can't do to itself, providing a kind of insight into language which is not immediately available.

This isn't a terribly populist, let alone popular, view, and, not surprisingly, Bakhtin's own discussions of the novelistic and the dialogical are criss-crossed by resistances to it. So, for example, one could read "Discourse in the Novel" as conflating the irony of the plebeian folk, their rustic native scepticism, with that more properly historical sense of language available in the nineteenth-century novel. Both of these are called dialogical, as if the public square was populated with peasant Balzacs and merchant Dostoevskys. In the same vein, Bakhtin's own history of the novel can never quite decide whether its mode is cyclical, depicting a high poetic literary language periodically engulfed by popular heteroglossia, or developmental, as in the chronotope essays, where the novel gradually perfects its narrative technique, the better to depict so-called real history and social struggle. One cannot help thinking that behind these ambiguities lies a "populist" unwillingness to admit that dialogism may itself be the fruit of a long developmental process, that it might be linked to the specific historical conditions of modernity and might require its peculiar resources — a concept of historical record-keeping, high rates of literacy, a varied and cosmopolitan urban social life, historical consciousness, democratic and secular beliefs, and so on — none of which would be available to the peasant, however refined his or her irony in the public square.

The novel itself, therefore, as a peculiarly modern genre, has work to do, yet Bakhtin, in keeping with populism, will only justify it with reference to the values of "the people". He thus avoids confronting all the different respects in which the novel and popular speech are uneven, incapable of entering into a real dialogue: the unevenness, for example, between print technology and oral speech, the unevennesses which result from differences in literacy and from the time and resources necessary for reflection on language, the unevennesses that correspond to social position and range of audience. In each of these respects the novel as speech, as that which accents or orchestrates heteroglossia, is constitutively different from that heteroglossia itself. And this unevenness, I will shortly argue, is not peculiar to this situation, but is a constitutive historical feature of our linguistic life.

If it turns out, then, that novelistic or dialogical writing can't embody the values of dialogue, is this a problem? Is dialogism just a sham rendering of dialogue, a case of novelists and intellectuals trying to cash in on the accepted values of dialogue or the notional vitality of plebeian sociability? Why doesn't Bakhtin revel in the distinctiveness of novelistic writing, in its difference from the everyday conversations of the people? The answer is that from his populist perspective, the constitutive, ineluctable unevenness of novelistic dialogism must appear as a limit on the possibilities of discourse, as the point at which the brute facts of modern life make real dialogue unworkable, for better or worse. This would be bad news indeed, for it would mean that to have novels — forms of discourse which cite and represent — we have to give up on the ideal of a free and democratized language. The price of modernity, as represented by that peculiarly modern genre, the novel, would be loss of pure dialogue and plebeian sociability. And the absence of pure dialogue, so the argument would go, leads inevitably to authoritarianism, monologism, oppression, inequality.

Unless, of course, there is something wrong with the assumption that dialogue represents all we should hope for in the political and social life of language. That, needless to say, is my point. Or, more precisely, it is Bakhtin's point, even though he does not seem to know it. In describing the relation of the novel to "everyday language" as a dialogue, Bakhtin intended to extend the realm of dialogue. In fact, by pointing out to us all that novels can do, even though they aren't dialogues, he revealed to us the limitations of the idea of dialogue. And a good thing too: for in the modern age, the age of print, of mass media and culture, of ostensibly democratic principles, dialogue would seem an impoverished ideal. It misses out too much about our speech life, it proposes models and aspirations unrealizable in all but a few situations. It would be a pity if all we could say in response was: too bad for modern life. Better to admit that there might be something to those genres which cite and represent, something they have that the public square lacks. Perhaps dialogism, to coin a phrase, reaches those parts dialogue cannot reach.

For dialogue, after all, does depend upon a rather peculiar model of language. It envisages language as an endless series of one-on-one encounters, encounters between speaking subjects who could in theory be evenly matched. The believer in dialogue naturally divides the stream of language into millions of roughly equivalent linguistic exchanges, each modelled on that famous Saussurean diagram in which two heads pass between them the lonely linguistic sign. It is the combination of this model of language with the political ideals of individual autonomy and respect for others which gives the claims of dialogue such force. If language were at bottom composed of such exchanges, then our social and political ideals would surely demand that they all aspire to the exalted state of dialogue.

From the perspective of 1991, however, such a description of language appears a bit out of date. In fact, it is more of a fantasy than a description, for language, I would like to argue, has never corresponded to this model. Its fatal defect is that it takes no account of what I will call hereafter the *uneven structuring of language*, that is, the fact that the discursive world consists, not only of speaking individuals, but of a series of interacting structures or forms of discourse, which vary according to the durability of the utterance, the size and nature of speaker and audience, the degree of literacy required for participation, as well as the social factors highlighted in Bakhtin's own work. To use the face-to-face conversation as a model for the TV broadcast, the government directive, the religious service or cultic ceremony, the written record or the literary text is wrong-headed and restrictive, for all these forms must appear deficient to the extent that they make impossible the pure relations of dialogue. Not only do such discursive structures often entail some kind of internal unevenness, such as a clear and irreversible distinction between speaker and listener, the relations between them are likewise uneven. Writing, then print, then the electronic media of the twentieth century have endowed certain speech acts with a force unavailable to others; conversely, face-to-face conversations often have a flexibility unavailable to the more durable utterance. As I will briefly indicate below, the unevennesses run along many different axes, such that no one form of speech holds the trump card. Nor do these unevennesses necessarily run parallel to divisions of a social and political kind. The critical point is that the linguistic world always has and always will consist of such a hodge-podge of structures, and that between those structures relations of citation and representation as well as of dialogue obtain. To describe language as a vast ocean of utterances, all more or less alike, entails homogenizing a much more complicated process.

Bakhtin, the champion of heteroglossia, is, alas, one of the villains in this drama. For while he acknowledges the diversity of language he irons out the kinds of unevennesses I am talking about when he argues that "there is a common plane which [...] justifies our juxtaposition of these languages: all the languages of heteroglossia, no matter what principle lies at the base of their particularization, are specific points of view on the world" (DN, 291/104). The difference between a newspaper and a shout in the street, however, cannot be described as a difference of point of view, and it would be silly to expect or desire that difference to be ironed out in a dialogue.

Neither, however, should we imagine that, having accepted the pervasiveness of citation and representation in the linguistic world, we can then expect this new, enlarged model of language to deliver some updated social and political ideal, capable of replacing dialogue in our politico-sentimental life. As I said at the beginning, I would doubt that we can draw social or political standards from an account of language alone, however nuanced. Bakhtin himself only gave the idea of a dialogical novel political flesh by combining it with his own quasi-Nietzschean populism. But the starting point for our reflections, wherever they may lead, should be a vision of language as unevenly structured, full of forms which don't respond, as in a dialogue, but cite and represent. Any modern politics of language has to acknowledge that *Gesellschaft* is the order of the day, even in speech.

Of course, even to mention that ugly word is to set people on edge, to seem to prescribe an endless diet of linguistic alienation and homelessness. Needless to say, the aim of this paper is not to reassure people, to say: actually this modernity and all its citation is quite a good thing. The point is that it appears as a bad thing when people indulge in a kind of sociological romanticism about language, and that Bakhtin certainly does his bit to encourage such romanticism. But at the same time his effusions about the novel, the people and the public square develop in his readers an enthusiasm for modernity which they may not want to own up to. When we become excited or inspired by his model of the novel, we recognize the possibilities or virtues not only of irony and sarcasm, in principle accessible to all, but of extensive historical knowledge, narrative sophistication, range of linguistic reference. These aren't modern features, but they're not something people are born with, either. If dialogism seems to require a certain level of literacy, cosmopolitanism and access to informational resources, then by rights we should look with pleasure, or at least hope, upon these products of modernity, even if they are bound up with the loss of linguistic *Gemeinschaft*.

If, then, dialogism isn't quite what we thought it was, if it isn't dialogue writ large, we should not despair. We ought to acknowledge the ineluctability of citation and representation in the social life of discourse. If we do not, we condemn ourselves, not to the past, which is, after all, irretrievable, but to a somewhat hypocritical populism, in which we forever pretend that the fruits of novelistic practice are available to all in their everyday dialogues. When we abuse dialogue, when we expect too much of it, we neglect those other forms of language and social exchange which tell us about virtues and possibilities besides those of dialogue, and tell us about the responsibilities of intellectual work, alas, not always reducible to the maintenance of dialogue. Dialogism is, I suppose, for real; for us, it seems, it is too real, for our fantasies of dialogue too often render it invisible.[1]

NOTE

1. My thanks to Bruce Robbins for his generous and thoughtful help with this article.

WORK CITED

Bakhtin, M.M. 1929. *Problemy tvorchestva Dostoevskogo* (Leningrad: Priboi).

CHATTER, BABBLE, AND DIALOGUE

Anthony Wall, University of Calgary

Perhaps one of the nicest things about writing a paper on a topic like chatter is that such a topic allows me to speak legitimately about almost anything and everything. I had originally thought about writing a paper composed of one single and drawn out sentence, but I already tried that once before, and the joke fell completely flat. Thus I began to look at a second idea about something that I might wish to speak about, perhaps about a chattering literary character, and the hero from Dostoevsky's *Notes from Underground* seemed just about fit the bill. But then again I have to back away because of all the Slavists who have contributed to this volume, and readers of this text who know Dostoevsky's piece so much better than I do. Besides, I don't even speak Russian. So I am left with really nothing at all to talk about, something which leaves me in a perfect position to chatter in a paper which pretends to be on chatter rather than in chatter.

Let me give a preliminary definition of what I mean by chatter, or rather what I *shall* mean by chatter, because before defining what I intend to talk about I am not entirely sure what exactly I intend to talk about. I shall define chatter as the act of speaking about the fact that you are not going to be talking about certain things, such as Dostoevsky's *Notes from Underground*, but then turn around and speak about it anyway despite having said, or rather *through* having said, that you were not going to speak about that. Chatterers thus manage to latch on to a very small discursive and semantic space and to spread it out so smoothly and widely, but also so thinly, that they make it cover as many other discursive spaces as possible.

So this was just about where I stood when I was preparing this paper — i.e. I had thought about writing a paper steeped in chatter itself, but then I chickened out, and then I thought about writing about Dostoevsky, but I chickened out again — there I was without very much to say when I read Gary Saul Morson and Caryl Emerson's *Mikhail Bakhtin: Creation of a Prosaics* (Morson and Emerson 1990), and then I really didn't know what to think any more. And then when I had finally decided upon what I was not going to write about and managed to start writing a paper on that subject, just before reading that paper I heard a number of provocative papers that I would have wanted to quote but those ideas have been lost in all my misplaced and incomprehensible notes. But Maroussia Hajdukowski-Ahmed, as I remember, read a provocative paper on hysteria and Charcot, and she quotes from Trillat who quotes Charcot when he says that hysteria "is much ado about nothing" and that epilepsy is "far more serious" because it is "more silent" (see Hajdukowski-Ahmed 1993, 188). Indeed, had I been able to find it in the proper reference book, I would have wanted to place that quotation at the beginning of my paper as an epigraph, but alas my paper is already written and there just isn't enough room left on the top of my first page between my title and my text so I shall have to be content with the observation that, if indeed hysteria is the disease of saying a lot for nothing, then females definitely do not have a monopoly on that disease.

It does seem true, though, that, as Caryl Emerson recently remarked in the late 1980s, "Baxtin Studies have come of age" (Emerson 1988, 503), and I propose to explore the meanings that the truth of this observation entails, meanings not at all explored in Emerson's piece. The surest sign of the maturity of Bakhtin Studies, or perhaps of their decadence, is the unfathomable volume of material that has been published in the past ten years. Since approximately 1984 we have had bumper crop after bumper crop, and you can see from my flimsy metaphors that I've been working in Western Canada for a bit too long. Now the result of all this production should be obvious: no *one* person can possibly have read everything that has been written on Bakhtin and I even wonder whether anyone would ever want to read it all. We are to a certain extent caught in the middle of a burgeoning field of inquiry which has an amazing trait: no one can possibly know intimately what all the other people are talking about, and as a result the Bakhtins we are producing are growing further and further apart.

We have cultivated, whether we wanted to or not, a marvellously fertile field where chatter is now beginning to flourish almost unabated. Let me explain what I mean. By chatter I also propose to designate all forms of discourse which purport to speak about something when it turns out there is no fixed object of discourse to be had. When I seek to speak about Mikhail Bakhtin, I should by rights be encountering the numerous and widely divergent discourses that also speak about him this very minute from all quarters and from all political points of view. But I am compelled to chatter because the numbers of texts on Bakhtin that I have read are far outnumbered by those that I have *not* read. International Bakhtin conferences are indeed unique intellectual events because you no longer have to worry about reading all the stuff that all your colleagues have been writing during the past few years. For example, of the fifty-eight titles listed in the third issue of the *Bakhtin Newsletter* for the year 1989 (Thomson et al. (eds.) 1991), I have managed to read only thirteen titles. Were I inclined to chatter more than I already am, I might be tempted to produce an almost exhaustive list (and I say *almost* exhaustive because I am sure that there are many more titles that were missed) of all the texts that I have not read, and in my exhaustivity, I could perform the well-known Rabelaisian trick of multiplying long and unwieldy lists, those "laundry lists" as Samuel Kinser calls them, or those "enumerations, subverbal utterances and neologisms without end" which manage to "jostle and jar as well as explore the limits of verbality" (Kinser 1990, 45). Such a list — but don't worry just yet because I won't write out the forty-five titles I have not yet read — or should I? — actually I don't need to because I can probably keep on speaking about this list that does not yet exist for a very long time indeed, more than the time that a simple reading of the list would have taken — such a list would unfortunately reduce to insignificance a great number of articles and books which deserve better treatment. This semantic reduction would be caused by the sheer massiveness of all the signifiers so crudely strung together whereby something's significance is utterly decimated by the brutal accumulation of too many signifiers. Such a list reminds me again of Rabelais, of a passage in the *Quart Livre*, chapter LV, where Pantagruel during his long voyage to China, instead of hearing the deadly sirens that Ulysses heard, begins to notice the curious sound of many, many frozen words meaning nothing to anyone: "Compaignons, oyez-vous rien? Me semble que je oy quelques gens parlans en l'air, je n'y voy toutefoys personne. Escoutez" ("Companions, do you hear anything? Methinks that I hear people speaking in the air, though I see no one. Hark.") (Rabelais 1962, 203). "The very overabundance of signifying materials", as André Belleau notes about this same passage, "brings on an inevitable loss of meaning" (Belleau 1990, 137). Indeed we are not very far removed from the type of empty seductive practices that Jean Baudrillard analyses when he writes that "words and gestures are emptied of all meaning by untiring repetition and scanning: tire out meaning, wear it out, and exhaust it completely in order to release pure seduction from the empty signifier" (Baudrillard 1980, 105), and not very far removed either from Kierkegaard's Johannes in *The Seducer's Diary* who, in the first stages of Cordelia's seduction, decides to make himself "as unobtrusive as possible in order to observe her all the better" (Kierkegaard 1987 [1943], 338).

Thus when chattering in a mock-oral text that I am now committing to written form instead of standing up in front of you to deliver my talk in person, I am purporting to speak about all those Bakhtins that I have not yet read. And, secondly, I propose to speak about the concept of chatter, another topic on which in pragmatic linguistics, in sociolinguistics, and in the philosophy of language a growing number of pertinent texts that I have not read are also being written. Once again the number of texts that I have not read far exceeds those that I have. And just to prove that I am not joking, let me just list some of the material I am unfamiliar with: There's Edit Schlaffer's and Cherly Benard's "Männerdiskurs und Frauentratsch" printed in the 1981 volume of *Soziale Welt*; there is Angela Keppler's "Der Verlauf von Klatschgesprächen" published in the *Zeitschrift für Soziologie* in 1987; Klaus P. Schneider's *Small Talk* published in 1988 in Marburg, and there's the whole rest of Deborah Tannen's interesting book called *Talking Voices* (1989), and I mean "the whole rest" because I've only read the first introductory chapter and the fourth chapter entitled, significantly for us, "Constructing Dialogue in Conversation", where she explicitly uses Bakhtin and Voloshinov to ground her analysis. And by the way, this latter chapter, the fourth one, is one of the many 1989 titles that were missed in the *Bakhtin Newsletter*. These are but four titles in a large number of publications recently appeared on such topics as gossip, bantering, small talk, phatic communication, and chatter, not to mention all those publications that we might imagine on such topics as prattling, babbling, prolixity, gab, jabber, verbiage, blather, poppycock, claptrap, verbosity, balderdash, flatulence, logorrhoea, gibberish, blarney, drivel, twaddle, incoherence, delirium, word-spinning, wordiness, vapouring, longwindedness, superfluity, padding, verse-fillers, digression, chinwag, palaver, gush, gammon, humbug, baloney sausage, rubbish, rot, gas, fustian, piffle, hot air, rigamarole, tommyrot, bilge, flap-doodle, gobbledygook, admininistratese (please forgive my rather unsubtle plagiarism of Roget's *Thesaurus* for significant parts of this list), and even a further technical concept that I'm not sure I shall be able to pronounce correctly, as it apparently belongs to the British dialect: "pi-jaw". I really believe that I must be dealing with something very important when I start studying chatter because, in accordance with a well-known linguistic principle, any concept that can generate as many synonyms as does chatter in a given language must be culturally significant for that linguistic group (cf. Yaguello 1981, 181).

Chatter, it would well seem, is a lot like ideology, considering, as Terry Eagleton once put it, that ideology is always a way of describing what other people do, but not what you yourself do (Eagleton 1983, 211). "Someone who accuses someone else of chattering is guilty of even worse chatter himself", according to Maurice Blanchot, "worse because his accusation is both pretentious and authoritarian" (Blanchot 1971, 145–146).[1] And at the risk of having myself accused of being a chatterer, I should nevertheless point out that chatter is no stranger to philosophers as diverse as J.L. Austin and Mikhail Bakhtin. Let's look at Austin first, then we shall return to Bakhtin — finally:

> A disagreement as to what we should say is not to be shied off, but to be pounced upon: for the explanation of it can hardly fail to be illuminating. If we light on an electron that rotates the wrong way, that is a discovery, a portent to be followed up, not a reason for chucking physics; and by the same token, a genuinely loose or eccentric talker is a rare specimen to be prized. (Austin 1970, 184)

In other words chatterers can teach us a lot about language, and by looking at chatter we stand to learn a lot about Bakhtinian dialogue. Compulsive chatterers talk about just about anything, and when they have nothing else to talk about, when they have no real object of discourse, then they can really begin their chatter for now they will begin to talk about the very act of talking in order to give themselves something that resembles an object for their discourse. Bakhtin had great admiration for one such eccentric chatterer, the Underground Man. Indeed this chattering hero is doubly effective. First he constantly tells us that he is writing about his own talk, that he is talking about his own talk, and that, even more perversely, he is also lying about his own talk. Allow me to give a few examples of this kind of chatter:

> A bad joke but I will not cross it out. I wrote it thinking it would sound very witty; but now that I see myself that I only wanted to show off in a despicable way, I will purposely not cross it out! (Dostoevsky 1969 [1864], 4)

> No doubt you think, gentlemen, that I want to amuse you. You are mistaken in that, too. I am not at all such a merry person as you imagine, or as you may imagine; however, if irritated by all this babble (and I can feel that you are irritated) you decide to ask me just who I am — then my answer is, I am a certain low-ranked civil servant. (Dostoevsky 1969 [1864], 5)

> I'll bet you think I am writing all this to show off, to be witty at the expense of men of action; and what is more, that out of ill-bred showing-off, I am clanking a sword, like my officer. But gentlemen, whoever can pride himself on his disease and even show off with them?
>
> However, what am I talking about? Everyone does that. They do pride themselves on their diseases, and I, perhaps, more than any one. There is no doubt about it: my objection was absurd. Yet just the same, I am firmly convinced not only that a great deal of consciousness, but that any consciousness is a disease. I insist on it. (Dostoevsky 1969 [1864], 6)

Notice that in the last example, to return briefly to Austin, we have a true example of a performative utterance: "I insist on it." Chatter that speaks about the very act of speaking has to be performative because without the very performance of chatter that the chattering itself provides there would be absolutely nothing to talk about, not even the possibility of talking about the act of talking. But unlike what the common view says of chattering, the act itself, the performance of speaking about nothing in the act of speaking about itself while it speaks, is not an empty act. Amongst the numerous other examples of chatter that I could have chosen from the opening pages of *Notes from Underground*, we notice that the Underground Man also insists on the fact that he is lying: "I was lying when I said just now that I was a spiteful official. I was lying out of spite" (Dostoevsky 1969 [1864], 4). The performance of lying is neither fuller nor emptier than any other performative chatter, but it allows us to see that all chatter, however empty we might believe it to be, is in reality a speech act of vicious aggression. I shall return to the aggressive side of chatter a little later.

For the moment I wish simply to remind you that there is a second level of effectiveness to the Underground Man's chatter. This second level is related to the fact that the hero himself is, in the words of Michael André Bernstein, the "endless chatter of already uttered utterances" (Bernstein 1989, 208), the epitome of the novelistic hero functioning within the novel genre where "languages throw light on each other" (EN, 12). The novel is the ideal genre of chatter because it is the constant function of the novel itself to speak about the languages of which it is composed. The state of chatter is thus arrived at when we speak about what we are now saying. "Along with the internal contradictions inside the object itself, the prose writer witnesses as well the unfolding of social heteroglossia surrounding the object, the Tower-of-Babel mixing of languages that goes on around any object, the dialectics of the object are interwoven with the social dialogue surrounding it" (DN, 278). As David Carroll has aptly put it: "This *autocriticism of discourse* is one of the distinguishing features of the novel as 'genre'"

(Carroll 1983, 77). But if the novel can contain chatter, chatter can also contain novels. Chatter is aggressive and predatory. The distinction of primary and secondary genres gets all messed up. Once again by looking at chatter alongside dialogue we see that the eccentric has much to teach us.

And so if it is true that, as Bakhtin says about the Underground Man, "there is nothing to say about him" (*PDP*, 151), I can nevertheless wish to interpret this phrase not as Bakhtin does in conjunction with the infinite powers of the Underground Man's self-consciousness and with the infinitely rich problem of the loophole, but rather in its complex paradoxical nature of saying that it is impossible to say anything about the Underground Man and thereby to say something about him. Chatter is now again the act of speaking about what you are not going to speak about when you have nothing else to say. And it is on this note of the paradox of speaking about that which it is impossible to speak that we can examine another angle of the Underground Man's chatter.

Let me continue by requoting Morson and Emerson requoting Dostoevsky in his *Notes from Underground*:

> Oh gentlemen, after all, perhaps I consider myself an intelligent man only because all my life I have been able neither to begin nor to finish anything. Granted, granted I am a babbler, a harmless annoying babbler, like all of us. But what is to be done if the direct and sole vocation of every intelligent man is babble, that is, the intentional pouring of water through a sieve? (Dostoevsky 1969 [1864], 16–17)

It is claimed by Morson and Emerson in their gloss of this passage that the problem of the Underground Man is that he "fully embodies the life of 'abstract content'" and that "he truly lives a life of 'empty potential'" (Morson and Emerson 1989, 19). But notice that the Underground Man formulates his musings on chatter in the interrogative mode. "Philosophy is perceptive faith", writes Maurice Merleau-Ponty, "which interrogates itself" (Merleau-Ponty 1963, 139). And yet, despite the interrogative mode of these remarks formulated by Dostoevsky's chattering character, we do not really believe for a single second that he has not already decided long beforehand what the answer should be. This chatterer feigns an opening in his discourse, feigns to imitate the openendedness of the world with an open and interrogative discourse, but we know that his questions are not those of the infinite question and answer of which Bakhtin writes in "The Problem of the Text": "The word wants to be heard, understood, responded to, and again to respond to the response, and so forth *ad infinitum*" (PT, 127). For the infinity of the dialogic exchange is the unending to and fro of taking turns, whereas the unending flow of the chatterer's discourse derives from the fact that it is impossible to get a clean start, and especially to make a definitive end. The hypocritical openings in the chatterer's discourse are cruel tricks that he plays upon us because the pretence of providing us with real holes in his discourse would constitute a false gesture toward recognizing our otherness. Chatter aggressively digests all otherness within itself and spews it out in a never-ending flow of aggressive logorrhoea. Chatter flattens out all otherness. You literally can get sucked into the semantic vacuum that chattering sets up, and thereby become objectified. The aggressiveness of the chatterer is transmitted by his refusal to stop. Even at the end of *Notes from Underground* we know that we are not really at the end. We could say that being subjected to a chatterer's talk is one of the rare experiences we have of eternity, that moment where a compulsive talker is infinitely adding on to what he has already said a hundred times (Blanchot 1972, 97). Or as Marina Yaguello observes: "Some people feel great anxiety when phatic contact is broken, because that means that everyone must now get back into themselves, and we all know the type of person who, standing in the doorway, starts up the conversation over and over again when each time he is about to leave" (Yaguello 1981, 27). Let it be said in passing that an examination of chatter helps us to get another view of what Bakhtin calls the chronotope of the threshold. The doorway of the chatterer is not the Dostoevskian doorway that Bakhtin analyses as a symbol of something new and different about to happen. It is rather the instrument of a constant and mean-spirited teasing whereby the outside is briefly glimpsed only to be cruelly shut off again. It is the instrument of the perpetual closing-off of all the possible openings in speech towards otherness or towards something new that otherness might provide. Compulsive talkers need to fill the silences that sometimes threaten to settle in around them. The inveterate chatterer can permit no outside to accompany the internal flow of his own discourse. The Underground Man's question, to sum up, is not a window into another's speech but a painful illusion whereby he manages to keep on filling the silence of his loneliness by answering his own questions.

Emile Benveniste in his *Problems of General Linguistics* cites Malinowski who speaks about chattering as a classical phatic situation where several people can get together and chit-chat without any particular goal in mind (Benveniste 1974, 87). Such situations are noteworthy, for they exist simply to provide a general "atmosphere of sociableness" where what is said is supposed to be much less important than the type of phatic speech act involved (see Malinowski 1972 [1923], 313–314). What is done here, i.e.

forging or sustaining social links and contacts, is much more significant than the sweet nothings that are being proffered. Benveniste goes on to say in the last paragraphs of his famous essay "The Formal Apparatus of Enunciation" that the phatic situation thus depicted by Malinowski is at "the very limits of dialogue" (Benveniste 1974, 88). And although I could not agree much more strongly than I do now that chatter does indeed present a limit case for dialogue, I am not entirely sure that the benign use of gregarious and harmless chatter is the best model available if we intend to see how such babbling language activities can be related to Bakhtinian dialogue.

For starters, I believe it is imperative to counteract a growing number of commentators, of different political stripes, but often of one political stripe in particular, who claim that Bakhtin as a theoretician overstresses the nice ways in which we dialogically agree with one another and drastically understresses the hard issues of disagreement and discord. I respectfully challenge this observation put forward several times in the Morson and Emerson collection *Rethinking Bakhtin*, by Michael André Bernstein (1989) and by Aaron Fogel (1989) in particular, and confirmed by Morson and Emerson in their book (1990) and by Emerson herself in her "Problems with Baxtin's Poetics" article, where she writes that Bakhtin "presumes no conflict in principle between an organism and its surroundings, just as he presumes no conflict in principle between self and society" (Emerson 1988, 516). Even Michael Holquist acquiesces — grudgingly, mind you — in this same point of view when he concedes in the final pages of his "Introduction" to *Art and Answerability* that "the lack of a more carefully considered treatment of conflict and power relations in self/other dealings is something of a limitation in Bakhtin's thought as well" (Holquist 1990, xxxix). At least he goes on to add the qualifier "particularly in these early works", something the other commentators we have just cited do *not* do. We shall return to this point shortly.

As we have seen, chattering and babbling, the eccentrics of talking, are rarely benign and benevolent, just as dialogue is not always the fruit of peaceful coexistence, even in Bakhtin's writing. Bakhtin is not a philosopher of the ideal speech situation and Bakhtin is not a philosopher of agreement. In comparison with someone like Dell Hymes, for example, Bakhtin is clearly much more aware of the conflicts between speaker, interlocutor, and speech situation (see Cazden 1989, 122). Bakhtin *does* lack insights into the ways in which speakers must function within institutionalized social spaces when they confront the discourse of others in their social environments (see Hirschkop 1986, 100, and Hirschkop's contribution to the present volume), but this is an entirely different matter from the criticisms of the American right, which seeks to use the assertion of an absence of conflict in Bakhtinian dialogism to re-emphasize the contradictory needs for constraints and for an introduction of a kind of social Darwinism where organized political opposition to reigning power is labelled as a species of theoretism directed against the freedom of the individual. But it does not take very long to find what, for upholders of this view, must be politically tainted words in the writings of Bakhtin, and we need not look in the disputed texts to find them. I'm thinking for example of the word "struggle". This is a word Bakhtin uses to describe the relationships between speaking subjects and the words that enter their consciousness:

> One's own discourse and one's own voice, although born of another or dynamically stimulated by another, will sooner or later begin to liberate themselves from the authority of the other's discourse. This process is made more complex by the fact that a variety of alien voices enter into the struggle for influence within an individual's consciousness (just as they struggle with one another in surrounding social reality). (DN, 348)

What I wish to show from this single example, and I could quote others, the example of the peasant, for one, who realizes the powers and the contradictions of the many languages that he is capable of using, languages that "in no way could live in peace and quiet with one another" (DN, 296), what I wished to show from this example, one that Cazden quotes for similar purposes, is that it is simply not true to say that there is no struggle in Bakhtin's conception of dialogism. It *is* true to say that there is no struggle in the early essays, and to a large extent in his very last writings, texts that he never intended for publication. But I strongly resist the kind of conservative book-end theory of Bakhtin that we are presently being subjected to, particularly in North America — the theory according to which everything essential in Bakhtin is to be more clearly understood if we concentrate our attention on the early and the late Bakhtin and a theory that says that, like empty chatter, or insignificant books, everything that comes in the middle simply has nothing to do with the real Bakhtin. I resist this theory's claim to literalness and truth for a position that is, in essence, nothing more than a crafty use of rhetorical metonymy.

What has happened in our mature Bakhtin studies is thus a little bit frightening. Certain periods of Bakhtin's multifarious thought are given undue weight in an attempt to find the real Bakhtinian canon. In a curious kind of anachronism, the earlier texts are deemed to be so very important precisely because they have been the last to be translated and because many readers of Bakhtin are desperate for a key and are willing to accept these "new" texts as such. Specifically targeted areas of Bakhtin's thought are raised to the status of representatives of the totality. In a kind of philosophical chatter, the otherness of other Bakhtins is declared to be be invalid and versions of that otherness are flattened out into a respectable, apolitical and ethically two-dimensional picture. Chatter occurs here when a restricted zone of all Bakhtin's discourses, i.e. a restricted zone of Bakhtin's multifarious intellectual developments, is spread out so widely, like a fine but deadly plastic sheet, that it smothers all the other zones that it has thus managed to cover. We are all chatterers in a sense when we study what we call Bakhtin because we really are not talking about the same thing at all. We are certainly not talking about the same object. This is the most probable explanation for the fact that we do not even need to read each other any more. There is a lot of chatter out there in the land of Bakhtin studies. I'm afraid that we've created a monster.

NOTE

1. The generally accepted condemnation of chatter is no doubt linked to Aristotle's condemnation of the Sophists in his *Metaphysics*. "Le titre *Le Plaisir de parler* reprend l'expression *légein logóu khárin*, 'parler pour parler', 'parler pour le plaisir', soit le chef d'accusation sous lequel Aristote, au livre *gamma* de sa *Métaphysique*, parachève la condamnation platonicienne et relègue le sophiste hors de la philosophie: en instaurant à la fois le principe de la non-contradiction et le régime de la signification, sous lequel nous vivons et parlons depuis lors (on ne parle pas pour parler, mais pour 'signifier quelque chose pour soi-même et pour autrui'), il forclôt le discours de la sophistique et nous interdit désormais de l'entendre directement" (Cassin 1988, ix).

WORKS CITED

Austin, J.L. 1970. *Philosophical Papers* (Oxford: Clarendon Press).

Baudrillard, J. 1980. *De la Séduction* (Paris: Gallimard).

Belleau, A. 1990. *Notre Rabelais* (Montreal: Boréal).

Benveniste, E. 1974. *Problèmes de linguistique générale*, vol. 2 (Paris: Gallimard).

Bernstein, M.A. 1989. "The Poetics of *Ressentiment*", in G.S. Morson and C. Emerson (eds.), *Rethinking Bakhtin: Extensions and Challenges* (Chicago: Northwestern University Press), 197–223.

Blanchot, M. 1971. *Amitié* (Paris: Gallimard).

________. 1972 "La parole vaine", in R. Ouellet (ed.), *Les Critiques de notre temps et le Nouveau Roman* (Paris: Garnier), 94–98.

Carroll, D. 1983. "The Alterity of Discourse: Form, History, and the Question of the Political in M.M. Bakhtin", in *Diacritics*, 13/2, 65–83.

Cassin, B. 1988. *Le Plaisir de parler* (Paris: Minuit).

Cazden, C.B. 1989. "Contributions of the Bakhtin Circle to 'Communicative Competence'", in *Applied Linguistics*, 10/2, 116–127.

Dostoevsky, F. 1969 [1864]. *Notes from Underground and The Grand Inquisitor*, tr. R.E. Matlaw (New York: E.P. Dutton).

Eagleton, T. 1983. *Literary Theory* (Oxford: Blackwell).

Emerson, C. 1988. "Problems with Baxtin's Poetics", in *Slavic and East European Journal*, 32/4, 503–525.

Fogel, A. 1989. "Coerced Speech and the Oedipus Dialogue Complex", in G.S. Morson and C. Emerson (eds), *Rethinking Bakhtin: Extensions and Challenges* (Chicago: Northwestern University Press), 173–196.

Hajdukowski-Ahmed, M. 1993. "The Framing of the Shrew: Discourses on Hysteria and its Resisting Voices", in D. Shepherd (ed.), *Bakhtin: Carnival and Other Subjects* (Amsterdam and Atlanta, GA: Editions Rodopi), 177–195.

Hirschkop, K. 1986. "Bakhtin, Discourse and Democracy", in *New Left Review*, 160, 92–113.

Holquist, M. 1990. "Introduction: The Architectonics of Answerability", in *Art and Answerability: Early Philosophical Essays by M.M. Bakhtin*, ed. Holquist and V. Liapunov, tr. Liapunov and K. Brostrom (Austin: University of Texas Press), ix–xlix.

Keppler, A. 1987. "Der Verlauf von Klatschgesprächen", in *Zeitschrift für Soziologie*, 16/4, 288–302.

Kierkegaard, S. 1987 [1943]. "The Seducer's Diary", in *Either/Or, Part I*, tr. H.V. and E.H. Hong (Princeton: Princeton University Press).

Kinser, S. 1990. *Rabelais's Carnival: Text, Context, Metatext* (Berkeley: University of California Press).

Malinowski, B. 1972 [1923]. "The Problem of Meaning in Primitive Languages", in C.K. Ogden and I.A. Richards (eds.), *The Meaning of Meaning: A Study of the Influence of Language upon Thought and of the Source of Symbolism* (London: Routledge and Kegan Paul), 296–336.

Merleau-Ponty, M. 1963. *Le Visible et l'invisible* (Paris: Gallimard).

Morson, G.S., and C. Emerson 1989. "Introduction: Rethinking Bakhtin", in Morson and Emerson (eds), *Rethinking Bakhtin: Extensions and Challenges* (Chicago: Northwestern University Press), 1–60.

________. 1990. *Mikhail Bakhtin: Creation of a Prosaics* (Stanford: Stanford University Press).

Rabelais, F. 1962. *Oeuvres complètes*, vol. 2 (Paris: Garnier).

Schlaffer, E., and C. Benard 1981. "Männerdiskurs une Frauentratsch: Zum Doppelstandard in der Soziologie", *Soziale Welt*, 32/1, 119–136.

Schneider, K.P. 1988. *Small Talk: Analyzing Phatic Discourse* (Marburg: Hitzeroth).

Tannen, D. 1989. *Talking Voices* (Cambridge: Cambridge University Press).

Thomson, C., et al. (eds.) 1991. *Le Bulletin Bakhtine/The Bakhtin Newsletter* (Queen's University, Department of French Studies, Kingston, Ontario, Canada), 3.

Yaguello, M. 1981. *Alice au pays du langage* (Paris: Seuil).

INDEX

A

B

C

D

G

H

I

J

K

L

P

R

S